Advance Praise for *Something Big*

"An eye-opening and detailed account of one of the most horrific crimes in Illinois history. It's an unforgettable telling to an unforgivable crime."

—Nic Edwards, host of the podcast *True Crime Garage*

"The Brown's Chicken Massacre sent ripples through suburban America. *Something Big* takes the reader back to when this horrific crime happened and tells the stories of the people involved, making this a true crime book you won't be able to put down."

—Charlie Worroll, host of the podcast *Crimelines*

"This book by Patrick Wohl is the first real deep dive into the Brown's Chicken Massacre, a case so fascinating any true crime fan will want every detail."

—Kristin Williams, host of the podcast *True Crime Creepers*

SOMETHING BIG

The True Story
of the
Brown's Chicken Massacre,
A Decade-Long Manhunt,
and the
Trials That Followed

PATRICK WOHL

A POST HILL PRESS BOOK
ISBN: 979-8-88845-900-3
ISBN (eBook): 979-8-88845-901-0

Something Big:
The True Story of the Brown's Chicken Massacre, A Decade-Long Manhunt, and the Trials That Followed
© 2025 by Patrick Wohl
All Rights Reserved

Cover design by Cody Corcoran

This book, as well as any other Post Hill Press publications, may be purchased in bulk quantities at a special discounted rate. Contact orders@posthillpress.com for more information.

This is a work of nonfiction. All people, locations, events, and situations are portrayed to the best of the author's memory and knowledge. Although adequate research was undergone concerning criminal cases, real-life people and perceptions, and authentic situations and incidents, the author and publisher do not assume and hereby disclaim any liability concerning any legal or criminal details present in this book.

No part of this book may be reproduced, stored in a retrieval system, or transmitted by any means without the written permission of the author and publisher.

Post Hill Press
New York • Nashville
posthillpress.com

Published in the United States of America
1 2 3 4 5 6 7 8 9 10

To the Victims:
Michael Castro
Lynn (Wiese) Ehlenfeldt
Richard Ehlenfeldt
Guadalupe Maldonado
Thomas Mennes
Marcus Nellsen
Rico Solis

To the Palatine Police
And Other Law Enforcement Who
Doggedly Pursued This Case
For Nearly a Decade

&

To the Prosecutors and Defense Attorneys
Who Finally Brought Justice
And Ensured a Fair Trial

TABLE OF CONTENTS

Preface ix

Part 1
Chapter 1 — Belva & John 3
Chapter 2 — Lynn & Dick 14
Chapter 3 — Kristin 29
Chapter 4 — Rico & Michael 39
Chapter 5 — Marcus, Lupe & Tom 47
Chapter 6 — Eileen 59

Part 2
Chapter 7 — Jane 71
Chapter 8 — Martin 80
Chapter 9 — Michelle 93
Chapter 10 — Anne 105
Chapter 11 — Jerry 116
Chapter 12 — Rita 129
Chapter 13 — Chuck 155
Chapter 14 — Frank 163
Chapter 15 — Casey, Todd & John 175
Chapter 16 — Jennifer, Dana & Joy 187

Part 3
Chapter 17 — Juan & Jim 197
Chapter 18 — Melissa 205

Chapter 19 —	Bill	213
Chapter 20 —	Alesia	221
Chapter 21 —	Vincent	232
Chapter 22 —	Juan	240
Chapter 23 —	Juror 56	257
Chapter 24 —	Jim	263

A Note on Sources & Dialogue 277
Notes 279
Acknowledgments 305
About the Author 306

PREFACE

America has a fixation with true crime. Who among us hasn't binged the latest Netflix miniseries or blown through a chart-topping *Serial*-style podcast? Ask a fan of the genre for their thoughts on the latest story making waves and chances are they'll have a theory of the case or excitedly rattle off some true crime recommendations of their own. A book you've just *got* to read. That podcast you'll love. A documentary that'll keep you guessing.

Perhaps it's strange that one of the most popular categories of books, audio, and TV—mediums that people use to take their minds off the chaos of the world—involves grisly tales of murder or notorious criminals who wreak havoc on their victims. In an odd way, reading or watching a true crime story can serve as an escape because it's far from anything most people will ever experience. But for those who were actually there, the depiction of a tale involving the murder of a loved one can also be an exercise in re-traumatization. Herein lay my own moral dilemma in writing this book. People love true crime—but at what cost?

In 1993, the so-called Brown's Chicken massacre made national headlines, and it was something that people in Chicagoland followed closely for years. I certainly did as I got older. As someone who was raised not far from where it occurred and grew up eating fried chicken from the chain for which the crime is eponymously referred, it always stuck with me. But the story was distant, something I read about in the papers and followed on the news as a kid. As I began digging deeper nearly thirty years after the murders while starting my initial research for this book, I was struck by the videos taken just hours after police arrived on the scene on that cold January morning in 1993, with cameras eyeing the victims' family members and friends, their faces painted with pain and some shrieking in an understandable, gut-wrenching agony. When the time came to actually conduct interviews with community members, friends of the victims, and even unflappable attorneys who'd presumably seen and heard it all, many broke down in tears. *How could I possibly approach others to talk about this story?* I thought to myself. Was this *really* something I wanted to write about? And more importantly, what would be the point?

Is true crime ethical? I googled naively, searching for answers in all the wrong places. Every thought piece or niche blog post on the subject had an equally certain yet completely contradictory take.

Can true crime be ethical? Yes. Take, for example, a case gone cold only to be revived from an engaging book or podcast. Other times a story might serve to put pressure on law enforcement in the event something has been overlooked.

Can true crime be unethical? Also, yes. And, sadly, all too often. With distance from the crimes depicted, it can be easy for a filmmaker or writer to harp on too gratuitously about the violence of a murder, attempting to entertain fans of the genre while also forgetting about those whose lives they're portraying. Other tales might overly humanize a monstrous killer or provide a platform to a person who would otherwise be better off fading from society.

SOMETHING BIG

So what exactly would my purpose be in writing a book about the Brown's Chicken massacre? The crime was indisputably solved, so giving it more attention had no investigatory purpose. Contrary to the opinion of many over the years, there were no credible errors from police that merited this case to be visited anew nor any prosecutorial missteps or deficiencies in the legal defense. Most importantly, more than thirty years later, the families of the victims still suffer from the horror of January '93. Why bother?

This story is in many ways a part of the history of the northwest suburbs of Chicago where I grew up, and I'm hardly the first person to touch on the subject. Put simply, people talk about this case. Podcasts are pumped out nearly every year. News articles mark anniversaries. Other books have been published. But of everything that has been made on the infamous Brown's Chicken massacre, I was struck in my early digging by the many deficiencies of past retellings.

Books written on the subject speak far too much about the legal procedure involved in the case and leave out the narrative. Many podcasts, while well produced, are done by people with no connection to the story or to Illinois; they mispronounce the names of important places and figures, leave out key context about the area where this takes place, and recount the story with significant factual errors. Other storytellers harp on about the gore of the killings, something I think is both disrespectful to the victims' families and downright uninteresting. Most importantly, nearly every past retelling lacked sufficient context about each victim and the impact on the community where this took place. No one thus far has fully addressed the magnitude of what many people to this day consider the worst massacre in Illinois history.

If you ask a casual news observer in Chicagoland what they think of this case, a common refrain is that it was botched by police and that a small suburban police force was unprepared to handle something of this magnitude. From my vantage point and with the clarity of hindsight, this is simply not true. To be sure, there were errors and distractions, like there are in any criminal investigation, but on the whole, the Palatine police consistently made the right moves.

In writing this book, I sought to remedy the deficiencies of past retellings by focusing on the stories of the people involved and the human element of this tragedy. Who were the individuals consumed by this case and how did this come about? In particular, I sought to tell a genuine story about the life of each person killed and what they were like as individuals, not just victims. Much of this is informed by my own discussions with family members, friends, and trial testimony from those impacted about their loved ones.

When reaching out to people for interviews, I was always clear that if they did not want to speak, I would not bother them further. And yet, I fully recognized that an out-of-the-blue email or a text from myself, a complete stranger, could itself trigger horrible memories. Who are you? What business do you have writing about this? So I tried my hardest to go about researching this case in the most respectful way possible. Fortunately, most people were more than willing to speak and incredibly gracious with their time. In fact, most people *wanted* to speak. For their openness, I am exceedingly grateful.

People trusted me with incredibly intimate stories about this awful event that profoundly impacted their lives. Many of them still live with this tragedy day in and day out. To them, it's not just a story.

SOMETHING BIG

I promised to write this book in a way that is different from other tales, respecting the families while still managing to tell a compelling narrative for readers with no connection to Palatine, Illinois. Ultimately, the people impacted by this case—the families, the past suspects, police, and attorneys—will be the ones to judge whether I kept that promise. I hope they feel that I was true to my word and that this book does their story justice.

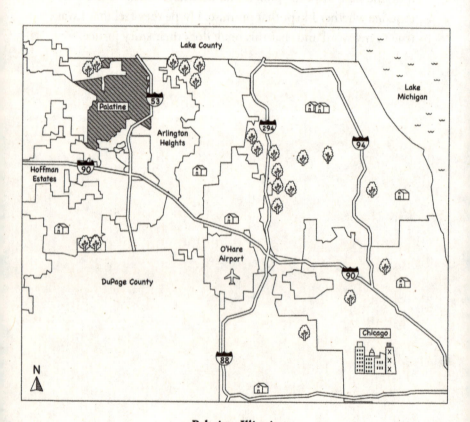

Palatine, Illinois

PART 1

PART 4

"When someone shows you who they are, believe them the first time."

Maya Angelou

CHAPTER 1

BELVA & JOHN

By the time he placed the gun in his mouth, there was little that could dissuade John Brown from pulling the trigger. He'd built a successful business and made mountains of money. By every measure, John Brown had achieved the American Dream. And yet, something was still missing inside the founder of Brown's Chicken.

Belva and John Brown were both products of the Great Depression. Perhaps it's trite to say—everyone who lived through that time, after all, was in some way a *product* of the era—but it instilled in them a deep sense of contentedness. The two were happy with what they had but always willing to work for more.

When he moved to Chicago from Indiana in 1938, John Brown purchased a small plot of farmland that came with a flock of chickens.[1] The couple met during the height of the war when John was working his farm and Belva was laboring away in an automobile factory. When things became serious, John was clear with his prospective wife about what their future would entail. "I can't marry you, Belva, unless you can grab a chicken and wring it by the neck."[2] That was no problem for Belva, so the two wed in 1943 and settled into life on the farm. They had no money for a wedding celebration and little savings for a home. But despite the lack of material possessions, their early years were happy ones.

The couple was roughly the same height and each wore glasses. From the right angle, John could easily be confused for a young Dwight D. Eisenhower. And what the balding John lacked in hair coverage Belva made up for with her long black curls.

For the first five years of their nuptials, the Browns' living arrangements were humble and they lived much of the 1940s in a sectioned-off part of a chicken coop on a five-acre farm that was also home to poultry, hogs, and other farm animals.[3]

These were the years just following World War II, where Americans began populating the suburbs and sparking a baby boom. The Browns were no exception to this wave, and they'd soon require more space than a chicken coop to grow their family, eventually constructing a proper home out of cinder blocks in the summer of 1948 where they'd bring four children into the world.

They continued sustaining their livelihoods as farmers, but in time, the fowl business proved foul for Belva and John, and the couple was in need of some extra income to support their family. Instead of searching for a job with a steady paycheck, they opted to create their own work. Like many ambitious young Americans, they understood the best job is the one you create yourself. That, and they had a lot of chickens.

In 1949, the Browns sold Belva's beloved piano and bought a trailer used for carnival concessions.[4] Instead of popcorn or cotton candy, they decided to sell another comfort food—fried chicken. The trailer was made of metal and had rounded edges at the top, with collapsible awnings and sliding windows where customers could walk right up to and place their orders. Parked on the edge of their farm, the trailer was surrounded by oversized black sandwich boards displaying the prices for customers. Around their setup were acres of untouched Illinois prairie. After outfitting the trailer with two large deep fryers, Belva Brown's recipe was slowly perfected.[5] Fresh chickens would be taken directly from the farm and prepared for their destiny.

There are many ways to butcher a chicken. A sharp axe to the neck pressed against a chopping block or tree stump gets the job done in one clean hack. Swiftly and sturdily breaking the bird's neck and spinal cord is another option. (Less gushing blood, more snapping sounds.) And of course, a good old-fashioned sharp knife to the neck will do the trick too.

After the bird is done wiggling around like a chicken with its head cut off—which in this case is more of a literal observation than an expression—its feathers are plucked from the body until an unrecognizable beast becomes the familiar pink-colored protein staple that a grocery shopper places in their cart each week. Little do they know.

From there, the Browns sliced their whole chickens into eight pieces—two wings, two drumsticks, two breasts, and two thighs—then dunked and dredged them through rich and creamy buttermilk, coated them in breading for that extra crisp, then deep fried the meat in cottonseed oil.

The recipe was simple, and so was the taste. Customers bit into a golden crispy outside then sunk their teeth into juicy chicken—both white meat and dark—that wasn't overpowered with spices. It was balanced, the perfect taste for the clientele in the area who were mostly of Irish, English, and German stock, cultures where mild flavors were customary. Culinary snobs might call it bland, but for the Browns' audience, it was the perfect blend. Not to mention, for just cents on the dollar, customers could take home an entire fried chicken to feed their family.

Belva and John's trailer operation was unassuming. No frills, just great fried chicken. In short order, that simplicity turned into sustained success. The Browns' trailer became a popular attraction in their nice corner of the western Chicago suburbs.[6]

The operation continued with that consistency for many months until the Browns had a run-in with the local health department. The trailer setup lacked a proper toilet or running water, something that persnickety bureaucrats said couldn't stand. "Well, if nature's calling, we've got plenty of prairie," Belva responded to their demands.[7] Still, it was not enough, and the Browns were forced to ditch the trailer and shut down in 1951.

Despite the setback, Belva and John were determined to continue. After a search, they purchased a piece of land in nearby Bridgeview, another suburb just minutes away. The land included both a site for the new establishment as well as room for a new home just feet away from where they'd raise their four children. The day-to-day management was a family affair, with the Browns' kids pitching in to clean, prep potatoes and meat, and serve customers.

Bridgeview had experienced rapid growth like many suburbs outside of Chicago during that decade, and it was a fitting location for a new, family-friendly restaurant. For just sixty-nine cents, customers were served a tray with fried chicken sitting on a slice of fresh white bread that soaked up the savory drippings. Each platter was accompanied by a side of coleslaw mixed with homemade French dressing.[8] The eatery was a triumph.

After finally getting the hang of things, John Brown decided the new Bridgeview restaurant could be designed more efficiently to meet his needs, but he needed a permit for the renovations.

Obtaining that document required blueprints. And while John Brown was skilled at farming and frying, a draftsman he was not. So John Brown looked around the community for some help. By a stroke of good fortune, he mentioned his desire to renovate the restaurant to an old fishing buddy. *My son can help you!* the friend suggested.[9] The business would never be the same.

A draftsman by training, Frank Portillo Jr. started his first job out of high school with the Northern Illinois Gas Company. He worked his way up, receiving a promotion to the level of a field engineer, but he remained deeply unsatisfied with his prospective career. He yearned for something more, and without a college degree, he felt one of the few paths to success would be starting his own business.[10] Born to a mother who immigrated from Greece and a Mexican father, the Portillo children quickly dropped the silent *L*s from their name in favor of a more Americana pronunciation—*Por-till-oh*. It was an early sign of the family's instinctive marketing genius.

Frank Portillo and his siblings lived their early years in a subsidized row house that was part of the Mother Frances Cabrini housing project. They grew up poor. Eventually, Portillo's father made enough money to move the family to a new neighborhood and plant more permanent roots in suburban Bridgeview.[11] This upbringing formed Portillo into a young man hungry for success. Sensing an opportunity, Portillo agreed to take the referral from his father and help his fishing buddy, a man more than twenty-five years his elder, with his restaurant renovations.

While still working full time during the day at the gas company, Portillo spent his nights and weekends laboring away at the Bridgeview Brown's Chicken. He marveled at the crowds that gathered at the restaurant day in and day out.[12] For Portillo, it became clear this could be an opportunity to make a smooth exit out of the utility business and become an entrepreneur.

Portillo approached John Brown with a proposition. For $1,000, he asked for the rights to open a second restaurant. John agreed, and when Portillo had trouble scrounging up a loan to start the business, John went a step further and arranged instead to form a partnership on the second venture. John Brown would quickly become a source of mentorship for Portillo, and the two embarked on an entrepreneurial journey.[13]

In June of 1958, the second location of Brown's Chicken opened in suburban Elmhurst, about fifteen miles northwest of the Bridgeview location.[14] Together with his wife, Joan, Frank would lead the operation and learn the ropes, from preparing the food to handling the accounting. Frank Portillo was enthusiastic, confident, and ambitious. John Brown was old and wise. Together, they formed a balanced team. And after the second restaurant proved to be a success, the pair decided to further expand their operation.

Scaling up provided a unique opportunity, and the two men were intrigued. They'd built their business by creating a slow but steady stream of reliable patrons, crafting handmade coupons, and frying up some damn good chicken. But Portillo in particular was keen on expanding. The two started by officially forming their company in 1964, Brown and Portillo Inc.[15] By that time, they had already earned a respectable amount of money, and John Brown began spending his winters in Florida. While snowbirding, he deferred to Portillo to manage the expanding business. On the side, he helped his brother Dick Portillo with an investment in a hot dog stand out of a twelve-foot trailer that they dubbed "The Dog House." It would soon be renamed Portillo's.

The owners of Brown's Chicken began by opening five restaurants with customers who'd approached them about their desire to expand the chain. Portillo and Brown retained a 52 percent ownership of each establishment.[16] They still had skin in the game and enough equity to ensure full control of the restaurants. Quality, consistency, and proper management were all key. Quickly, the business that had started off in a humble trailer parked near a farm exploded. People took notice, and the company was inundated with potential partners for new franchises. Business in those early days was handled through the power of relationships. No fancy sales brochures or slide decks, just person-to-person contact with potential franchisees.

The decision to franchise involves an entirely new calculus for a business. Franchising can be a sign of success and an indication the market wants more of your product. But franchising also creates great challenges. For Portillo and the Brown's Chicken team, it meant shifting their focus to things like training new operators on how to manage their business, raising brand awareness through advertising, and ensuring that the quality of their business was maintained. Simply put, the Brown's Chicken name would be on all the new restaurants, but the routine management of these establishments would mostly be out of their hands.

While the business was succeeding, the same could not be said of the union between Belva and John. Accusations of infidelity flew from both sides and the restaurants they'd built together proved not enough to sustain the marriage. In 1969, the couple divorced, with Belva giving up control of her part of the business. She would later take ownership of the original restaurant in Bridgeview and run it as her own, while her husband and his business partner would move the chain in a different direction.[17]

John Brown and Frank Portillo continued expanding well into the 1970s. Portillo hired new staff and worked from a corporate headquarters in suburban Oak Brook.[18] While handling the business, John Brown would fly back north to Chicago in the summers and, in Portillo's words, "raise hell."[19] Frank Portillo might have been in charge of the day-to-day, but John Brown was still part owner and the company's founder. Not to mention, it was his name on those restaurants, after all.

Profits soared. In 1974, the company had less than $9 million in sales. Just a decade later in 1983, that number reached $71 million.[20] Both men were now earning more money than they could have ever fathomed. And by 1987, Brown's Chicken boasted more than one hundred franchises.

Brown's Chicken remained a regional force, something the company insisted was to their advantage. Aside from a handful of locations in the Kansas City area and Florida, the chain focused on the Chicagoland market. They worried rapid expansion might lead to the company's ruin. "I can firmly write the names of 15 chicken chains that no longer exist," Frank Portillo once observed.[21] There was Minnie Pearl's Fried Chicken, which collapsed after an embarrassing SEC investigation. And Mahalia Jackson's, named after the Queen of Gospel who hawked "glori-fried" chicken in hopes of empowering Black entrepreneurs, which failed to turn a sustainable profit. Even Popeye's declared bankruptcy in 1991. By focusing on their regional strength, Brown's Chicken would grow swiftly but sensibly.

Year after year, Kentucky Fried Chicken remained their strongest competitor. During its early days, KFC was run by John Y. Brown, a coincidence that perfectly encapsulated

Brown's Chicken's perpetual silver medal status in the Chicagoland market.

Aside from the obvious, John Brown and John Brown had little in common. The John Brown who made Colonel Sanders and his eleven herbs and spices synonymous with fried chicken was a lawyer from a wealthy and well-connected political family who would go on to serve as governor of the commonwealth of Kentucky. The John Brown who spread Brown's Chicken franchises throughout Chicagoland was a self-made man who started by raising and plucking his own chickens.

Despite lagging in market share behind KFC, the Brown's Chicken restaurants were a model for other franchises. With homey vibes, vinyl tablecloths, and comfortable red booths, the brand's atmosphere was consistent. The chain's logo—a yellow stick-figure-like drawing of a chicken with a horseshoe-shaped bottom, wings peeking out on both sides, and a triangle beak—at first glance appeared ambiguous. On the second look, one might deduce it's a chicken. On the third glimpse, one might second-guess that second assumption. Whether or not customers actually knew the logo represented a chicken didn't matter, because it nonetheless became an instantly recognizable symbol throughout Chicagoland. It was the company's equivalent of the Golden Arches.

Even more recognizable than its logo were the company's advertisements that blanketed radio and TV waves.[22] An ad agency hired by Brown's conducted extensive research for their various ad campaigns, including running focus groups. During one session with consumers who were tasting fried chicken meals from other restaurants, the focus group facilitator asked participants why they preferred Brown's Chicken over its competitors. "It tastes better!" one of the attendees exclaimed.[23] And just like that, the simple-yet-straightforward response from an everyday customer became the slogan that would become synonymous with the company for decades to come. "*It tastes better!*"

In TV and radio advertisements, a catchy jingle would repeat those words in different formats, in different settings, and with a different cast of characters each time. A lead actor in one such Brown's Chicken commercial was a young comedian named Steve Carrell, an up-and-coming performer at the famed Second City Theater in Chicago. In 1989, TV producer Lorne Michaels and other scouts from *Saturday Night Live* came to Chicago to seek out new talent. But they were disappointed to learn that Carrell wasn't at the show they were attending that night at Second City. When they inquired, they were informed that Carrell had recently landed a gig filming an ad for a regional chicken chain, Brown's Chicken. Carrell had chosen the restaurant over his chance at landing a spot on SNL. He needed the money, and the ad was a guaranteed source of income over a not-so-certain chance for TV fame.[24] Despite missing a potential spot on SNL, his career would eventually pan out.

By the late 1980s, in roughly thirty years, Brown's Chicken had gone from a modest trailer equipped with deep friers to a bustling operation with over one hundred restaurants. John Brown and Frank Portillo, both starting from humble beginnings, had created a company that was quintessentially Chicago.

John Brown continued his life in the Sunshine State, operating franchises in Florida to keep himself busy, and reaping heavily on what he had sown. In time, he became more of a corporate figurehead than a manager. A mascot of sorts. While he was quick to be called on for interviews about the company or for appearances in advertising, a great distance began to grow between corporate management and the business which bore his name. His problems compounded in his personal life, too, as his children complained about his obsession with money and unshakable ego. To them, he was a man so poor that all he had was money. Never remarried, John Brown was now alone, and he began to feel a profound dissatisfaction with life set in.

Two days after Christmas 1992, John Brown wrote a final note to his family on a sheet of yellow lined notepad paper in pen. "A new finger of pain is creeping up my neck," it read. "I can see nature and God telling me that it is time for me to leave this troubled world. I'm so sorry," he wrote, underlining his apology for emphasis in a squiggly line that itself appeared to be a worrisome manifestation of his profound unease.[25]

A few days later, on December 30, 1992, eighty-five-year-old John Brown placed a gun in his mouth and pulled the trigger.[26] It was a tragedy. And yet, in just a matter of days, the unexpected suicide of its founder would be by far the *second* worst thing to happen to Brown's Chicken.

CHAPTER 2

LYNN & DICK

It was a church basement much like any other. The congregation used it for their usual functions—coffees crowded around folding chairs and card tables after service on Sunday, the occasional no-frills wedding, and programming aimed at students on campus from Bible studies to AA meetings. Surrounded by imposing stone academic buildings, the two-story church served as a refuge for students at the University of Wisconsin-Madison campus.

For Lynn Wiese, this unassuming spot at Wesley Methodist had a particularly important significance beyond the ordinary activities of church life. Many years ago, her parents had met in that very same basement as students.[1] It's said that history doesn't repeat itself but that it can rhyme. In that sense, life, which had brought Lynn to Madison as a Badger in 1961, was about to weave an unexpected rhyme into her own story.

Lynn was born in Clintonville, Wisconsin, a small town with less than five thousand residents roughly an hour west of Green Bay and the shores of Lake Michigan. The daughter of a lawyer who became a county judge and a homemaker who later became an elementary school teacher, her parents were always encouraging their three daughters to dream.[2]

Methodism was a central part of the Wieses' lives in Clintonville. The faith called for more than just perfunctory attendance on Sundays. It was church choir and Bible study. There were potluck meals and prayer. Plus lots and lots of volunteering. For Methodists, works of mercy are central—and the Wiese family was no exception. Feeding the hungry. Clothing the poor. Providing shelter to the homeless. As the name suggests, Methodism is about the methods—the action—not just talk.

Immersed in this altruistic attitude from her childhood, Lynn, with her quintessentially sixties cat-eye glasses and dark black hair that she wore in a bob, found a slice of home at Wesley Methodist.[3] She was a calm presence, always soaking in what others had to say in a genuinely interested way. She had empathy. And despite a faithful Christian upbringing, she was not doctrinaire about her beliefs in any way. Lynn was straight-laced and a rule follower, but she was open to new ideas, and Madison had plenty of them for a young person to absorb.

At Wesley Methodist, students gathered weekly at a supper club. It was the standard event found at many churches on campuses across the country, a chance for genuine fellowship and an opportunity to meet like-minded students who might otherwise be hiding among the crowd of indistinguishable faces in classrooms across campus.

Lynn mixed and mingled with Badgers at the supper club. And then, she had an encounter that was mostly unremarkable at first. Lanky, with a prominent nose, Richard Ehlenfeldt was attractive, but he was just another guy. Not to mention, Lynn was taken. Had she known the things they had in common, she might have better understood just how serendipitous that encounter would turn out to be.

Richard Ehlenfeldt also hailed from rural Wisconsin. The town of Columbus was roughly twenty-five miles north of Madison. There, his parents ran a laundromat business which they lived above for a time until they could afford a two-story standalone home in the area. They later moved to the town of Beaver Dam and opened a laundry business where clothes were cleaned on-site or delivered across town.[4]

One of two kids in the Ehlenfeldt home, most people called him Rich. And for the Ehlenfeldts, life was classic Wisconsin. Family was always not far by—cousins, aunts, uncles. Summers were spent working at the local Dairy Queen, doing odd jobs for neighbors, and on occasion, hunting.[5] Unathletic as a teen, Rich tried his hand at football too.

Rich Ehlenfeldt was smart enough to know early on that Lynn Wiese was unavailable, so things began as just an innocent, light-hearted rapport. On a mission trip crammed in the back of a car, they goofed around and were giddy, the kind of playfulness that precedes love whether a young person recognizes it or not. On campus, Rich walked Lynn home to her dorm room, waiting until she got inside and turned on the light in her window to signal that she was safe. It was the gentlemanly thing to do. Eventually, things went his way when Lynn broke things off with her long-distance boyfriend.[6] She fixed up Rich's name too—and Rich became "Dick" Ehlenfeldt on campus.[7]

As the state's flagship school, Madison was home to thousands of young students from across the Midwest. In the early sixties, the campus was a hotbed of activism, holding true to the moniker that some used to praise or deride it as the "Berkeley of the Midwest." When Civil Rights activists in Greensboro,

SOMETHING BIG

North Carolina, organized sit-ins at segregated lunch counters in the South, hundreds of students in Madison showed their support from miles away by picketing the Woolworth store on the nearby Capitol Square. As nuclear proliferation became a hot-button issue, students protested outside the school library against alleged new nuclear testing in Vietnam. And when the military draft began to be implemented, sit-ins were organized around campus in protest.[8] The decade was marked by grand displays of idealism, and universities like UW-Madison were the paragon of that trend.

Lynn and Dick shared many of the same cultural, moral, and religious touchstones. Both were born in small towns. They had similar religious upbringings. And they both found themselves immersed in the political ideals that some at the time disparaged as radical. To them, nothing was radical about fighting for a more just society. It was merely an extension of their lifelong understanding that they were called to do good as Methodists.

Some impassioned advocates are all talk, no action. But Dick and Lynn led by example. When protests erupted on campus, the couple joined in as part of the action. When an administrative building was occupied by students on campus, Lynn and Dick were there in the thick of it.[9] Things were happening in Madison, and there was a sense that they were living in an important moment in history.

Still students, Lynn and Dick's relationship blossomed quickly, and in 1964, they decided to elope.[10] The bright-eyed couple headed southwest to Dubuque, Iowa, where obtaining a marriage license on a whim was possible without burdensome paperwork and blood tests. They exchanged vows and took each other as husband and wife in a Methodist church just across the border from Wisconsin.[11]

Dick's family took easier to the elopement given his parents had wed the same way. Lynn's side, understandably, needed some warming up to the idea. Were they sure about getting married? Had they rushed into this? What about a wedding? For the family, such important life events were not to be done in haste. Eventually, things were smoothed over when the Wiese and Ehlenfeldt families met and became close.

Dick and Lynn resumed their lives as students, spending their first two summers together with his family in Beaver Dam and their days laboring at the local Green Giant canning facility.[12] Lynn finished her undergraduate degree in 1965 then pursued a master's degree in vocational rehabilitation; Dick paused his schooling to support them while she finished. The two became house parents for a time at a Baptist dormitory on campus during Lynn's final year.[13]

Eventually, they moved to the city of Oshkosh, Wisconsin, where there was another university campus for Dick to finish his studies. On the side, he worked with several Methodist congregations as a student pastor and deacon while Lynn devoted her time to social services.[14]

In November of 1968, racial tensions in Oshkosh reached a fever pitch. Mostly white, the town's residents had long faced prejudice in the city as demographics changed. When a group of nearly one hundred students began protesting these disparities, the campus erupted on what became known as "Black Thursday." While he finished the studies that he'd paused, Dick again became a student activist, eventually heading up the campus's chapter of Students for a Democratic Society, a group inspired by left-leaning causes and opposition to the war in

Vietnam.[15] Before things got out of hand, the local Methodist bishop encouraged Dick to be involved. As an older student who had credibility with the group, there was hope he could keep the demonstrations peaceful. And he did.[16]

Leading marches across campus, he dressed in a black suit, a uniform that betrayed the criticism of him and his compatriots as radicals. He pumped his fist and chanted with other students. He stood on soap boxes and gave speeches.[17] Lynn too met with campus leaders to try and find a solution to the problem.[18] Dick talked to the press and his name was splashed throughout newspapers and his face lit up on local TV which the Ehlenfeldts—staunch Republicans—could see back home. Nervous and slightly embarrassed at first, Dick's mother became proud that her son had kept the peace.[19] And eventually, the Ehlenfeldts became loyal Democrats because of their son's impassioned activism.

In July of 1969, Lynn and Dick had their first daughter, Jennifer, and decided to head east to Boston. There, Dick would pursue the seminary at Boston University School of Theology.[20] He was to become a Methodist minister, an aspiration he'd had since high school. In Massachusetts, Lynn ran a halfway house for women leaving the Framingham Prison located in the suburbs of Boston. Living on the second floor with parolees, they combined their love of helping others while also managing to stay afloat financially.[21] She cooked meals, took women to appointments, and coached them through their new transition to civilian life.

In 1972, their second daughter, Dana, was born, and the halfway house proved to be an interesting place to raise a child. On one occasion, Lynn's sister was helping babysit their two daughters. While Dick and Lynn were out, a woman appeared upstairs in their apartment with a gun and began yelling while the children slept. "Where's the money!?" the woman demanded while recklessly wielding her weapon. Lynn's sister calmly pointed her to the lockbox in the closet, then went to the other room to quiet down one of the crying girls.[22] The women left them unharmed.

As Dick knew well, man plans and God laughs. And what started as a mission to become a minister eventually was sidetracked when the seminarians were instructed to find a volunteer project as a learning experience. In 1972, the country was in the throes of a presidential election between South Dakota senator George McGovern and incumbent president Richard Nixon. Attracted to the populist candidate because of his strong opposition to the war in Vietnam, Dick found his project: working on McGovern's campaign. McGovern had also dabbled with becoming a Methodist minister, and the two had a lot in common.

Dick thrived in the fast-paced life of a campaign. He humbly boasted to friends that he was the highest-ranking unpaid person on the presidential campaign. Then, when he officially was placed on the payroll, he became the lowest-ranking paid person.[23] Despite the loss to Nixon, it was a formative learning experience for Dick that piqued his interest in politics and opened new doors. He left the seminary for a life in politics, viewing it as an even bigger opportunity way to make a difference.

After the presidential campaign, McGovern ran for re-election to the United States Senate in 1974 and the Ehlenfeldt family picked up and moved to South Dakota, where Dick would work on the senator's press team. That same year, Lynn had their third daughter, Joyce.[24] After the successful reelection in South Dakota, the family uprooted again to Rockville,

Maryland, just outside of Washington, DC, where Dick took a job in the senator's Capitol Hill office. But even among the halls of power, Wisconsin was calling, and Lynn and Dick's goal of returning home was finally made a reality when he received work in 1976 as a legislative staffer for the lieutenant governor, Martin Schreiber, who would later serve as governor.

As Dick pressed on with his political work, Lynn managed the home front and volunteered at places like the local Association of Retarded Citizens chapter helping differently abled youth. In the eyes of their girls, family life was like a scene from *Leave it To Beaver*. Hot breakfasts in the morning. Notes in the girls' lunch boxes each day.[25] Attending school field trips when parental help was needed.[26] Their mother, with her curly hair and big square glasses, cheering on the girls from the sidelines during soccer games—loudly, and often with a cowbell—each time they scored.

As parents, Dick and Lynn were complements of one another. Lynn was the nurturing caretaker, difficult to upset and rarely one to raise her voice. Dick was an advocate for his girls, had a sense of humor and a love of pranks, but also a bit of a temper. As the easygoing one, Lynn embraced the clutter that came with a life with three kids—piles of papers from school, messy clothes and shoes strown about. Dick, on the other hand, put a high value on tidiness, preferring things in order and in their place and sometimes trashing belongings the girls left behind if they sat idle for too long.[27]

For Lynn and Dick, raising daughters meant instilling in them a sense that they could do everything a boy could. When their oldest daughter was seven and they were living with Dick's sister in Columbus, Wisconsin for six months, parents were instructed in a letter home from the principal that a Memorial

Day parade would take place and each child would have roles. The boys were to carry small American flags, a sign of patriotism, pride, and strength. The girls were to carry flowers, a sign of meekness, tameness, and timidity. Needless to say, Lynn was incensed, and she went to chat with the principal, forcefully explaining to him the subtle but demeaning lesson he was sending his students. When the parade took place, the Ehlenfeldts' daughter and niece were the only girls carrying Old Glory. The next year, parade organizers made an adjustment—both boys and girls carried flags.[28] Even with the little things, Lynn and Dick endeavored to affect change.

In Wisconsin, Dick worked at all levels of government and politics. He'd been in the trenches of the campaign, living the life of a staffer with a trunk filled with yard signs and balloons, working nonstop to elect or re-elect the boss. When he staffed a chaotic and failed bid by Schreiber for governor of Wisconsin in 1978, he crisscrossed the state extensively and became close with Doug La Follette, the nominee for lieutenant governor.[29] A frugal politician, La Follette even moved in with the Ehlenfeldts, living in their basement and occasionally babysitting the girls so Lynn and Dick could have a night off.[30] Over the years, Dick would continue to do advance work for key figures in the Democratic Party including Bobby and Ted Kennedy and an overseas trip to Germany with Jimmy Carter.[31] Dick lived for the behind-the-scenes action.

With a family to raise, the couple had had enough of the chaos and instability of government and politics. It was a young man's game, in his view, so Dick took an executive-level job in government affairs at Group W Cable in 1979, a company based in Chicago.[32] At first a temporary position, Dick rented an apartment that he would commute to on Monday morning then head back north to Madison on Friday.

The arrangement, as it would be for any parent, was rough on Lynn.[33] Left to raise the kids alone during the week, friends and family would pitch in where possible. The girls bickered as siblings do. But Madison was home, and it was where the family wanted to remain after so many moves.

Dick's temporary job eventually became a more than two-year commitment of traveling back and forth.[34] *I think your parents are divorced*, friends of the girls would joke. But the family made it work as best they could. To keep up with the lives of the girls, Lynn would tape dinner-table conversations and give it to Dick to listen to as if he was in the room. They'd visit Chicago here and there, touring the city as a family and seeing the sites. And eventually, the decision was made to dispense with the back-and-forth and move the whole clan to Chicago.[35]

As expected, the move was not well received by the girls. The Ehlenfeldts had roots, and the daughters, with their eldest about to be a sophomore, were not pleased. To sweeten the deal, Dick and Lynn bought the girls a cat, breaking their long-held opposition to owning a pet. Dick did extensive reconnaissance on all the best suburban soccer teams so the girls would have a place to compete.[36]

Settling into Arlington Heights, a suburb northwest of Chicago, the Ehlenfeldts bought a four-bedroom, two-story house that was painted blue and situated in a quiet subdivision that would serve as their new home base.[37] It was the summer of 1984, and life as usual resumed.[38]

As in Wisconsin, the church became a center of their life in Illinois, and the Ehlenfeldts quickly found a community at the Kingswood United Methodist Church in Buffalo Grove. They convinced the church to participate in the local PADS program, which provided shelter for the homeless. Lynn helped with the local Meals on Wheels program, planning delivery routes about town. She put together youth camps in the summer. When a suggestion was made to spend money on upkeep for a cemetery, Lynn became comfortable enough in the church community to speak her mind. "I think this money needs to be spent on the living," she politely objected.[39] Others agreed.

Group W started as a stable job outside of the on-and-off work of government, but corporate restructuring led to layoffs, and Dick was out of work in 1989.[40] With their oldest daughter in college in Wisconsin and the two youngest in high school, it was a particularly painful period for the family. Dick searched for new roles, but it proved difficult finding a proper replacement at his level. He tried hard to find a plan to fix things, walking around the house at night stressed and agonizing over how to pay the bills. Months turned to years, and the strain on the family was hard. Lynn worked jobs wherever she could to keep the family afloat, including a role as a volunteer services coordinator at a local nonprofit.

Dick began pondering other avenues and started to do research about the restaurant business, an idea that had always piqued his interest. During their time in Oshkosh, Dick and Lynn had lived across from a diner that he worked at briefly.[41] The establishment fascinated him, and it was the perfect outlet for his implacable need to organize. He was always finding new ways to improve systems, clean messes, and better serve the customer. In one instance, he came up with a pay-as-you-eat pancake special for the after-church crowd. With this in mind, a lightbulb had gone off for Dick—mostly out of necessity.

SOMETHING BIG

The family looked into opportunities to purchase a restaurant in Wisconsin and move back north again, but knowing the business was unpredictable and harsh, they decided against it. Dick turned his energy toward the restaurant franchise business, a path they thought would provide more stability given a franchise has already shown proof of concept. Eventually, they came across an opportunity with Brown's Chicken, a fried chicken chain owned by prominent Chicago businessman Frank Portillo. There was an existing franchise in nearby Palatine (pronounced like Palestine without the "s"), a suburb bordering their hometown of Arlington Heights that had a somewhat absent and underperforming owner looking to sell. There was also an opportunity to open a franchise anew in Milwaukee, but the Palatine location was less risk given the built-in customer base.[42]

The Brown's franchise in Palatine seemed like a fit, so Dick and Lynn went ahead putting things in order. They borrowed money from family and scrounged up $300,000, a sum that represented their life savings—and then some.[43] It was a total leap of faith, but Dick felt excited by the opportunity to do something new. It was a chance to have something that was entirely their own, their small fiefdom, one of 115 plots in the Brown's Chicken kingdom.[44]

Once the deal was signed in May of 1992, the Ehlenfeldts became the proud owners of a new business.[45] Brown's Chicken corporate sent Lynn and Dick through a training process, showing them how to run the business, cook the food, and understand every aspect of their new livelihood.[46] They took it seriously, seeing openings in the catering business with hope to potentially expand to other restaurants if all went well.[47] As new operators, they were visited by Frank Portillo from Brown's Chicken corporate regularly, and the couple got to know the company's president as they got their business off the ground.

The location of their franchise sat in a large strip mall shopping center on an island by itself at the corner of two busy thoroughfares. It was a standalone, square building surrounded by other shops like an ethnic grocery store, a deli, and an armed forces recruitment center.[48] The Ehlenfeldts slowly made changes to the layout like a new counter and a self-serve soda machine.[49]

Lynn and Dick each had different skillsets that they brought to running a business. Reasonably handy, Dick was able to keep up with the unexpected hiccups that came with managing a restaurant, and his insistence on perfection helped keep things organized. The nurturer, Lynn had a knack for dealing with the employees, most of whom were teens. For her, it was a way to use her social work skills and mentor the employees. The workers they inherited from the previous owners were mostly teenagers, all paid the minimum wage of $4.25 an hour then $5 after six months, a surefire way to incentivize success.[50] The restaurant was chaotic, a constant source of stress with never-ending problems and needs. Mentoring employees was one of the few positive outlets for Lynn amidst the pandemonium. In contrast, Dick thrived on the energy. He loved the rush of customers and busy peaks that characterized their nonstop sixteen-hour days.

Running a restaurant provided the Ehlenfeldts with an income and new sense of purpose, and it also rooted them further in the community. They became engaged in the local chamber of commerce. They hired new staff from the local high schools. And they continued giving back.

One night, a nun entered the restaurant wearing her full habit with covered hair and a large cross draped around her neck. She approached the counter while one of their daughters was working. *I'd like to redeem these meals*, she told her, proceeding to present fifty coupons for free two-piece chicken meals. Dick explained to the nun that the coupons were an offer from the previous owner, and they were apologetic but simply couldn't honor them. But Dick had a solution. *How about we give you the leftover chicken each night?* he suggested. After that, each night a member of the Little Sisters of the Poor of Palatine would pick up the chicken or have it dropped off by someone at the restaurant.[51]

The franchise proved all-consuming, and the couple poured their heart into making it a success. Putting forth all their effort meant leaving other things behind. Lynn had long been the parent roaring on the sidelines at soccer games for her girls, but the couple missed the state championship game to tend to the restaurant. When their youngest graduated from high school, the Ehlenfeldts threw a graduation party at their home but were mostly absent, briefly stopping to drop off chicken and pasta and return to the busy restaurant to handle catering orders for other graduation parties.[52] The business was becoming a success, but more success meant more stress.

Perhaps nowhere was that stress made manifest more to their girls than around Christmastime 1992, about eight months after the restaurant had been open. The Ehlenfeldts took Christmas seriously. Each year after Thanksgiving, the family would go up to Wisconsin to be with aunts, uncles, and cousins and bake cookies. Thousands of cookies. Spritzes, sugar cookies, ginger snaps, pecan balls and everything in between. Throughout the season, it was a joy to hand them out to friends and colleagues on holiday trays. Dick decorated the exterior of the house with lights and Christmas wreaths. Inside he decorated with antique wax villages accompanied with mini yuletide carolers.[53]

But Christmas 1992 was different. When the Ehlenfeldts' middle daughter came home for winter break she was welcomed to an empty house. No garland or colorful lights. No Christmas villages or holiday tunes on the radio. Not even a tree. Things were just too busy at the restaurant, even for tried-and-true traditions. The boxes that housed the family's decorations sat untouched and collecting dust. *I'm so sorry we didn't decorate*, Lynn said apologetically.[54] The girls were more concerned for the stress their parents were facing, in particular their mother.

While her parents were busy laboring away at Brown's, their middle daughter, a senior at the University of Illinois, went out with her boyfriend and bought a big Christmas tree. She wrapped it in white lights and covered some branches with small red bows. It looked nothing like their usual Christmas centerpiece adorned in homemade ornaments marking life events, barely space to see the green—but it would do.[55]

When Lynn returned home from work that night, she burst into tears at the sight of the tree. She was exhausted, both mentally and physically. Keeping up with the day-to-day of the restaurant—the orders, the scheduling, the bookkeeping—was like trying to escape from quicksand. Through the sniffles and tears, Lynn was filled with joy again.[56]

For most of their lives, Lynn and Dick had taken care of others, always going out of their way to be as generous and caring as possible. Now, they were the ones struggling. But their daughters were Ehlenfeldts, after all. They recognized this. And perhaps there is no better testament to the strength of a person's parenting than how their children act in times of tribulation, both big and small.

CHAPTER 3

KRISTIN

Had she foreseen being tied up and forced into the trunk of her boyfriend's car, Kristin Lennstrom probably would have never dated him. Jim Degorski was boorish and combustible, but he could also be charming. For sixteen-year-old Kristin, his charisma was alluring, and the two began dating midway through her junior year in high school in May of 1991. Two years her senior and a recent high-school dropout, dating Jim was in some ways an act of rebellion.

A stoner, Jim found the rigid environment of Fremd High School in Palatine to be uppity. For most students of Fremd, the path was the same—finish high school, head to college or find a job, get married, and raise a family. Conforming to this rigid expectation proved less interesting for others. Jim Degorski had trouble paying attention in school and rarely did his homework. He found comfort in listening to heavy metal bands like Metallica, drinking to excess, and getting high with friends.[1] The moon-faced Jim was plain-looking. Six feet tall, he had a full head of brown hair that showed early signs of receding in the corners. A supportive mother might say he was big boned. Others would probably just say he was a bit chubby. He wore jean jackets and T-shirts, often a souvenir found at a concert he'd attended.[2] He could be extraordinarily cocky. *I'm gonna be famous some day*, he'd tell Kristin.[3]

The Degorskis lived in a split-level house on a peaceful cul-de-sac in suburban Hoffman Estates called Dover Court, the kind of name given by developers in suburban areas to zhuzh up an area otherwise lacking in character or distinction architecturally.[4] Jim was the second oldest of five kids. His father, William, was a schizophrenic. When Jim was in high school, his mother, Patricia, filed for a protective order alleging domestic abuse. Home life was chaotic.

Unfortunately for Kristin, her boyfriend had inherited many of his father's less desirable traits. Things started off affectionately. Jim could be sweet.[5] But he also had a trigger that would shift at a moment's notice. Some things just set him off.

One afternoon, Jim and Kristin were hanging out at his parents' house in Jim's basement bedroom. In a house full of people, Jim took his privacy very seriously. The basement was his own little curtain of solitude.

The day dragged on, and Kristin, with her wavy blonde hair, dark roots, and bangs that nearly covered her sky-blue eyes, decided it was time to go. *Can you drive me home?* she asked. Jim refused. Always in control, he didn't want her to leave just yet. The two continued hanging out when Kristin went upstairs from the basement to use a home phone and call Jim's sister for a ride. *Can you pick me up?* she asked, explaining to her friend that she and Jim, her brother, had been arguing. From the basement, Jim listened surreptitiously from an extension in his bedroom. When she hung up, he was furious.

The two began arguing. But Jim put an early end to things, punching his sixteen-year-old girlfriend in the stomach. The blow made her winded, temporarily unable to breathe. Kristin was stunned, but her misery was unfortunately only beginning. A furious Jim then proceeded to throw her down the six-step flight of stairs that led to his bedroom, later causing bruises all over her body.[6] When Jim's sister came home, the beating stopped, and she drove Kristin in her truck back home. She'd narrowly escaped her boyfriend's abusive wrath.

As the first instance of Jim's abuse, Kristin found simple explanations for his behavior. A manipulator always apologizes, appearing more sincere and sorry than ever. Then, he'd be sweet, the caring boyfriend who she'd fallen for from the beginning. In time, however, these occurrences grew more frequent.

Jim worked at a restaurant called Jake's Pizza, a delivery and by-the-slice joint located in a strip mall less than a five-minute drive from his parents' house. Also employed at the pizzeria, it was there where Kristin first met her boyfriend. As an employee at Jake's, Jim spent most of his time making pizzas, putting red sauce on dough, sprinkling mozzarella cheese about, then placing toppings.

Kristin and Jim had been dating a few months in 1992 when she was at Jake's where they both worked and to no one's surprise, they began arguing. Fed up, Jim led his girlfriend out the back door of the restaurant. It was the same route that workers took to bring out the trash or relax for a cigarette break, surrounded by dumpsters and overlooking a manmade retention pond encircled by prairie flowers and weeping willows. Just on the other side of the pond, Kristin's house was visible just yards away.

Jim closed the back door that led to the alley. Then, he punched Kristin in the stomach. It was a quick hit to the gut, an easy way to get her to stop talking and end an argument. For Kristin, beatings like these became more frequent and more violent.

Five months into their relationship, Jim took his own unpredictability to a new level when he and his friend Greg stole a car and brought it back to his parents' garage.[7] His friend wanted to swap transmissions with his car, but their mechanic skills proved faulty. When they couldn't put the stolen car's transmission back into place, they decided to break it up into little, tiny pieces and place each bit in a dumpster near a local 7-Eleven convenience store. They'd dispose of the car in the same way a cautious person rips up a check or credit card before it's thrown in the garbage. Except instead of a piece of plastic, the two men were hiding an entire motor vehicle.

When Jim's mother became suspicious of the activity in her garage, Jim and Greg fessed up. They explained that they'd stolen the car and were trying to cover their tracks. Leaving them with no choice, Jim's mother turned him over to the Hoffman Estates police where they admitted their wrongdoing and were charged with possession of a stolen car.

Jim's record included more petty crimes as well. When he received a traffic violation, Jim was summoned to appear at a Cook County courthouse in nearby Rolling Meadows. Kristin accompanied her boyfriend along with his friend Juan Luna, a fellow Fremd classmate in the same grade as Kristin. Always conscious of appearances, Jim wanted the two of them to join so that he'd look more wholesome.[8]

When they walked into the crowded courtroom awaiting Jim's name to be called to face the judge, there was no space for the trio to sit together. They were late. Faced with a decision to sit with Jim or Juan, Kristin squeezed into a row with Juan across the aisle. After facing the judge, the friends left the congested courtroom for the echoey hallway where Jim proceeded to punch Kristin again in the stomach. *What the fuck were you thinking?* he carped. Jim was angry she hadn't sat next to him. Standing immediately by, Juan did nothing to dissuade his friend's abuse.

Juan Luna and Jim Degorski met at Fremd High School in a vocational training program and became close buddies. Two years younger, Juan was more subdued. At 5'9", the Mexican-born teenager was shorter. Juan was also quieter than his friend. And yet, he also had a tough-guy side. He liked to brag to friends about owning a pistol and getting into fights before he moved to the suburbs.

After a year of dating, Kristin decided she'd had enough of Jim's abuse. In May of 1992, she penned her boyfriend a letter breaking up with him.[9] She believed that was the end of her and Jim. But leaving her shift one day at the daycare center where she worked, Kristin was greeted in the parking lot by Jim and Juan. Standing outside the driver's seat of Juan's black compact four-door, Jim begged to speak with her.

Kristin was totally uninterested and rushed to her car.[10] *I'm going home*, she insisted. *Please, let's just talk*, Jim begged her. After much prying, she eventually agreed to give Jim a ride home so they could chat. Juan left them alone. On the drive home, the two argued about the year they'd spent together. It was typical high-school breakup drama, except Jim seemed to really believe the end of this relationship was the end of something essential for him. He was simply not willing to let go.

When Kristin pulled into the driveway to Jim's parents' house, he told her to wait. *Just let me grab something, I want to keep talking*, he told her. When he hopped back in the car, he convinced his ex-girlfriend to drive by a new subdivision that was under construction where they'd have more privacy to talk. When they arrived and parked, Jim noticed a picture of another guy hanging from Kristin's keychain in the car's ignition. *Who the hell is that?* he demanded. She'd already moved on, and that enraged him.

You fucking whore, he screamed at her. Filled with rage, he punched Kristin in the mouth. She immediately sensed the iron taste of blood which began flowing. Petrified, she tried to escape and opened the driver's side door and put her feet out of the car. He reached over the console, grabbed the door handle, and began slamming it on her legs repeatedly, forcing her to drag her body back into the car where he continued raining blows upon her.[11]

Within a few minutes, Jim took her outside of the car and pulled out a roll of duct tape. He forced Kristin to hold her wrists together which he wrapped up, then opened the door to the hatchback trunk of the car where she sat down. He fastened her ankles together and forced her to lay down in the trunk, proceeding to put a piece of duct tape over her swollen mouth. He then had second thoughts about the necessity of covering her mouth, quickly removing the tape from her lips.

Kristin's vision was blurry from the hits she'd taken. *Don't move and stay down so nobody can see you*, he instructed her. He explained that he'd be taking her on a trip around the area to all of his friends' houses. They were angry that she'd broken up with him, he said, and wanted to hurt her even worse than he had. *I'm doing you a favor*, he insisted, saying that his friends would leave her alone once they'd all seen he'd beaten her up pretty bad and gotten what she deserved.

SOMETHING BIG

After closing the door to the hatchback, Jim returned to the driver's seat and began navigating. Huddled in the back, Kristin feared for her life. *He's going to kill me*, she thought. As he made turns and stops, she followed along in her head but eventually lost track of where he might be taking her. After a few stops where Jim went in and out of the car, she convinced him to let her take the duct tape off. *If you can get out of it, go ahead*, he said, offering no help. Using her teeth, Kristin gnawed the duct tape off her wrists to free her arms. She then pulled off the rest from her ankles and climbed in the back seat of the car.

Jim pulled into a dingy motel in rural Harvard, Illinois, roughly an hour northwest of Hoffman Estates and just five miles south of the Wisconsin border. *If you try to leave, I'll find you and I'll kill you*, he warned her as he left to use the phone in the motel office. In short order, he returned with a key. *The old guy at the counter was really nice and let us have a room so I can use the phone*, he told her. *Let's go*, he said. After all this, Kristin didn't know what to believe.

Inside the motel, he turned on the TV and flipped to the news. One of the segments was covering a local murder of someone Kristin happened to know. "I'm going to do the same thing to you," he warned, looking at her ominously.[12] The conversation again turned to their relationship, and Jim still wanted to get back together. Sensing this as a life-or-death discussion, she agreed. *You're right*, she assured him. *I'm so sorry, I never should have broken up with you*, she apologized with all the sincerity she could muster. Jim was assuaged by her contrition and finally agreed to let her go. But escaping wasn't as simple as just walking away. With her vision inhibited badly from the beatings, she asked him to drive her home, which he agreed to. During the hour-long drive back through the bucolic prairie surrounding

Harvard to suburban Hoffman Estates, Jim made sure Kristin had her story straight. *Tell your parents you got in a fight with another girl*, he instructed. She agreed.

As they got closer to home, Jim decided he didn't want to be seen dropping her off, so he stopped at the strip-mall parking lot of Jake's Pizza just around the corner from Kristin's house. After five treacherous hours, she was free. When Kristin frantically pulled into the driveway, her mother was waiting anxiously. Her daughter had never come back after work nor had she phoned home. Kristin's parents were horrified at what they saw. Their daughter had been battered and beaten. The next day, the family spoke with police and eventually pressed charges against Jim.

Because he was not caught in the act, the justice system took time to do its thing. Police needed to investigate and gather further information from Kristin. But even knowing the threat of police intervention loomed, Jim was undeterred, frequently threatening Kristin with the help of his buddy Juan. Occasionally, those threats came in the form of voicemails on her family's answering machine.

Juan: Hello, Kristin?
Jim: She answer?
Juan: No. Umm, I have good news and bad news. Good news is nothing is gonna happen to you.
Jim: Don't leave no threats!
Juan: What?
Jim: Don't leave no threats!
Juan: Oh.
Jim: Cool.

<u>Juan</u>: Nothings gonna happen to you if you drop the charges.
<u>Jim</u>: No, don't say...
<u>Juan</u>: Good. Just joking. Kristin, uhh, what's going on? Not much here. Have fun. Party.

The two men had a hard time heeding Jim's own warning not to make threats. In another voicemail, the intimidation escalated. "If they, if those bastards touch my friend or threaten him or his family or any of his friends, that's a bad motherfucker. Have you got that, bitch?" he yelled. "So you better lay off it. If you lie in court I'm gonna kick your fucking ass, you little ho," Juan continued. The intimidation extended to her family as well. "Man, I'm gonna get someone else to beat the fuck out of your family and your fucking mom and your brother and yourself, bitch. Especially your old man, I'll fucking kick his ass. Later, ho." Before Juan hung up the phone, Jim could be heard laughing from nearby.

In July of 1992, Jim Degorski pleaded guilty to misdemeanor battery, and his charge for felony unlawful restraint was dismissed.[13] Kristin's nightmare was over. Juan and Jim disappeared from her life after the ordeal was finished in court. Yet a feeling of insecurity still lingered for Kristin. She took the cassette tapes from her family's answering machine and put them in her dresser drawer for safekeeping. It was an indisputable piece of evidence should anything ever happen to them.

That same summer, fresh off a growing record, Jim learned of an enticing offer from a friend of his brother. The friend was looking to sell a stainless steel-colored .38 Smith & Wesson revolver with wooden grips he'd stolen from a friend's mom. Purchased legally at a gun shop in California, the woman was given the weapon by her ex-husband after they divorced. It was a source of protection for her and their son. She kept it in a shoebox, which her son showed off to friends on occasion. One day, her son's friend snuck into the house when no one was home, crept into the spare room where she kept it, and swiped the gun. Later, when the woman was cleaning her house one day, she noticed the weapon was missing, but she did not report it to police.[14]

The friend who had stolen the gun saw it as a liability and worried about the illegal weapon getting him in trouble. So he decided to pawn it off and make a few bucks, and Jim Degorski was an interested buyer. The two met at a White Hen Pantry convenience store to discuss, and Jim asked him about the gun. The Hen, as they called it, was a hangout spot for local kids, a place to grab candy, snacks, and cigarettes. *Can I see it?* Jim asked. The seller agreed to follow Jim into an undeveloped subdivision where they'd have more privacy. Jim approached the car window, and the friend reached under his seat and handed Jim the weapon.[15] Holding the gun, Jim was giddy. The friend threw in about fifty bullets for free. The fifty-dollar price tag was too much. "I'll give you fifteen now and the rest later," he haggled. Jim stiffed him on the remainder of the money.[16]

When he returned home, Jim went to his bedroom in the basement and put the six-chamber revolver on some crates next to his bed. Jim Degorski had no use for it just yet.

CHAPTER 4
RICO & MICHAEL

The 1980s and early 1990s were decades of great uncertainty in the Philippines. For Rico Solis, that turmoil was more than just an idea for historians or political scientists to analyze from a distance, but a reality that he'd seen up close. Growing up in Manila, things were changing all around him. Swanky condos and shiny office buildings sprouted up around the city as new investment poured in. At the same time, stark contrasts of poverty abounded.[1] Rolling blackouts sometimes left residents in the dark for long stretches of time.[2] A nation with a nascent democracy facing growing pains, there were periodic assassination attempts on the country's leaders and failed coups that threw the country into instability.

At the age of twelve, Rico Solis's father was stabbed to death in Manila.[3] It was a tragedy, a further mark of insecurity. That same year, his mother remarried and immigrated to the United States. Left behind under the care of their grandfather, Rico Solis took on an inordinate amount of responsibility helping care for his younger sisters Jade and Jizelle. He was their protector. So when his mother, Evelyn, was finally able to bring the children to America in May of 1992, Rico was thrilled. It was the place he'd read about in books and seen on TV. The land of opportunity people spoke of so longingly.

Acclimating to a new place would be difficult for anyone, but Rico Solis was fortunate to already have family who had preceded him. Living there now for five years, his mother and stepfather could help the three children better assimilate. Heading to America was a chance to do something new, an opportunity that excited the tall, rail-thin, jet-black-haired seventeen-year-old. The family lived in an apartment complex in suburban Arlington Heights, a three-story red brick building not far from a busy highway and open forest preserve. In comparison to Manila, the suburbs of Chicago were calm, far removed from a bustling metropolis. Yet for the naturally more shy and reserved Rico, the change of pace fit. He appreciated the new setting.

Rico was fortunate to have time to adjust, and the summer months of 1992 let him get acclimated for his sophomore year at Palatine High School. It was a new place with a new culture and a new language. But the mind of a seventeen-year-old is young and malleable, and Rico was up to the challenge. He played video games. He listened to alternative music. He watched action movies like *Die Hard*. Rico Solis did everything he could to adjust to life in America.[4]

The Filipino community in Chicago was tight knit. For many, it provided a source of comfort, a network of support, and the ability to be understood by others who'd undergone the same experience of immigrating to America. With a long history of immigration from the Philippines to Chicago, the community was robust and there were plenty of like-minded people to learn from both in the city and suburbs. Rico was trying his best to fit in, but his roots would serve him well almost immediately as he began his sophomore year.

Palatine High School had the traits typical of any high school in the early '90s. Think *Saved by the Bell* but if the characters had thick Chicago accents and wore winter coats. There were cliques, like the band kids, church goers, star athletes, and stoners. The style and clothing found in the hallways was no surprise—a mullet here and there or blonde highlights, baggy T-shirts and acid-washed jeans, and lots of neon colors as a sort-of holdover fashion statement from the '80s. To kill time, kids in Palatine went to the movies or the mall, hung out at fast food places, went to the football games to cheer on the Palatine Pirates or tried getting drunk while hiding from parents in basements across the city. For Rico, year one was about finding his place in this environment.

Each morning, Rico hopped on the bus and headed to Palatine High School, its hallways filled with strangers.[5] But almost immediately, Rico found comfort. He was placed in classes with a boy named Michael Castro whose parents had immigrated from the Philippines. Like Rico, Michael had dark black hair, thick eyebrows, and the kind of reedy mustache you'd expect of a sixteen-year-old kid. The two clicked immediately. In gym class, they became drill partners, forced to keep track of one another's reps and stay disciplined. In their social studies course, the two sat in the back row and had the opportunity to work on projects with one another in class.[6]

While the two boys shared similar ethnic backgrounds, they also had big contrasts. But opposites attracted. Rico was shy but driven. Still perfecting his English, Michael helped him master the language. In contrast, Michael was outgoing and gregarious, the kind of kid who said hello to everyone in the hall and joked around with his friends. No stranger to a dance floor, some buddies dubbed Michael Castro "MC"—like

MC Hammer—because of his confidence.[7] He was mature, the friend who was a favorite of the adults. Michael shoveled snow for neighbors in the winter. He'd chat up the elderly woman who lived down the block. And true to form, he wasn't too cool to ask an old lady sitting alone if she'd like to dance at family parties.[8]

Both Michael and Rico shared a desire to serve in the military after high school and a love of cars. They talked about saving money, suping up their vehicles, and what they might buy if cash were no obstacle. Michael's father had bought him a Nissan Sentra coupe which became his pride and joy, and he joined the auto club at school to learn more about how to care for his vehicle. A lover of music, he wanted a new stereo to blast tunes from in his room, so he worked nights as a cashier at the Brown's Chicken franchise, slowly working toward the purchase one shift at a time.

Michael was immensely proud of his work at Brown's and his hard-earned money. His bedroom at home had the normal trappings of a high-school teen—posters, like one of Michael Jordan and expensive cars including a red Porsche and black Lamborghini.[9] There were huge stereo speakers on which he'd blast music. But hanging most prominently on the wall was a framed dollar bill with his first paycheck from Brown's.[10]

Rico had expressed an interest in working, so Michael suggested his friend apply for a job at Brown's Chicken and he could help guide him. *How about I introduce you to the owners?* Michael suggested. Rico obliged, and just four months after coming to America he went through the application process.[11] New applicants came into the restaurant and filled out a form with the basics—name, past work experience, age, availability. They'd typically then be interviewed by one of the owners in a cushioned booth at the restaurant. Often that job fell to

Lynn Ehlenfeldt, who handled much of the scheduling and employee-related affairs.

In October of 1992, Rico Solis started his new job at Brown's Chicken in Palatine. He went through the normal training that all employees had to endure. He received an employee uniform and instructions on how to dress—a code the new proprietors actually enforced in contrast to the apathetic previous management. Rico met the other employees he'd be working with. He was walked through how to clean the front of the restaurant, where to stack dirty trays, and how to properly wash the dishes. There was a proper method for baking the restaurant's signature buttery biscuits which were always fresh, never leftover, and required a steady supply.[12]

Working shifts after school, Rico would start mainly by washing dishes and baking biscuits. Michael manned a cash register at the front, punching in customers' wholesome-sounding meal combos like the Farm Basket, Bounty Basket, and the Heart Basket. There were other popular items too, like the mushrooms (fried), gizzards and livers (fried), and onion rings (also fried). And of course, there were plenty of sides to keep track of as well, from fresh coleslaw and crispy French fries to creamy mashed potatoes and classic baked beans.

In the back of the restaurant, the older employees would do most of the prep work and cooking, coating chicken in flour and batter then hopping it into the deep fryer. Not to mention the pasta dishes that were popular for catering, an addition to the restaurant's menu in the '80s. The scent of the cottonseed oil was pungent and nearly impossible to get rid of, seeping into your clothes and lingering for hours. If you'd just left a shift from Brown's Chicken, chances are someone could smell you from a distance.

Aside from the pay, there were other perks to being an employee of the Ehlenfeldts. The couple gave their staff half off meals while they were working. The benefit had been slimmed down over time after some holdover employees from the previous owner took advantage of their generosity.[13] With a crop of workers that was mostly local high-school kids, overindulging in free food was to be expected.

Michael and Rico were fortunate to often work together along with other classmates from Palatine. The two talked about things happening at school, their classes, and made work in the restaurant as fun as possible. Occasionally, the boys would chat in Tagalog so others couldn't join in on their inside jokes.[14]

For Rico, the work wasn't all that fulfilling. He hated the grease smell that clung to his clothes and hair after work from the fryers.[15] He appreciated the money, using his first paychecks to buy a 1986 Dodge Charger from his stepfather and purchase new clothes.[16] Rico valued his independence. Still, he wanted something different, so he applied for a job at the local Menard's hardware store. Sensing he was unhappy, the Ehlenfeldts promoted Rico to the job of cashier and gave him more hours.[17] It was enough to get him to stay, and leaving Brown's would have meant he would no longer be working with his friend Michael.

By December, the semester ended and winter break began for Michael and Rico. Even for a teen, Michael took his Catholic faith seriously, and Christmas marked a reflective time of year. It also was a chance to spend some quality time with family without the obligation of school. The 1992 holidays were ordinary by most standards for the Castros. This year, there wasn't a ton of money for gifts or nonessentials, but Michael and his siblings made do. His sister Mary Jane always made it a point to bake Christmas cookies with her brother. The two were six years apart but still very close. They bickered about the kinds of silly things that seem important to siblings. They teased each other.

Baking Christmas cookies was a joyous tradition, but it was also a total mess. That was part of the fun. Flour would be strewn throughout the kitchen while they mixed together the ingredients for sugar cookies. They'd roll out the dough in different shapes, trying to get in the festive spirit. Michael took one blob of dough and put together a heart-shaped cookie. *Ohhh, is that for your girlfriend?* Mary Jane needled her brother. When they got tired of baking from scratch they'd dispense of the homemade routine and cut corners with a Pillsbury bake-and-break block.[18] Nobody would know the difference.

December 1992 marked the first Christmas and first major holiday in America for Rico Solis. He'd survived a semester in a new country and begun making new friends. He'd even found a job that was bringing him new money and independence. Rico rang in New Year's Eve with his family by attending mass at St. Edna's Catholic Church.[19] It was officially the beginning of his first full year in America.

Heavy snow blanketed Chicagoland in those early days of January 1993. For the adults trying to get to work and go about their normal lives, it was that unlovable quality of Mother Nature that they learned to tolerate. For kids on break from school, each heavy snowfall was like a winter miracle. And in the Philippines, Rico had never seen snow. It was his first time witnessing the joy of winter in Chicago, the season celebrated with snowballs, sledding, and hot chocolate.

During one snowfall, Rico and his younger sisters ventured outside their apartment complex and sat on the porch. They gazed at the flurries that began sticking to the ground.[20] The three of them decided to suit up in their winter gear and venture out into the open, trotting to a spot in the whitened lawn and playing around for more than an hour. They plopped down on their backs to make snow angels, rubbing their arms and legs back and forth to make the outlines stick.[21] When they hopped back to their feet, Rico and his sisters marveled at their creation. "Isn't this nice?" Rico asked, thoroughly enjoying this first-time experience. After a chaotic few months, he was finally getting the hang of life in America.

CHAPTER 5

MARCUS, LUPE & TOM

It didn't take long for Marcus Nellsen to know she was the one. When he spotted Beverly Goff in the Navy cafeteria where he worked in 1983, he approached her and asked her out.[1] She said no at first, uninterested in him and uninterested in settling down. But the chatty Navy cook persisted, and eventually she agreed to meet him out for dinner.[2] He was a talker and extroverted, the kind of guy who'd never met a stranger. Handsome with a cleft chin and rounded nose, Marcus liked to look his best, dressing well in his street clothes or when sporting his Navy service uniform.

Marcus was infatuated with his new girlfriend, and things moved quickly. After just two months, he proposed. Beverly said yes, and the two were married in San Diego, where they were stationed in November of 1983, exchanging vows at the picturesquely named Stardust Motel. The groom was twenty-three and the bride twenty.[3]

The Nellsens settled down in a small apartment in Ocean Beach, California, not far from the Pacific Ocean and an hour north of the US-Mexico border. The early years of marriage were smooth, with Beverly giving birth to a daughter, Jessica, in March of 1987. Fatherhood was a big shift for Marcus, and he was nervous about the daunting new task. The first time he changed his new daughter's diaper, he was terrified, so nervous about hurting his new angel and just wanting to do things right.

The Navy had been more than just a job for Marcus, and he was immensely proud of his service to his country. He'd been inspired to enlist by his uncle, Fred, who'd thrived in the Navy, viewing it as a gateway to opportunity like it is for so many young men and women.[4] The branch's unofficial tagline for new recruits—"Join the Navy and see the world!"—became a reality for him. It afforded Marcus the chance to travel the globe to far off places and spend his day-to-day perfecting his passion for cooking. As a high schooler in Tennessee, he enrolled in ROTC then enlisted at the age of seventeen.[5] His early service began with cooking for other enlisted members, providing three square meals a day to keep them fueled. He excelled, eventually cooking for some of the bigwigs on base. He'd later commemorate his service by getting an elephant tattoo with a Navy hat, a permanent reminder of the work that'd fueled his mind, body, and soul.[6]

Marcus could cook a meal for a crowd with ease, but whipping up dinner for his small family of three was a different challenge. Sometimes the food came out undercooked. Other times it was burnt. But he tried his best to adapt to serving three instead of three hundred. "No, no, it tastes great!" Beverly would say encouragingly.[7]

A desire to serve his country ran in Marcus's family, but so too did the scourge of alcoholism, a struggle that quickly led to troubles in their marriage. The drinking accelerated during his time in the service, and he'd underwent a brief stint in rehab the year before he met Beverly.[8] When returning to port during a deployment, he liked to let loose. Marcus Nellsen partied a little too much. And just a year after their daughter's birth and around the time he was ending his nine-year stay in the Navy, Beverly and Marcus divorced.[9]

The split was devastating for Marcus, and he blamed himself and the drinking for the breakup.[10] In time, he left California and headed back to Tennessee to be closer to his mother, eventually making his way back to his home state of Illinois. Marcus returned to the north side of Chicago, the place that'd always felt like home to him. It was where so many of his lifelong friends lived and where he loved to attend a ball game at Wrigley Field.[11] He quickly found work at a factory then an ice cream plant before it moved to another state. He was then hired as a cook in a suburban retirement home.[12]

There was physical distance between Marcus and his ex-wife and daughter, but there was no distance between them in his mind. Reconciling his past life was all he thought about.[13] He sent money back above what the alimony from the divorce required. He cut down on his expenses where he could, opting for a can of tuna or fast food instead of indulging in the freedom of life as a bachelor.[14] Marcus began working on himself, taking sobriety seriously after suffering from depression and getting real medical help in 1992 to kick the addiction.[15] He started attending Alcoholics Anonymous meetings and devoting himself to a rigorous twelve-step program.[16] He tried praying, reading the Bible, and began building up his confidence.

Marcus had been on the move more than he would have liked. He lived with his brother for a time when he first returned, then at two different YMCAs as temporary refuge.[17] Eventually, at an AA meeting one day in 1992, Marcus met a woman named

Joy McClain who he became close with. Quite a few years his senior, the gray-haired McClain had a proposition.

"Why don't you come and live out here?" she suggested. At the time, he was working at a retirement home in nearby Arlington Heights as a cook. "I'd feel safe, and it would help with expenses."[18] The move made financial sense, so Marcus moved in to a spare room in McClain's townhome. The two became close companions.

Without a car, Marcus' previous commute was arduous, requiring him to walk to the closest Metra station, hop on the train, then walk another few blocks.[19] Instead of slogging it every day, he decided to look for another job closer to home. Just a few blocks from the townhouse in Palatine with Joy, the Brown's Chicken at the corner of Northwest Highway and Smith seemed like a good fit. With a background as a cook, the Ehlenfeldts agreed that he was a match. And when they weren't around, they soon came to trust the retired sailor to man the ship.[20]

Marcus thrived at Brown's Chicken. He loved the people. He loved the work.[21] And he quickly saw Brown's as more than just a gig, but a career. Soon, he was on the management track. In January of 1993, he was set to start attending trainings at Brown's Chicken corporate, an opportunity that excited him despite the jest from other employees.[22] *Have fun at Brown's Chicken University!* the other workers would joke.[23] His focus, as always was on his now five-year-old daughter, Jessica.

At work, Marcus got along well with all of the other employees. He chatted with everyone, always wanting to learn more about their lives. But surrounded by high-school kids, he became particularly friendly with his colleague Tom Mennes, who was roughly the same age.

SOMETHING BIG

It was the second week of January 1993, and Tom Mennes had contemplated calling in sick for his upcoming Friday night shift at Brown's. "C'mon, let's go hunting!" his friend Dirk prodded him.[24] Tom was an avid bow hunter, but in reality, this hobby was more about being outside in the open air then getting a kill. On one instance when out with friends, he zeroed in on a clear shot of a deer in the foreground just twenty yards away. He loaded his arrow, then purposefully missed, shooting just above the target. He froze.[25] Tom couldn't kill—not a fly and certainly not a deer.

An identical twin, Tom was one of five kids in the Mennes family.[26] He was reserved and quiet, but not necessarily shy. Tom was just discerning about who he opened up to.[27] Some might call Tom Mennes quirky. Others eccentric. The thirty-two-year-old was slender, with his hair slightly thinning in the front and a horseshoe-shaped mustache. As a child, life had not always been easy, with his mother passing away from cancer when he was just fourteen. His brother John died from a heart attack four years earlier.[28]

Tom Mennes didn't drive, opting instead for a bulky black bike to get around Palatine when meeting friends to bowl a few frames at a nearby bowling alley or throw some rounds of darts at a local bar.[29] His aversion to driving was attributed to a moment he never lived down. Years earlier, he had taken his brother Larry's car out for a joyride, proceeding to crash it into his house.[30] After the incident, he vowed never to drive again.

The offer from Tom's friend to skip work was tempting, but he knew he was needed that night. "I can't," he told his friend. "There's something big going on at the school, so they're going to be shorthanded."[31] That big event was the cross-town rivalry basketball game between Palatine High School and Fremd.

Palatine's equivalent of Alabama vs. Auburn, Army vs. Navy, or Florida vs. Florida State. The excitement about town was palpable, and Brown's Chicken would no doubt be facing a Friday night rush as a result.

When he was in high school, Tom struggled. Academics were not his thing, and he never finished his degree. But he managed to hold down a job even as life threw new obstacles at him. He'd worked at a diner called Perkins Restaurant in Palatine as a dishwasher, only to show up one day to find the place closed. The restaurant had been sold, but nobody bothered to tell Tom.[32] He had a brief stint at a roofing company.[33] Tom tried working at other restaurants. He bagged groceries at the local Dominick's store, often helping elderly or disabled customers to their cars.[34] After so much change, the stability of Brown's Chicken was a relief.

The job at Brown's was a good fit for Tom. He worked as a breader, mastering the important art of dunking the restaurant's raw chicken into buttermilk then coating it with breading before the cooks tossed it into the fryer for a grease bath. That Friday night, Tom would be working with was forty-seven-year-old cook Guadalupe Maldonado, known as Lupe to friends and family.

Lupe had first come to America from central Mexico in 1975 when he was thirty years old, living in the northwest suburbs with siblings and working with his brother-in-law as a dishwasher at Ye Olde Towne Inn restaurant in suburban Mount Prospect, an establishment that served pub food, pizza, and often hosted live bands. For four years, Lupe and his brothers crammed into an apartment together, put in hours at the restaurant, and saved as much money as they could to send back to their hometown of Celaya, a city of about three hundred thousand surrounded by picturesque farmland and a stopping point for trains on their way to Mexico City. The family had a plot of land where they would spend their days working outside, often planting corn.[35] In Chicago, home was always on their minds, and the brothers joked with each other about heading back to Celaya to find wives.

The third of nine children, he was one of the older Maldonados, honing his skills in the kitchen as a child by helping his mother cook for the family. With a full house, life was always a team effort, and Lupe was used to hard work. When he moved to America, he started off washing dishes at the restaurant, then was promoted to a cook.[36] His reputation as a diligent laborer meant the owners did not hesitate when he asked early on if they'd hire his brothers. In the evening, he took English classes at a local high school.[37]

After four years in Chicagoland, Lupe and his brother Pedro decided to head back to Celaya. It was time to fulfill the goal of finding wives. Pedro found a match in short order, and it was her sister to whom Lupe took a liking. Despite an age gap, thirty-four-year-old Lupe and seventeen-year-old Beatriz clicked. Physically fit, Lupe had a square face and a clean mustache. When they married in 1979, Beatriz was pregnant with their son Juan Pablo, and two years later in 1981, their second son, Javier, arrived.

During this time, the Maldonado family lived on their farm near Celaya. The economy began to falter in Mexico, and sensing potential insecurity on the farm, they made the decision to return to the northwest suburbs of Chicago, again uprooting their lives. But the two brothers knew how to navigate life in America now, and they returned in 1982 to their jobs at the restaurant in Arlington Heights where Beatriz would also take up work. Lupe tried to be generous with others coming to the United States, lending friends money when he could and helping them find new places to live and work.[38] He'd been through it before, and he felt he could mentor others.

The Maldonados' days were filled with family time in Chicago. They'd gather for meals, celebrating birthdays and every life event of the sort. In the local parks in Palatine, the families would play soccer with one another on Sundays and meet up with friends. They'd begun to build a community of their own. But again, Mexico called, and when Beatriz became pregnant with their third son, Salvador, in 1987, they returned to Celaya and the family farm.[39] Beatriz was pleased about being closer to family and friends and a larger support system for her three kids. The couple raised their children at home near the lush hills of central Mexico and Lupe worked on the land. This peaceful pace of life resumed for about five years until the Mexican economy again weakened, prompting the necessity of another move back to Palatine to reunite with Lupe's brother Pedro, whose family had remained in America.

Travel with a family of five from Celaya to Chicago came with a hefty price tag. Conscious of saving money, Lupe was set on taking the bus, a nearly thirty-two-hour journey not factoring in stops or changes. With three kids, such a trip would have been miserable. So Lupe's brother Pedro suggested they fly instead and arrive in time for Christmas to celebrate their new reunion with family. Beatriz and Lupe obliged, borrowing more than $1,000 for the plane tickets and making arrangements to arrive two days before Christmas. They booked the tickets and boarded a plane, and just hours before Christmas, the family arrived at O'Hare Airport and were picked up by Pedro for the short drive to Palatine, where they'd stay until they found a place of their own.[40]

Having spent a small fortune on tickets, there was little money left for Christmas presents for the kids. So Beatriz and Lupe asked their oldest boys, ages thirteen and eleven, to sacrifice so their youngest brother could have a present.[41] The gift of family was more than enough for everyone else.

Lupe's plan had been to return to Ye Olde Towne Inn where he'd worked during his last stay in America and pick up where things left off. But when he went to inquire about a job, his old boss delivered him the news that there was no room, and he'd have to wait a few months until things picked up with summer festivals and other events.[42] It was back to the drawing board. He crisscrossed town, applying for jobs and putting in applications at half a dozen different fast-food restaurants.[43] Lupe was willing to work anywhere to support his family. Except, perhaps, a Mexican restaurant. He laughed at the cuisine from his home that he found in America, finding it to be totally inauthentic. Tasteless salsa that looked more like water with red food coloring. Steaming plates of fajitas that customers ogled at as they were plopped down on their table. Rubbery yellow queso.

What's more authentically American, on the other hand, than fried chicken? The father of three applied for a job at Brown's Chicken in Palatine and met with one of the owners, Lynn Ehlenfeldt. She took a liking to him instantly. In a place surrounded by immature and often unreliable high school kids, she appreciated that he was older and more mature. He had extensive experience cooking in a restaurant, which was a huge plus. And while his English wasn't strong, he spoke enough to get by, having honed it living in America in the past. On the nights he wasn't working at Brown's, Lupe also put in shifts at a local pizzeria in Palatine where his brother worked.[44]

Lupe Maldonado was hired by the Ehlenfeldts shortly after Christmas 1992. He learned the ropes at Brown's—how to fry the chicken, where to find the right boxes for the two-piece versus four-piece meals, the proper method for the pasta dishes that were popular for catering. Lupe had returned to the kitchen, back in his element. Fast food was different than a full-service restaurant, but it would do for now.

His first week of work started on the day shift. This week, he was working the dinner rush and he'd agreed to cover a shift for another seventeen-year-old worker at the restaurant. In the apartment, Beatriz and Lupe ate a late lunch—pork ribs—with his brother and sister-in-law. He then played with his sons, teasing them and roughhousing. Then, just before 4:00 p.m., it was time to head to work. *Los quiero, chicos*, he said to his sons, kissing them goodbye. *Nos vemos!* Lupe and his brother both headed off to work.

Friday was payday. It would be the first for Lupe, and it couldn't come quick enough.[45] He was hoping to start paying back his brother for the plane tickets. The $230 paycheck wouldn't quite cover it, but it was a start.[46]

Rico Solis came in that day like so many others to pick up his paycheck after school. Like Lupe, he hadn't been on the schedule that night, but he picked up a last-minute shift from Casey Sander, a girl who he went to high school with and often worked alongside on nights.[47] Michael Castro came in to work the cash register, and when his sister called him that afternoon and tried to get him to ditch and come to a party instead, he insisted.[48] Lynn Ehlenfeldt hadn't been scheduled to work, but obliged when her daughter Dana asked her to fill in for her shift so she could have dinner with her boyfriend and his parents.

Throughout the night, things were busy as anticipated. Customers came in and craned their neck upwards toward the menu to order chicken dinners to dine in. Others came in for takeout to bring home a bag of hot chicken for the family. The clicking of the pop machine they'd installed could be heard throughout the night, filling drinks for thirsty customers. Metal fryer baskets were lifted up and down with chicken and sides, with the food then placed under the hot lights that separated the kitchen from the registers. The cash register had a microphone stiffened straight that employees used to shout orders and was covered in a placard promoting half-priced cold chicken. Staff in the front grabbed orders from the metal slots behind them as the meals magically appeared from the back, then placed them on green trays with paper Brown's Chicken liners. Lynn and Richard Ehlenfeldt were busy all throughout the restaurant, filling in gaps and doing office work in the back.

The pace slowed as the night crawled closer to the 9:00 p.m. closing time and temperatures outside dropped. The Ehlenfeldts and their five employees began their routine as final customers finished their meals. The last remaining customer was a woman accompanied by two men from the Little Village residential home for people with disabilities. She was caring for two residents who were both in their thirties, nonverbal, and in wheelchairs. Outside, the van from the home was the only vehicle left in the Brown's Chicken parking lot other than employees' cars. When the three of them finished, the woman wheeled each man out of the restaurant with one hand each, then loaded them into the back of the van with the heater on full blast and strapped them in safely.[49] Needing a little caffeine jolt, she retraced her steps back into the restaurant to order a cup of coffee, which she took with cream and sugar, using a black plastic coffee stirrer to swirl it around then toss the refuse in an empty garbage can with a swinging door that had just been replaced with a fresh liner. She hopped in the van, then drove the residents back to the facility.

With the restaurant empty, the closing routine commenced for all seven people gathered, a symphony that operated with precision, each employee knowing their precise place. Dozens of trays were gathered from atop the garbage cans and on tables and thrown in the sink, sprayed down with a hose, then patted dry with a towel.[50] Rico Solis began mopping up. The tables were cleaned with soap and water from a spray bottle.[51] The countertops and booths were wiped. Lupe Maldonado cleaned the deep fryers. Garbage was taken out back to the dumpster and bags were replaced in the cans. Lynn Ehlenfeldt counted up the cash haul from the night, sorting through the stack of receipts, with a key hanging on a coiled loop wrapped around her wrist.[52] Dick Ehlenfeldt and Marcus Nellsen started loading food back into the cooler and taking inventory.[53]

As the process continued, two men arrived outside the double glass doors at Brown's. The restaurant made it a habit to serve customers even after the doors were locked if there was still chicken under the heat lamps. So the two young men were let inside the restaurant. One of them approached the counter and ordered a Hearty Basket, a four-piece chicken meal. With his food on a green tray, he walked to a booth in the corner of the restaurant and met his friend who was sitting alone. Around them, the five employees and two owners of Brown's Chicken in Palatine continued their closing routine.

CHAPTER 6

EILEEN

To the rest of the country, Chicago pizza evokes images of heavy deep dish with mounds of gooey mozzarella, a single piece enough to sustain you for a meal. To those who live there, however, the iconic dish is more of a rarity. Chicagoland residents' Friday night go-to pie is tavern style, a thin pizza with a crispy cracker crust that's buttery and adorned with toppings. Each pizza is cut in squares—not slices—a method that somehow seems to make things go further. A culinary optical illusion.

In the northwest suburbs, everyone had a reliable pizza shop they could count on. There was Rosati's, a staple and tasty enough to get the job done. Or Lou Malnati's, a trustworthy name. Those daring for a more decadent pie might have ventured to Barnaby's, with its delicious crust and old-timey feels.

For many of the locals in Hoffman Estates, that dependable spot was Jake's Pizza. The name *Jake* is not exactly one that rings "great pizza," but the restaurant's steady stream of customers would beg to differ. The Jake's in Hoffman Estates was nothing out of the ordinary, one of multiple franchises in the area located in an otherwise dull strip mall off busy Algonquin

Road. Yet the owners of this franchise took particular care of their business, helping it stand out from others.

Pat and Reg Kroll were a husband-and-wife team. A skilled cook, Pat added new menu items aside from just pizza—homemade soups simmering in the back kitchen, baked lasagna filled with melted cheese and meat sauce, and fish entrees for lighter fare.[1] At Jake's, there was something for everyone, and the Krolls tried to make their franchise into something more than just a takeout joint in a strip mall.[2]

Jake's Pizza was a gathering spot. Coaches took their little-league baseball teams for a slice after a game. Local parent-teacher organizations met up for monthly meetings over cold beer. Hungry high schoolers stopped in to satisfy their cravings, both the kind that is innate in every growing youth and the kind that stalks a stoner with the munchies after toking up.

Like many restaurants, working at Jake's Pizza was a popular first job for high schoolers. There were cooks needed in the back to prep the food and put together pizzas at a moment's notice. Delivery drivers kept the orders coming out the door. And waiters in the front of the restaurant served those dining in at a small collection of tables.

For a group of stoners from Fremd High School in Palatine, Jake's was the perfect spot to work. Owned by the parents of their friends, they had some freedom that wouldn't exist working for strangers. The group could commiserate there about the horrors of high school life and hang out when not working. Many stayed working at Jake's even after finishing high school. Together, the group dubbed themselves the "Pizza Burns."[3] Nineteen-year-old Eileen Bakalla was a proud member of the Pizza Burns.

Eileen started working at the Hoffman Estate's Jake's location in high school as a waitress, also doing prep work and filling in other duties where needed. Her routine usually began by opening up the kitchen in the afternoon, then waitressing at night. Among her friends at the restaurant was Jim Degorski, who started the same day as her.[4] The two had been close for a while, first meeting four years earlier in 1989 on the school bus when she was a sophomore and he a junior, and their relationship took off when they started together at Jake's.[5] They became best friends. And Eileen would hang out in Jim's parents' basement along with people like Juan Luna, the Kroll kids, and other Pizza Burns.

The two friends understood one another. Like Jim, Eileen was a little rough around the edges, sometimes crass. Her curly brown hair helped soften her up in comparison to her friend. The two smoked pot together on an almost daily basis. They'd hang out in the forest preserve, chill by a local dam, and drive around to kill their free time, the kind of free time that gets wandering youths into trouble. For Eileen, Jim was also a love interest.[6]

It was just another Friday night for the employees at Jake's Pizza. Orders were called in around the clock as delivery drivers came in and out shepherding pizza in insulated bags. Diners placed their orders and sat down at tables adorned with parmesan cheese and red pepper flakes. Waitresses picked up empty plates and cleaned up tables for the next rush of customers. During lulls, employees listened to music and chatted or played video games.[7] Eileen waited tables during her late shift, well past dinnertime.

At 9:30 p.m., Eileen put her time card into the machine and punched out to finish her shift. But Jake's was more than just a work environment, it was a hangout spot. The other employees were her friends, not just colleagues. The Pizza Burns stuck together. So Eileen waited for her friends to finish up working, playing darts as others readied themselves to depart for the

11:00 p.m. close. Outside, a full moon peeked in periodically from the scattered clouds in the dark sky and the snow still laying on the ground hardened from the frigid cold.

A few minutes before 10:00 p.m., the phone rang behind the counter. *Eileen, it's for you!* one of the other employees said.[8] Eileen walked to the phone. *Hello?* she asked. On the other end of the line was her friend Jim Degorski. *Come pick us up at the Jewel in C'Ville*, he told her, instructing her to meet at the grocery store in a nearby suburb. "We did something big," he said nondescriptly.[9]

Without delay, Eileen put on her coat and ventured outside into the frozen night and went to her car. The twenty-minute ride was ordinary, passing through the dark forest preserve and busy roads only to make her way to another unimaginative suburban strip mall filled with snowbanks from the plows that had cleared it that day.

When Eileen arrived at the parking lot in front of the grocery store, she saw Juan's black compact four-door Ford Tempo and parked next to it. The parking lot was lit with overhanging light posts. When she approached, Eileen noticed green rubber gloves and a canvas bag like the one used at Jake's Pizza to carry cash from the register. *What's that?* she asked. Juan and Jim explained to her what they meant by "something big." *We robbed the Brown's Chicken*, they boasted.[10] It was the same restaurant where Juan had worked months before, a place he had an understanding of as a former employee. He knew the layout, how much cash was on hand, and where the owners kept their money. It was an easy target.

Juan and Jim packed up their things then climbed into Eileen's car. *Let's go to your place*, they told her. The three pals embarked on another journey thirty minutes south where Eileen lived with her friend in the nearby city of Elgin. Her roommate was out of town that weekend, and her absence provided them the privacy to discuss what had just occurred.[11]

When the three friends arrived at Eileen's townhome, they entered and headed to her bedroom upstairs. Things started off like a normal hangout session on any regular day. The guys chugged light beers while Eileen sipped on wine coolers. Around them were her roommate's cats who they played with as they meowed and meandered about. As the clock approached midnight, they packed a bowl with weed and passed it around. Then another one. And another one.

Finally, it was time to discuss business. They took the canvas bag full of cash and dumped it out on the floor, counting their haul from Brown's between them. In total, it was $1,800. They divvied the money up, skimming a little off the top for Eileen. *Here, I owe you this*, Jim said as he handed Eileen $50. She accepted the stolen loot.

Eileen, Jim, and Juan continued relaxing as the night crawled on. Worried about covering their tracks, they hatched a plan for how to clean Juan's car. The next day, Jim and Eileen would take it to a car wash for a proper suds.

After about three hours at Eileen's townhouse, it was time to leave. Trudging again through the snowy sidewalk, the trio piled into Eileen's car and headed back to the grocery store parking lot in Carpentersville. As she'd done hours earlier, Eileen drove another thirty minutes with her two pals who'd just professed to robbing a fast-food restaurant. It was late, and the roads were mostly empty. When they arrived, Juan got out and headed back to his Ford Tempo, while Jim and Eileen decided to drive back to his parents' house and spend the night.

With Eileen behind the wheel, Jim asked his friend to drive past Brown's. He wanted to show off what they'd done. As they approached the corner of Smith and Northwest Highway, there was a faint glow of flashing lights. When they passed the corner, the ominous signal of first responders came into view—police, fire, and paramedics. The parking lot was full, and people were gathered around the building. *We did a little more than rob the place*, Jim confessed.

***

It was getting late. Evelyn Urgena watched TV, fast-forwarding through the VHS tape she'd rented for her son, Rico. *Batman Returns* had been released on VHS just a few weeks earlier, and watching movies was one of the few comforts he had when he wasn't working or studying. Rico was constantly on the go.

As the night drew on, she began feeling uneasy. "Can you get me a glass of water?" she asked one of her daughters. Uneasiness turned to the kind of fear a parent can sense but is loath to verbalize, as if expressing something aloud would will it into being. "There's something wrong," she said to the girls. That night, Evelyn Urgena did not fall asleep.[12]

***

As the owner of a small silk-screen business, Manny Castro worked long hours. On Friday morning, he'd left his house at 4:00 a.m. before dawn to get ahead of his day. That afternoon around 3:00 p.m., he received a call from his son, Michael, after school. "Remember what I told you," he demanded of his son. "I'll be home on time," Michael said, acknowledging his request to return quickly from his job at Brown's Chicken after he was

SOMETHING BIG

let off. Manny told his son he loved him. "Love you too, Dad." Then they hung up.

When Manny Castro arrived home that night, he was exhausted. He and his wife, Epifania, a nurse, ate dinner, then he retreated to bed early. But by 10:00 p.m., Michael was still not home, and Epifania was stewing about the house, worried sick. She waited, knowing that the restaurant had closed an hour ago and there was probably a simple explanation. Then around 11:00 p.m., she gave up, entering the dark bedroom and waking up her slumbering husband. "Michael isn't home yet," she nudged him.[13]

Still groggy, Manny decided to venture out and search in the bitter cold dressed in boots and a heavy jacket. The streets of Palatine were desolate. On his drive to Brown's, he peered at each car that passed him by in the dark, hoping to catch a glimpse of Michael. He pondered scenarios in his head, like that his son's car broke down or was unable to start in the cold. He turned on the radio and listened to a newscast. As he turned into the parking lot around Brown's at Smith and Northwest Highway, he saw his son's Nissan Sentra. Snow covered the windshield. Manny got out and peered into the car, trying to open the doors. He then looked into the restaurant, seeing no one. He knocked vigorously on the doors but received no response.

With no sign of his son, Manny Castro returned home. "He's not at the restaurant," he told his wife. Together, they ventured out again, driving around Palatine aimlessly, hoping for any clue. "This isn't like him," Epifania worried. By 1:00 a.m., the Castros decided to call the Palatine police.

With Michael missing for only a few hours, it was too early to file a missing persons report, but the Palatine police sent a squad car to the restaurant. "No sense sitting here," Manny told his wife after they hung up. "Let's go to Brown's Chicken."

***

The driveway in front of the Ehlenfeldts' home in Arlington Heights was covered in fresh snow. It was untouched. No tire tracks, no footprints. And when Dana Ehlenfeldt pulled into the driveway, she saw no other sign of her parents.

It was late, well past midnight and well past their normal return home. That night, Dana had swapped a shift with her mother so she could have dinner with her boyfriend and his parents. Thoughts popped into her head, like perhaps her parents had a particularly successful night and went to celebrate. Or maybe it was something worse, like her dad having a heart attack.

When she arrived at the door, Dana was greeted by her grandmother, who was anxious. *Your parents never came home*, she said. They tried calling the restaurant to no avail. Around 3:00 a.m., Dana and her grandmother put on their coats and got in the car.[14]

***

The phone rang and rang at Brown's Chicken, but no one answered. Beatriz Maldonado hung up. Her husband was typically home by 10:00 p.m., and he was nowhere to be found. *Es tarde*, she said to her brother-in-law Pedro. *¿Dónde está?* Pedro decided to head to the restaurant and look for his brother at around 1:30 a.m.[15]

When he arrived, he spotted the Dodge Charger he'd lent his brother in the parking lot along with other vehicles. As he drove around, a police car appeared, pulling up beside him and motioning him to open his window. "What are you doing here?" the police officer asked him.[16] Pedro responded in English, trying hard to get his point across. "My brother did not come home from work," he said. The officer was unfazed. He was used to dealing with these sorts of calls. People were always worried when they spoke to a police officer, always insisting that their problem was the one that merited immediate attention. "Now go home," he told Pedro. "He's probably out drinking or hanging out." Pedro headed home and told the family what he'd heard. They all knew Lupe was not a drinker.[17] Not one to dart off from his family. With his sister-in-law, wife, and each couple's kids, they decided to stay up and wait.

***

Jerry Mennes startled awake suddenly. It was the kind of wake-up that disorients you in the middle of the night. He looked at the clock, and it was around 1:00 a.m.[18] Next to him in bed, his wife, Diane, was sleeping peacefully.

Perhaps it was just your average trouble falling asleep or a bad nightmare. Or perhaps it was something heavier weighing on him, like the anniversary of his mother's death from cancer eighteen years ago.[19] At the time, he and his twin brother, Tom Mennes, had been only fourteen years old, just starting their formative days of high school. The twins had grown up since then, but such a loss never faded.

Jerry fell back asleep.

PART 2

"Yet I was myself in no way prepared to accept this news as final: there was a level on which I believe that what had happened remained reversible...This was the beginning of my year of magical thinking."

Joan Didion, *The Year of Magical Thinking*

CHAPTER 7

JANE

Officer Ron Conley perused the outside of the Brown's Chicken restaurant on what was now Saturday, 3:11 a.m. The exterior of the building was brick that was painted eggshell white and blended in with the snow. Hanging from the end of the roof's green awnings that slanted downward hung plastic American flags that flapped in the wind. The Brown's Chicken lettering faced south on the street, its *R* missing. The doors to the front of the restaurant, the customers' entrance, were locked. Conley peered through the windows of the eatery, which was dark, trying to glean anything he could from what appeared to be an empty store.

Conley made his way around the back of the restaurant toward a green back door. He tugged on the door, and it opened. Officer Conley was responding to a call by himself, but he was not alone. Just behind him, a father who claimed his son was missing followed.

Officer Conley poked his flashlight inside to get a look. Immediately, he noticed a mop that appeared bloodied on the handle. *I need backup*, he called into his radio. "Back off!" he instructed the man trailing him. This was a crime scene.

Inside, the worried father caught a glimpse of his sixteen-year-old's winter jacket hanging from a coat rack.[1] Soon, additional help arrived for the officer to cover him as they searched the restaurant.

Officer Conley and Officer Kurt Saxsma entered the door with guns drawn. The two men were crouched low, prepared for anything. Inside, there were a few lights on, but it was dark. The faint glow from street lights and nearby businesses provided little clarity. Christmas decorations were still hanging around them.[2] Fans turned.[3] Gripping their flashlights, the officers guided themselves around cautiously. As they approached the kitchen, the heavy door to the walk-in freezer was slightly cracked open. A foot and arm was poking out.

Conley pulled his sidearm, again approaching guardedly.[4] The two men looked inside the freezer and were horrified by what they saw. *Jesus Christ*, one of them uttered in alarm. It was a mass of bodies, tangled up inside surrounded by shelving units full of food supplies. Some of the bodies were face down, others face up. Crammed in such a small area, it was hard to tell just how many were in there. The floor was covered in blood. A jug of frozen gravy had a bullet hole in the front. Some of the victims' eyelids were still open, staring back at the officers as they felt the cold air from the freezer breeze past them.

Saxsma and Conley exited the kitchen area, making their way to the bathrooms—one male, one female—and cleared them of any suspects. They checked under the tables for any signs of life, and then a call went out to other officers. "Code One, report of four people in the walk-in freezer at Brown's Chicken, 168 W. Northwest Highway," the warning went. "Unknown whether they are breathing or not."[5] There was no immediate sense of how long the bodies had been there.

All across Palatine, more officers made their way toward the intersection of Smith and Northwest Highway. It was all hands on deck for the suburban department. Another officer, Sergeant Bob Haas, arrived at the scene and entered the building. The three men regrouped in the kitchen, searching through the food preparation area for other signs. Noticeably, the restaurant was clean. There was no food on the counters or dirty dishes laying around. The garbage cans had been emptied.

As the three officers continued their search of the restaurant, they noticed a walk-in cooler just outside the kitchen with the metal door handle broken off and laying on the ground. The door was closed.[6] Sergeant Haas approached, opening the door as the other two men covered him with their guns. Inside he found two additional bodies, both men. One man's glasses were broken on the floor. There were bullet marks through the plastic strips meant to keep the cold inside. Officer Conley checked for a pulse, confirming that both men were dead.[7]

The building was empty. Whoever had done this had left hours ago. The lights appeared to have been shut off using the circuit breaker in the back of the restaurant. An analog clock, its glass broken, was stopped at exactly 9:48 p.m.

Sparing no time, the officers began securing the scene. Officer Saxsma was tasked with starting a crime scene log of everyone that came and went.[8] Officer Conley left the restaurant at around 3:30 a.m. and assisted another colleague unfurling crime-scene tape around the parking lot. Paramedics and fire finally arrived, and about a half dozen first responders entered to check for signs of life. For some of the fire and paramedics, it had already been an eventful day responding to a house fire earlier that evening.[9] Outside, with the sun still hours from rising, a TV news cameraman had already arrived and began filming the police activity in the parking lot. Word was spreading fast.

It didn't take long for crowds to gather. Additional family members arrived in a frantic search for any sign of their loved ones. Employees of the Ehlenfeldts came to see which friends and colleagues had survived. Reporters arrived ready to ask questions. Cars were sitting in the lot gathering frost on their windshields—Michael Castro's Nissan Sentra coupe with Marine Corps stickers on the back, Lupe Maldonado's beat-up Cutlass Ciera borrowed from his brother.[10] Some sat in the snow weeping. Others wandered aimlessly, a thousand-yard stare painted on their face. "That's my only son! My only son!" the mother of Rico Solis screamed as her husband wrapped his arms around her, with snow falling in her face.[11] Officers hadn't confirmed the deaths officially, but it wasn't hard to deduce who had been killed from the signs all around.

Law enforcement instructed the families of those gathered to head to the Palatine police station and wait for more answers. In short order, local hospital chaplains were notified to help guide the families through the process and help deliver the news. "If you haven't heard from him by now, you can probably expect the worst," one of them told a worried family member still holding out hope.

Inside the eatery, processing of the crime scene had already begun. Officer Saxsma videotaped the restaurant with a camcorder, capturing the clean and untouched front and kitchen, the lights cut off from the circuit breaker, and the horrendous scene in the cooler and freezer. Each person that entered was recorded. Phone calls were made to the chief of police and others, waking them up with the horrible news.

SOMETHING BIG

Around 5:00 a.m., the phone in the restaurant rang. Officer Bob Haas picked it up. *Hello?*, he said. *Hi, I'm calling from WBBM News Radio*, the voice inquired. *We received news on the police scanner that there's been bodies found at the Brown's Chicken location in Palatine and—* Haas hung up the phone.

It was an early sign of the chaos that was to come.

***

Jane Homeyer heard the news like most people, woken up at 4:00 a.m. by a call from a dispatcher at the Highland Park police department, a nearby suburb. She hopped out of bed, quickly got ready, then headed to the Northern Illinois Police Crime Lab where she worked.[12] On staff were nearly a dozen analysts working mostly as generalists handling a wide variety of jobs. At NIPCL, toxicology, serology, handling biological evidence, and most other roles were shared responsibilities. It was a team effort.[13]

The facility was housed in the second floor of the Highland Park police department. It had an evidence room to secure materials and labs to analyze samples. The temperature-controlled facility was secured by separate keys and separate alarms from the police department, which allowed it to maintain its independence. The lab functioned as a non-profit, paid for by police departments in the area through a membership fee based on the population of each jurisdiction.

When she arrived at the lab, Homeyer conferred with a colleague who'd also received the call, and they collected the necessary equipment to process a crime scene of this nature—camera gear and a 35-millimeter camera, a fingerprinting kit, flashes, scales for measuring, a tape measure, and envelopes to store film.[14] While the lab's staff were generalists, Homeyer was particularly adept at lifting fingerprints. Tall and thin with short black hair, Homeyer dressed plainly and wore little makeup.

Armed with a PhD from Northwestern, Jane Homeyer had undergone extensive academic training. This would be, however, only her second crime scene—and her first murder investigation.[15] The amount of pressure on this case was a new level, with little room for sloppiness. Eventually, a news helicopter flying above the restaurant, with its chopping wings audible from below, was a constant reminder of the high stakes.

At the scene, Chris Hedges and Jane Homeyer were accompanied by other colleagues from the lab including Robert Wilson and Charles Principe, the lab's director.[16] They would be aided by other departments including the Palatine police and Cook County sheriff's office.

The process was always consistent. First, medical aid was provided to victims if necessary. Then, the scene was secured to prevent contamination. After that, evidence was documented. This was followed by processing. Then more processing. And more processing.

The team from NIPCL first conducted a walkthrough of the restaurant, attempting to craft a plan to address things in the most efficient and effective manner. Police had already secured the site and were noting everyone who entered and exited so the DNA of those individuals could later be excluded.

Homeyer and the others began packaging and sealing materials. The pace was methodical. The team worked from the dining area and logged everything with the appropriate forms. On each evidence bag, Homeyer marked the initials of her maiden name—JW—to signify who had handled each piece of evidence.[17] The scene was a massive undertaking, and it quickly became clear it would entail a multi-day effort.

***

Standing in the cold, Eileen Bakalla watched as Jim Degorski got to work at Bill's Coin Wash, a do-it-yourself car wash in suburban Streamwood. The business was secluded, the perfect location for not raising any suspicions. With a dozen stalls, the operation was unmanned and tucked away among a tree-filled lot, with no one around to ask questions. Aside from the location, the two were protected by the veil of night.

Jim was meticulous, careful not to miss a step. This was all about covering he and Juan Luna's tracks. The mats were taken out then vacuumed to get rid of any debris. Jim scrubbed the red interior of his friend Juan's car, from the floor and seats to the dash and doors. He used a pressure washer to rinse certain areas completely clean, then a towel to wipe inside and the coin-operated vacuum to extract any leftover water.

It was Saturday night, and just hours before, Jim had explained to his friend Eileen exactly what they'd done. Mere minutes away, people were still gathered in the parking lot of Brown's Chicken in Palatine which they'd passed that morning. Police were scurrying across town chasing down leads. Evidence technicians were processing a horrendous crime scene unlike anything the northwest suburbs had witnessed before.

Eileen and Jim, meanwhile, headed to the mall after cleaning Juan's car. The shopping center had all the usual offerings, like department stores, kitschy boutiques, and hot pretzels. Eileen found a new pair of shoes and tried them on. They were a fit. She felt good about her new kicks. When Eileen went to pay, she used cash: the fifty dollars her friends had violently stolen the night before.

***

There were many unenviable tasks that fell to police and crime-scene technicians while processing the scene, but perhaps the most sorrowful job of all entailed placing each individual in a white body bag, zipping them up, then carrying them out on a stretcher to be placed in an ambulance. Making matters worse, each time the three to five individuals tasked with this job left the building, they were greeted with the blinding flash of dozens of cameras, their clicks filling the shocked silence of civilians gathered nearby. The crowd remained stunned, as one, after another, after another, after another, after another, after another, and a final body was removed from the Brown's Chicken building in Palatine at 6:53 p.m.[18]

When entering the scene, police placed plastic bags on their feet to prevent contamination.[19] The restaurant was cold, requiring everyone to wear winter coats throughout. Jane Homeyer and the team from NICPL dusted obvious areas for prints, like doors and handles. Given its cleanly state, many areas were void of clues. Aside from some crumbs on one table, the other areas were spotless. There were no shell casings left over from the bullets. Nevertheless, they found hundreds of prints and a shoe print on a coupon that had fallen on the tiled floors. Officer Bill Heche noticed a mostly empty garbage can filled with thrown-out food. He flagged it for others.

On Sunday, the investigation entered its second full day. They continued dusting for prints. At one point, a kerosene-powered heater was brought in from Soldier Field where the Chicago

Bears played to help melt snow in the parking lot and uncover anything obscured. Each night, a van owned by the NICPL was loaded up with evidence, then taken back to the lab.

On Monday, as people continued to stop by outside and the media frenzy intensified, a former manager of the restaurant was brought in to open the safe. In the bottom compartment of the safe was a spare canvas bag for cash, rolls of quarters, dimes, nickels, and pennies, and miscellaneous junk stored in empty Styrofoam Brown's Chicken containers normally used for mashed potatoes and coleslaw. The employee helped print out a receipt of the last item ordered at 21:08. The meal had cost $6.69 and matched the food found in the garbage can.[20]

Homeyer eventually turned her attention to the trash, which she and three other officers pulled out and sat on the floor, staring at what was inside.[21] Wearing gloves, she poked around the bag's contents: a four-piece chicken dinner, a black plastic coffee stirrer, French fries, coleslaw, untouched biscuits, honey packets, and some napkins.[22] The chicken was mostly untouched—one leg, another leg partially bitten, an untouched wing and another breast, all wrapped in a waxy paper and found on a Brown's Chicken placemat.[23]

"What are you guys doing digging through the garbage?" someone asked, skeptical that their methods had any value.[24] As anyone who'd been involved in processing a crime scene understood in 1993, there was little that could be done with evidence like half-eaten food. DNA technology required a much larger sample to be useful than a simple bit of saliva. But Jane Homeyer knew the field was advancing rapidly. Carefully, she placed the half-eaten chicken and other materials into an evidence bag, then labeled it with her initials.

One man's trash. Another woman's treasure.

CHAPTER 8

MARTIN

Being hit by a car had its upsides for Martin Blake. To be sure, the recovery was rough. He spent a month in the hospital with two broken legs, a nasty concussion, and a broken wrist. That didn't even take into account the cuts on his face, damage to his teeth, or the month of physical therapy that followed. According to some friends, the accident even caused his speech to slow.[1] No amount of damages or insurance money could make up for those life-altering changes, but a good chunk of cash certainly didn't hurt either.

Any crash is bad news, but Martin's 1986 accident was worse than most. To start, it wasn't a vehicle-on-vehicle collision. The then-high-school sophomore was just minding his own business, walking along a tree-lined street of two-story homes in suburban Palatine when a driver came barreling down the road.

For a teenager, the $158,000 settlement he'd receive was a lot of dough. And like any teen, he had a few ideas of how to spend it. In a twist of irony, Martin bought a car—a 1988 white Mustang GT, to be exact.[2]

Martin spared no time putting his hot rod to use, racing it around neighborhood cul-de-sacs and in one instance, driving it over his neighbors' lawn.³ Martin had been struck by a reckless driver, and yet he'd become the very thing which nearly ended his life. Within a few years, he'd rack up quite a collection of speeding tickets and other driving infractions. He was something of a loose cannon, but Martin Blake was determined to live his life to the fullest.

After graduating from Fremd High School in Palatine, Martin went to work at various odd jobs around the northwest suburbs. By 1992, he was twenty-three years old and living on his own in Elgin, Illinois, just a few miles from where he'd grown up.

Aside from the car, the settlement allowed Martin to buy a house in Elgin in a neighborhood filled with middle-class homes and well-kept green yards. Unlike most young people his age, he paid in cash—all $105,000.⁴

Someone might politely refer to Martin's house as a "bachelor pad." Someone with less patience for the idiosyncrasies of young men would probably just say it was a fucking mess.

From the view of a passerby walking their dog or jogging down the street, Martin's three-bedroom, two-story house wasn't much out of the ordinary. There was a wooden fence that connected his lot to his neighbors' homes. A driveway stretched up the lot toward an attached garage. And the front of the house was surrounded by simple stone siding.

The inside of Martin's house was a different story. Old newspapers were strewn throughout. Dirty dishes were piled in the sink just begging to be washed. A fish tank filled with pet bluegills was cloudy and unclean.⁵ Martin's two dogs crapped freely about the house. At Christmastime, instead of decorating festively with popcorn garlands and candy canes, Martin's tree was festooned with empty aluminum beer cans.⁶

Martin Blake had a mullet, a popular hairdo with his peers. Standing at five-foot eight inches, his eyebrows were bushy and his hair dark brown.[7] He was handsome, with a contagious smile and a youthful face.

A sociable guy fond of off-color jokes, there was always a steady stream of people around Martin's house. Oftentimes, Martin's booze-filled parties attracted crowds of forty or fifty people, and he relished his role as host. Sometimes, he let things get out of hand. On one occasion, likely after a few too many beers, Martin punched a hole through a wall during a party and the next day shrugged off the episode despite having a badly bruised and bloody arm.[8]

Despite his affable demeanor, Martin did not mesh well with some of his neighbors. Aside from the keggers he threw, he hosted lots of houseguests whose presence sometimes alarmed the neighborhood. Roommates came and roommates went.[9] For a few friends, Martin served as a benevolent landlord and rented out a low-cost bedroom in the house.[10] After he encountered a homeless couple living in their car one day, he invited them to take up refuge in his garage.[11] This was not the typical Elgin household.

The settlement had been a good haul for Martin, but he still needed a steady stream of income. There was, after all, home upkeep, groceries, and beer to pay for. Martin had no trouble finding work. Keeping those jobs proved to be a more difficult task, mostly because he was totally unreliable. In 1992, Martin was working in the kitchen of a Brown's Chicken restaurant in Palatine near where he'd grown up. It wasn't glamorous, and neither was the night shift which became his regular slot.

When Lynn and Dick Ehlenfeldt took over the restaurant from its previous owners in 1992, things began to change in the eatery. The couple had poured their heart and soul into making the restaurant a success, not to mention their entire life savings. There was no room for avoidable error, and that included mistakes from fickle employees. The Ehlenfeldts implemented performance ratings for their workers and tracked their progress. They required each employee, with the exception of a few kitchen staff, to wear a company uniform, a dress code they strictly enforced.[12] They'd invested in a brand when they bought the franchise, and they weren't about to let a bunch of teenagers decide how to run the show.

On New Year's Eve 1992, Martin Blake showed up to his shift in the kitchen of Brown's Chicken on time and got to work. And yet, the draw of hosting a New Year's party at his house was too alluring. So, he left work a few hours early to ring in the New Year with friends.[13] Martin was principally concerned with having a good time, and the minutiae of frying chicken and cleaning tables wasn't enough to overcome that.

On New Year's Day, Martin received a phone call. It was Dick Ehlenfeldt, who didn't mince words. *You're fired*, he told him, attributing the decision to Martin leaving work early. The newly unemployed party host was annoyed, but it also wasn't his first time being canned.[14] Martin was used to hopping from job to job.

Life went on for Martin despite his temporary unemployment. At the very least, he was lucky to have friends renting a room in his house that provided some side income. A week after being fired, Martin watched a movie with some friends, smoked pot, and drank a few beers.[15] He was ready to put the whole ordeal of Brown's Chicken behind him. No more cottonseed oil and smelly clothes. No more clocking in and clocking out. No more sweeping up and cleaning up empty vinyl booths. Other than a run to the liquor store for more beer, he stayed home that night to watch a made-for-TV movie called *Revolver*, a selection to which Martin objected. *C'mon, it'll be crazy!* he said to his friends, trying to convince them to watch another film called *Faces of Death* instead, a gory picture that depicts real-life killings on screen.[16] Martin's buddies weren't interested.

The following morning, Martin awoke with the familiar feeling of a hangover. He'd had a few too many the night before. By mid-morning, news of the massacre at Brown's Chicken was spread all across Chicago TV and radio. Martin's home phone rang, and his friend Melissa Benz was on the line. The two went back for years, old high school pals who'd stayed in touch. "Were you working last night?" she asked him, alluding to the killings in her soft voice. His friends all knew about his job at Brown's.

"No, I got fired a week ago," he told her matter-of-factly. The two discussed the likelihood that he'd be called by the police for questioning. Not only had Martin worked at Brown's, but he had also dated another employee's sister. They feared her brother, Michael Castro, might be among the seven killed.

"I bet you're pretty happy about it," Melissa continued, alluding to the firing. With the aftermath of the party from the night before still fogging his brain, Martin had still not made the connection. "What do you mean?" he asked her bewildered. "If you were there you might have gotten shot," she said. Martin laughed. "Yeah, I guess you're right."[17]

***

From the moment Chicagoland learned about the killings, the Palatine police station's phones began ringing nonstop. The rush of information was intense. Never before had this suburban law enforcement team seen such an influx. Within a few hours, staff at the station began installing extra phones just to keep up with the flurry of tips.[18]

Sorting through the early leads was a Sisyphean task. Each new call was like a snowflake in a blizzard, indistinguishable at first glance but increasingly complex on further inspection. Which were to be ignored, and which were essential to follow? Answering that question could be the difference between life or death, and it was something few members of the police force had the experience to respond to, a fact nobody held against them. This was a heinous crime which no amount of preparation could properly equip a person to comprehend.

As the phones continued ringing and police were called into the station for what quickly became an all-hands-on-deck exercise, a tip came in at 11:38 a.m. which seemed promising. It had been just nine hours since the bodies had been found, but police had their first real lead.

The call came from a woman who claimed to know the person who brutally murdered seven people at Brown's. *Look at Martin Blake*, she said. He's a disgruntled former employee. An unstable man. On top of that, he owns a gun that he's been practicing his shot on with phone books and the heads of his mother's old beauty-pageant trophies in his hallway as a makeshift target. He's armed and dangerous.[19]

Any law enforcement official investigating a murder feels the pressure to solve things quickly. A person has lost their life, the grief-stricken family is begging for answers, and the public is worried about a potential killer on the loose. In this case, that immense pressure was multiplied sevenfold.

Within hours, a group of officers suited up and prepared to arrest Martin Blake at his home in Elgin, roughly twenty-five minutes west of Palatine. They scoped out the neighborhood, which was covered in snow with streets still unplowed. Like a scene from a spy movie, law enforcement concealed themselves in utility vehicles from the local gas and power companies.[20] Martin Blake was armed, they were told, so they couldn't risk alerting him to their presence. Police cleared out neighbors from houses nearby. Then, they waited.

By late afternoon, Martin's head had cleared enough that he decided to venture outside and fix his car. In addition to his Mustang GT, Martin also owned a 1977 white Ford Bronco. Unfortunately, the SUV had become more a burden than a joy. It wouldn't start, and as a result, it sat in the driveway collecting snow. So Martin left the house in hopes of flipping the hood and tinkering around.

Unbeknownst to him, officers were just feet away with their guns drawn while neighbors observed the takedown from afar. Some law enforcement watched from inside neighbors' homes. When Martin finally lifted the hood of his Bronco at 2:56 p.m. on Saturday afternoon, more than a dozen police officers swarmed him with their guns drawn and aimed directly at him. *Put your hands on the hood!* they shouted. They handcuffed the twenty-three-year-old and took him into custody. "We got him," an officer nodded to a neighbor watching nearby.[21] Martin was stunned. "Is this about last night?" he immediately asked them as he was hauled away.[22]

In the early hours of the investigation, the Palatine police focused principally on former Brown's Chicken employees. The crime appeared to be a robbery gone wrong, and a person who had a connection to the restaurant would have known critical details like when the restaurant was busy, who would be present at closing time, and where the Ehlenfeldts kept their money. Of course, someone who could answer those questions and was *also* recently fired had all the qualities of the perfect suspect.

Martin was quickly whisked away to the Palatine police headquarters, where investigators began questioning him. Where was he last night? Why was he fired from Brown's? Where did he keep his weapons? For hours and hours, police grilled him about the circumstances surrounding his firing and the last time he had been at Brown's. Martin also matched the description of a man witnesses said they saw around the restaurant that night. Martin was administered a polygraph test to detect if he was lying to investigators. He passed.[23] When asked questions, his responses were slow, and he seemed uncertain, a pattern of speech that only made investigators more suspicious.

The fact that Martin had recently been fired by the Ehlenfeldts was enticing enough for police. Occam's Razor tells us to trust the simplest explanation. And yet, with this murder, the motive simply didn't add up. *I didn't need the money*, Martin insisted to investigators. He was still living off his accident settlement. Yes, some friends had mentioned he'd talked about retaliating against his former employer and was angry, but that was all hyperbole. Just stupid talk.

While not being interrogated, police put Martin in a small cell in the basement of the police station as a holding place. The police took his clothes to be tested for any traces of relevant DNA and gave him temporary garments, a white jumpsuit reminiscent of a hospital gown.[24] Noticing a surveillance camera monitoring him, he pleaded for help. "*Habeas corpus, habeas corpus!*" he repeated over and over, remembering the legal term requiring an arrestee to be brought before a judge to determine the legality of their detention that he'd learned in civics class years ago.[25] When it appeared that wasn't going to work, Martin began to pray. "God, if you get me out of here, I'm going to do something really good," he vowed.[26]

The Palatine police department had instantly become a hotbed of media activity after the seven bodies were found at Brown's. News trucks with satellites reaching toward the sky were staked outside where reporters provided live updates to viewers at the top of their programs. Print reporters buzzed around the area looking for anyone with a tip, approaching individuals with even a vague connection to the victims or alleged first suspect. There was no avoiding the press for Martin.

Sure enough, within a few hours of his arrest, the name Martin Blake would be known across Chicagoland. His image was splattered on TV news programs on every channel. Newspaper articles began describing him as the primary suspect in the case. He was a disgruntled employee who had threatened to retaliate for being fired, they said.

It didn't help Martin's case that he had a past arrest record. He was previously charged with theft of a radar detector in 1988 and reckless driving in 1992, misdemeanors to which he pled guilty and served community service. There was a litany of speeding offenses and one run-in with the law for drag racing. It didn't matter to the media that not one of these offenses were violent; Martin had a record. That was enough to ignite the public's imagination, which the press fanned over and over.

Within a few hours, one local TV station aired home video of Martin. "We have obtained the very first video tape of the man now in custody in Palatine," said Chuck Goudie, an ABC-7 News investigative reporter. The tape rolled, showing Martin hanging out in his kitchen at a house party with a group of friends two months before the killings. "'I've never been in trouble," Martin said looking directly at the camcorder while his friend recorded. For the media, the line was simply too irresistible not to play up.

"Martin Blake may not have been in trouble when this video was shot during a party at his home two months ago, but now this man is being questioned by Palatine police in connection with the restaurant massacre," Goudie said to thousands of viewers.[27] Friends of Martin came out of the woodwork to be interviewed. While Martin sat in jail, people claiming to be his friend spoke to reporters and informed the media of his past firings and run-ins with police.

Another friend told reporters how he'd joked about killing someone in the past. Just a joke, he insisted, not understanding how viewers would interpret this jest. Retracting words spoken during a live broadcast is like putting toothpaste back in the tube, and all that now lingered in viewers' minds was the image of a diabolical Martin Blake, the recently fired party animal with a mullet and a penchant for speeding, killing seven people and stuffing their bodies into a freezer.

From the beginning, the media got a lot wrong about Martin. Papers reported that he had a record of drunk driving. (Not true.)[28] They said he had a weapon he called the "hammer of discipline" (true) which he used to beat his dogs (false). Perhaps most damaging was the assertion that Martin Blake was now the investigation's primary murder suspect. (Police never *actually* named him a suspect.)

While the Chicago press corps dug deep into Martin's Blake's past, the police searched his home. With Martin now in custody for more than a day, law enforcement combed through his residence for clues. They emptied dresser drawers, looked in sink drains and pipes, and located his gun. With the media monitoring the proceedings from outside, police took out two large garbage bags labeled "Evidence" and hauled them away.[29]

Despite all the hope, the search bore good news for Martin. As the original tipster had mentioned, he owned a gun that could have been used as a murder weapon. But his .22 caliber pistol didn't match the one police believed the killer used at the restaurant.[30]

After hours with police and intense, on-and-off questioning, the Blake family enlisted the help of a lawyer to get Martin out of custody. A seasoned criminal defense attorney, Dennis Born went to the Palatine police station on Sunday night to speak with his client and explain to him how things would work. By law, police could only hold him as a suspect for a reasonable amount of time, something investigators were already butting up against, having held him for more than a day. Born was familiar with many of the police and officials from the state's attorney's office working the case, so he was able to negotiate calmly with the other side. *You either charge Martin with a crime or I'll have a judge order you to release him*, he explained. After two days in police hands, Born finally received word that Martin would be released.

Eager to clear his name, Martin wanted to speak to the press. "I want to go to the front steps of the station and shout '*I'm free!*'" he explained to his attorney.[31] Born quickly talked his client out of the ill-advised proposal and suggested a different idea. He requested that police sneak Martin out the back door to avoid the throngs of onlookers and press while Born exited from the front to give a brief statement. Police took him to a church parking lot two blocks away where Born picked up his client and took him to Martin's father's home in the affluent suburb of Inverness, Illinois.

When they arrived, it appeared their backdoor exit was futile. Cameras were waiting. Dressed in blue jeans and a plain white T-shirt, Martin exited the running car and sprinted through the snow-covered driveway into his father's open garage. His attorney walked to the gaggle of reporters gathered on the front lawn of the acre-and-a-half lot to answer questions. "He expressed remorse concerning the deaths of the individuals at Brown's Chicken. He expressed regret that he has been in custody for the last forty-eight hours. He is relieved to be home," Born said, his breath visible in the cold and microphones pointed in his face. "They have informed me that there are no holds on Mr. Blake. He is free to come and go as he pleases," he continued, discussing his eleventh-hour negotiations with the police.[32]

Martin Blake's nightmare was over, but his name had still been destroyed. Suspicion would forever linger upon him. He was the first suspect of the Brown's Chicken massacre. Reporters said all those nasty things about him on the news. People would always wonder whether he had been involved in the whole thing. If not Blake, then who?[33]

Martin would later sue the Palatine police department alleging a violation of his civil rights. Police denied any wrongdoing, and the two parties would settle for the small amount of $8,000 and agree not to speak of the matter publicly.[34] In part because of the intense attention he attracted, Martin moved out of state to escape the long shadow cast by being a suspect.

And therein lay the larger problem for police. The more time that passed from the killings, the less likely it became that a suspect would be located. After Martin's release, law enforcement held a press conference at the Palatine police headquarters. Standing between the backdrop of a black chalkboard and a wooden podium covered in wires and microphones, police and staff from the state's attorney's office faced the media for questioning.

With a sea of reporters in attendance, they addressed the Martin Blake situation. There was no reason to charge him, they said, but they stopped short of apologizing for the ordeal. His alibi held up.

Other than that, details were scant. No information was released about the crime scene or about what investigators found. Police said they had no other suspects. It was Monday, January 11. More than two days had passed since seven bodies had been found by police in the cooler and freezer at Brown's Chicken in Palatine. People were demanding answers.

In most crises, leaders seek to calm the fears of the public. Cook County state's attorney Patrick O'Malley, on the other hand, decided to follow a different playbook. The room was filled with a palpable sense of frustration. Police and prosecutors responded curtly to the relentless questioning from the media. Closing out the press conference, O'Malley provided little relief to the thousands of Chicagoans watching their TV sets at home. "We are not here to reassure the community," he said, sounding annoyed at the repetitive inquiries. "This crime has not been solved, and yes, there is a murderer or murderers on the loose."[35]

CHAPTER 9

MICHELLE

A student journalist crafting run-of-the-mill articles for the high school newspaper is a bit like a child eating their broccoli at the dinner table. Lacking in excitement but necessary for one's development. Student editors at Palatine High School's *Cutlass* certainly had their fair share of humdrum stories. There were pieces about the most recent victory for the Palatine Pirates against a rival football team. Interviews with administrators and faculty appeared, highlighting everything from the newest additions to the cafeteria menu to the ins and outs of the student work program. When the school's thespians put on productions of *Annie* or *The Sound of Music*, reviews of their latest performance encouraged students to see it for themselves.

Aside from the everyday stories, student editors at *Cutlass*, the Palatine High School student newspaper, were also unafraid to push boundaries. That certainly held true for Michelle Parke when she became editor-in-chief during her senior year. When she published a two-story edition on safer sex, she caused a commotion among more puritanical parents and staff.[1] Talk of condoms, birth control, and teen pregnancy was the kind of stuff people whispered about privately in the quiet suburbs, not something discussed at length between the pages of the student newspaper.

With black hair down to her shoulders and wispy bangs, the seventeen-year-old senior had counted down the days before she'd fill the editor-in-chief role during her final year on the paper. The previous summer, she spent time at Indiana University in Bloomington at a journalism camp, honing her interview skills and sharpening her prose.[2] Michelle was easygoing but confident, not afraid to assert herself as a leader in the new role.

On Friday, January 9, Michelle was just grateful to have made it through the first week back at school from winter break. After the bell had rang and her after school activities were finished, Michelle drove through the snowy streets to pick up dinner for her family around 6:30 p.m. Brown's Chicken was an easy and fast option, so she drove to the restaurant that proudly proclaimed "*It Tastes Better!*" and grabbed a greasy bag of crispy fried chicken to share with her family that Friday night while winding down from the week.

When Michelle awoke the next morning to a cloudy and frigid day in the upper twenties, she walked into the kitchen and was greeted by her father. "Something happened at Brown's Chicken," he informed her matter-of-factly after hearing it on the radio around 9:00 a.m. *I was just there*, Michelle thought to herself. Sparing little time, she got dressed and headed out to the place she'd been just hours before to see what was awry.

When Michelle reached the corner of Northwest Highway and Smith Street, she could see the parking lot surrounding the restaurant was cordoned off with police tape and a crowd of about thirty people were gathered in the area that Brown's shared with other businesses in the larger strip mall. The restaurant was off on its own on the corner, an island away from the lot filled with establishments like a hair salon, specialty foods store, and a deli. Banks of snow were still piled knee-high in parts of the lot.

After parking her car, Michelle made her way to the crowd of bystanders, immediately recognizing some classmates from Palatine High School, a few of whom were sporting their letterman jackets in the cold. Some were crying, others standing catatonic in the cold. The shock of the events surrounding them seemed to numb them from the elements. Palatine police and other law enforcement were on the scene, heading in and out of the building without speaking to the crowd. Each time someone exited, the collective anticipation of the group rose as they looked for further information only to be disappointed by the silence from law enforcement.

Whispers among those gathered pondered the unthinkable. Some of the students there from Palatine High School were employees at Brown's Chicken who'd had the night off. They were looking for their coworkers and classmates. A senior who ran in different crowds, Michelle didn't know either boy. She did, however, know one of the owners' daughters, who she'd played soccer with. Her heart broke for the news that had not yet come but seemed inevitable.

Michelle retreated to her car, blasted the heat, and began pondering her next steps. This was a huge story impacting her school, and she wanted to get more information. She drove home and called her newspaper advisor. *Figure out what's going on*, her teacher told her. So Michelle headed out to the Palatine police station to dig further. When she arrived, it was clear from the bevy of news trucks and reporters standing in the entranceway of the station that she wasn't the only one investigating. Crews were setting up their satellite links in the parking lot, and reporters from TV stations and newspapers who she regularly watched on the nightly news were all gathered. It was a veritable who's-who of Chicagoland investigative journalism, and Michelle was in the center of it.

At the Palatine Community Center which housed the police station, the usually peaceful building was filled with chaos. Media was pressing anyone and everyone walking through the building for questions. Officers now called back into work on their day off were still getting up to speed on the situation. *These guys are in over their heads*, some reporters mumbled to one another.

***

Theft comes in many gradations. On one end of the spectrum is the person who steals a loaf of bread to feed their family *à la* Jean Valjean. Perhaps it's wrong—technically criminal—but many would justify the act in the right circumstances. On the other end are the more disgraceful acts—like stealing from the collection plate at church or pocketing cash from grandma's purse. The innocence and purity of the victim makes the crime seem even worse. In that sense, one parent's decision to steal $100,000 from his child's high-school booster club was on the latter end of the spectrum. His acts would make even the more hardened criminals blush.[3]

The fundraising campaign to help the Palatine High School's symphonic band's trip to a 1991 competition in Hawaii took months. The money vanished, however, in a much speedier fashion. When the Suburban National Bank in Palatine called the high school inquiring about an $87,000 check that had bounced, officials were quickly led to the group's treasurer. A compulsive gambler, he used the money to pay off debts accrued from his addiction, a hunger fed mostly by ill-fated bets made at the local horseracing track. The parent volunteer was bad at both gambling and covering his tracks, and he'd eventually be charged, found guilty, and sentenced to four years in prison.

There were a few good things to rise from the ashes of this mess. For United Airlines, providing the Palatine High School band with free plane tickets to Hawaii proved to be a great public relations move. And for principal Nancy Robb, dealing with the media frenzy caused by this ordeal quickly taught her how to deal with the press. As she rose the ranks to become an administrator, there were no courses in crisis communications during her education nor had she anticipated the school to be so closely thrust into the spotlight.

If Palatine High School staff were asked to describe Nancy Robb in a few words, the responses would be consistent. Smart. Competent. Pragmatic. Thrown new challenges, she was calm and decisive, someone who led with poise but could also be trusted on a personal level. If cast as a stunt double based on looks, she'd be a stand-in for a young Jodie Foster—but taller and with auburn hair.

Robb's leadership had certainly been tested. There was the booster club theft, of course. Earlier in her tenure, a horrible electrical fire threatened to close the school for weeks. In January of 1993, a student tragically passed from muscular dystrophy.[4] Despite these instances, however, nothing in Robb's career had prepared her for the chaos that awaited her on the other end of the 6:00 a.m. phone call she received on Saturday, January 9.

She heard the horrible news in the same way many affected by the massacre at Brown's Chicken did. Filled with a rush of emotions. Robb thought of her daily commute. It was a strange feeling. Each morning on her way to school she passed the corner of Northwest Highway and Smith Street where the restaurant stood. *There but for the grace of God go I*, became a common refrain for many learning the news.

Prep for the week ahead could not wait, so Robb went immediately to her office at Palatine High School and called in her administrative team. In a pre-Columbine era, there was no playbook to follow. Robb merely followed her instinct. She instructed staff to call in counselors and prepare a plan for that Monday. Her immediate focus, on the other hand, would be preparing for a press conference later that day at the Palatine police headquarters. She was tasked with informing the press with the basics. Who were Michael and Rico? What were they involved in at Palatine High School? What was the school doing to help students cope?

Just hours earlier, Robb had been lying in bed on a Saturday morning with not much to do. Now, she was dressed in a white high-neck blouse with a dark blazer sitting in a holding room at the Palatine police station. On the other end of the wall, a mob of press was waiting anxiously. Robb would kick off the lineup of speakers, followed by the deputy chief of police, a local pastor, Frank Portillo of Brown's Chicken, Palatine mayor Rita Mullins, and Ann Ehlenfeldt, Dick Ehlenfeldt's sister.

When Robb walked into the press room with the rest of the group, cameras began snapping like a string of firecrackers, and lights blinded their vision of the crowd filled with reporters hungry for information. The podium was packed with microphones and recording devices. When Robb approached, the flashes began anew. She firmly gripped both sides of the podium, giving brief remarks then opening the floor for questions. The press corps peppered her nonstop for further details, which she couldn't provide. At this point, no one had the details the public was seeking. Mayor Mullins discussed the collective devastation of the community. Ann Ehlenfeldt told reporters that there were no known problems with employees. "I talked to Lynn on Wednesday, and she didn't express any concern," she said in response.[5] For Nancy Robb and the others, the press conference was less of a media event and more of a foggy daze. Some members of the press were aggressive and unrelenting, a stark contrast from how people in Palatine were handling things.

Aside from the press conference, the school calendar was creeping up on Robb. That very night, a basketball game was on the books against rival Schaumburg High School. To cancel or not to cancel, that was the question. On the one hand, moving forward might seem disrespectful, like the community didn't care about the horror which had just greeted it. On the other hand, cancelling would disrupt the students even further.

Left with no easy option, Robb and her team decided that the Palatine Pirates and Schaumburg Saxons would play on. The school gym filled that night with nearly 1,200 spectators. Flags hung high above the glossy basketball court marked at the center with an outline of the state of Illinois and the school's moniker on the courtside, a skull and crossbones on a scarlet flag being waved by a pirate's sword. Around the walls of the gym were banners in the shape of Illinois commemorating past teams who'd made it to the semifinals or state championship. The sounds of hundreds of conversations filled the gym as did the constant beat of basketballs hitting the court while the players warmed up. That night had all the signs of a normal game, but the side conversations in the bleachers were filled with hushed discussion of the murders, not who'd win the match.

When the teams finished their warmups, Robb walked toward the referees' table at the side of the court and faced the crowd. She looked up at the faces staring back at her in the bleachers. The noisy crowd became silent and the band put down their instruments as Robb grabbed the microphone. School cheerleaders stood straight on the side of the court and put their pompoms to their sides. "We are saddened tonight by the tragedy which has struck our community," she said as her voice cracked. Reporters crouched around her and snapped photos. "We extend our sincere sympathy to the family and loved ones of the victims," she continued. Finally, she bowed her head and asked the fans to observe a moment of silence. A long fifteen seconds passed, finally interrupted by clapping from the basketball team huddled around one another.[6]

On Monday, students dressed in scarlet and gray Pirates gear, colorful parkas, baggy winter clothes, and sweatpants returned to school with questions still unanswered. The carpeted hallways were wet from melting snow from students' shoes and stained white with sidewalk salt carried in from outside. Halls were painted in tones of beige and gray, with lockers lining the walls and glass display cases exhibiting works of art, trophies, and announcements of upcoming events. Outside, the American and Illinois flags flew at half-mast surrounded by evergreen trees still dusted with snow. The roof and awnings above doors were blanked in much the same manner. At 8:00 a.m., it was a cloudy morning filled with an unmistakable heaviness, a feeling that betrayed the otherwise cheery aura of the school's decor.

When students arrived at their first-period classes, they learned their daily routine had been scrapped for a discussion of the killings. Robb and her team had spent the weekend preparing scripts for teachers about how to talk about the issue and assembling a team of fifteen counselors from across the district as well as student helpers.[7]

A school of roughly two thousand students, most did not know Rico and Michael simply because of the sheer number of pupils. Still, the fear of a killer on the loose loomed large, especially for those who worked after-school jobs in retail or at fast-food restaurants.

Robb felt emotional, drained from the chaos of it all and intense sadness that swirled around her. Classrooms and hallways across the campus paused as they heard the long buzzer signaling an announcement on the PA system. As she spoke to students offering counseling services to those who needed it, Robb's voice again cracked. "We at Palatine High School feel most intimately the loss of two members of our school family," she said. "Mike Castro, class of 1994, and Rico Solis, class of 1995, will be greatly missed by their families, their friends, and their teachers."[8] She ended with another moment of silence in memory of the victims.

The press continued to ask questions, and Robb quickly learned the attention was unavoidable. She received a sage piece of advice from one reporter. "You know, Nancy, you're new at this, but here's what's going to happen," he said to her bluntly. "I'm going to get my story one way or another, so either you provide the information, or I'll go across the street and talk to students."[9] In an effort to control the message and avoid a paparazzi-like atmosphere outside the school, she assembled a group of students to speak to the press in a more organized fashion. They'd be peppered with questions about the victims and the feelings of students with a killer on the loose.

Throughout the halls that day, students could be seen sobbing as they still registered the news.[10] As friends and classmates of Rico and Michael made their way through the day, two empty desks served as a surreal reminder of the loss. A fellow Brown's Chicken employee and classmate shook his head thinking about Michael. "He just got a new stereo system for the truck, but we never got a chance to put it in," he lamented.

***

If there were a list of golden rules in reporting, "don't become the story" would probably be at the top. For Michelle Parke, however, adhering to that rule was virtually impossible through no fault of her own. She continued attending press conferences, interviewing people in the community, and standing shoulder-to-shoulder with the press corps. Between sessions, reporters would play cards or venture outside in the cold for smoke breaks to kill time. Michelle would use the lulls to mingle. *What paper do you work for?* one of the reporters asked. When they heard her response, tape recorders and cameras were quickly pressed in her face and she was hounded with questions. Police were giving them scant details, so the story of the local student newspaper covering the killings at Brown's Chicken provided another angle of coverage on the tragedy.

During each press conference rooms were packed. Most of the police's responses were repetitive. *We can't answer that at this time. No comment. The investigation is ongoing.* Reporters understood why investigators were so tight-lipped, but their continued questioning did little to recognize that. Much of the work dealing with the press fell to Walt Gasior, the Palatine police's deputy chief of support services. A civilian, he was apt

SOMETHING BIG

at working with the press, and most journalists respected his professionalism. Still, his hands were tied.

Among the media, there was a great deal of skepticism toward the Palatine police's ability to handle a case of this magnitude. And when police rebuffed questions about handing off the investigation to other authorities, they reasserted that the Palatine police would take the lead. It was their investigation. *Oh, this'll go over well*, was the collective thought of many in the press corps. Big-city reporters thumbed their noses at suburban cops despite the fact that the Palatine police had quickly brought in outside help. Tons of outside help.

With so many developments happening the week after the killings, Michelle pushed back the planned publication date of their January 1993 issue. When a first draft of the paper came out, she tore it up and started over. She would take her time and get things right. Luckily for her, it was the first year the paper would use a computer. No more laying out the front page with scissors and glue.

Dozens of stories were published every day on the killings, and Michelle didn't want to just regurgitate the same repetitive details other outlets were covering. She decided to focus on the students, Michael and Rico. Interviews were conducted with friends of the two boys, and when she was unable to find pictures of the two of them given the yearbook had not yet come out, she had a friend create very rudimentary—perhaps crude—sketches of their faces. As the days passed, she pulled all-nighters putting together the copy and skipped class where necessary.[11] "Stop playing Little Ms. Reporter," a teacher admonished her, a warning that went unheeded.[12]

On the morning of Friday, January 20, *Cutlass* was sprawled out in bundles on tables throughout the hallways of Palatine

High School. Walking to and from class, students grabbed copies and flipped through the pages all over campus with sketches of Rico and Michael on the front cover. "January 9, 1993, is a day that Palatine High School will never forget," Michelle wrote in a piece titled "Road to Recovery."[13] She tried to depict Rico and Michael as two humans with diverse interests and complex stories rather than the cloying portrayal of victims often found in stories following a death.

Aside from the murders, the other big story that day was the presidential inauguration happening seven hundred miles away in Washington. From the west steps of the United States Capitol, President-elect Bill Clinton took the oath of office and became president at noon, warning in his inaugural address of times when "when fear of crime robs law-abiding citizens of their freedom." His reference to rising crime wasn't aimed at the massacre in Palatine, but the line nonetheless rang close to home for many. Seven innocent souls were robbed of their freedom for no apparent reason. Police had no motive. There were no suspects. Leads continued pouring in but failed to materialize any solid evidence.

People in the community yearned for more information, and a fear of the *unknown* gripped many residents. For some people, however, the opposite was true. There was also a fear that came with knowing *exactly* what happened that night—and Anne Lockett knew too much.

CHAPTER 10

ANNE

When a person decides to kill themself, there are a menu of options available to accomplish the task. Some people try a gun. Others turn to pills. Someone looking to cause a scene might hop off a building. Anne Lockett opted for Nyquil tablets, a choice that's sort of like slitting your wrists with a butter knife. Sure, it could work, but it's more likely to just make a painful mess. Fortunately for Anne that was the case, and she survived.

After getting her stomach pumped and being revived, Anne Lockett ended up in the Forest Hospital in suburban Des Plaines. The psychiatric facility would serve as a refuge, a chance to put life's pieces back together without the distractions of the outside world. It was only a few days into January of 1993, but Anne Lockett had already had a hell of a year.

Her reasoning for this attempt seemed sound at the time. Anne had been struggling in school, unable to focus and uninterested in being around her classmates during the day. She thought about dropping out. Then, she had the idea of attending night classes, which she proposed to a counselor at Fremd High School. Her hopes were dashed when the school informed her she had too many credits to transfer to the night program. She'd have to just stick it out.

Anne Lockett was an outcast. She had a couple friends, but not a ton to spare. Drugs controlled her life. It started with just smoking pot, which became a daily habit, and she was arrested for possession the summer heading into her junior year. Anne became a frequent cigarette smoker, which calmed her down. Then she started experimenting. She used acid with some regularity, distracting herself with an out-of-body trip here or there. She tried angel dust—PCP—and other hallucinogens. Anne drank heavily. Drugs and alcohol were a release, a distraction from her disordered life.

With a pale complexion, Anne Lockett had green eyes and long brown hair that she wore straightened. At 5'3", she was short. The petite teenager was often falling asleep in class, taking caffeine tablets to stay awake. Headaches were a constant occurrence. She often appeared lethargic to her friends and teachers, uninterested in the minutiae of school life. Anne could be forgetful, letting schoolwork fall through the cracks. Her attendance record was spotty.

While she struggled going through the motions of high school, Anne Lockett was not dumb. She was bored, uninterested in what went on in world history class or that week's chemistry lab. Anne had a softer side, and she could be creative. While not paying attention during a lecture, she'd be found scribbling poetry in a notebook.

The Lockett household had been stable growing up, but things changed as Anne got older. In his mid-fifties, her father's health was poor, suffering from bad emphysema and COPD. An oxygen tank confined him to home. And when he lost his job in sales and marketing, his drinking accelerated. Anne's mother, Kaye, took care of her husband and supported the family by finding work as a teacher's assistant. Her older sister was off at college at University of Illinois, so Anne was the only kid at home. All alone to deal with the drama herself.

When her father's condition worsened, he became vicious around the family. He was verbally abusive, and the stress at home affected Anne and her mother. Even more necessary than his oxygen tank was his booze, and he continued drinking heavily, slowly but surely killing himself.[1]

For Anne, there was no control at home. Outside, as an adult, she had agency. Anne donned dark lipstick, black fingernail polish, black clothing and used gloomy makeup to bolster her goth persona.[2] She wore rings with skulls.[3] Heavy metal was her go-to choice of music, with bands like Venom, Megadeth, and Suicidal Tendencies among her favorites. She attended concerts in the city with friends when she could, throwing herself into a mosh pit to try and seem hardcore.[4] Her outward appearance created a picture of an unapproachable goth teen confident of who she was, but Anne Lockett was actually quite reserved. She was shy and had a dry sense of humor.[5]

Like a lot of teens, drugs and drinking were an act of rebellion. So too was dating. And for Anne, dating a guy a few years older than her—now out of high school—was another way to get her mind off the chaos at home.

Jim Degorski and Anne Lockett became a couple midway through her school year in 1992. But if she sought to escape the drama of homelife, choosing to date Jim Degorski was a poor choice. Their social life was normal at first, hanging out at Jim's house in the garage or the basement, drinking with other teens in the area, and listening to heavy metal bands. They'd go to house parties and imbibe sometimes too heavily, which on one occasion meant Anne blacking out after a half bottle of whiskey followed by a half bottle of vodka.[6]

The two had met at Fremd High School in 1990 when she was fourteen and he was seventeen.[7] Jim and Anne traveled in similar social circles and shared some of the same friends. When they started dating, however, the dynamic changed. Jim Degorski was controlling. If Anne had friends he didn't like, he'd forbid her from seeing them. On a whim, he'd use her truck, taking it whenever he pleased.[8] He made sure to assert his dominance even with everyday interactions. One day, Anne and Jim were deciding where they wanted to go to dinner that night. *I'm not sure*, Anne, the quiet girl, replied. Jim spat in her face.[9]

He was erratic. He called the shots. But Jim Degorski could also be a compelling personality. He was fun to hang around, and when he screwed up, he always seemed sincere when he apologized.

Anne had been in the hospital recovering from her suicide attempt just a few hours. It was Saturday, January 9. The facility was a controlled environment, with check-ins every fifteen minutes for the patients.[10] Patients were to focus on their recovery, not the chaos of the outside world.

Near the nursing station in the hallway, a pay phone rang on Anne's floor.[11] It was a call for her. When she got to the phone, she heard her boyfriend's voice. *It's Jim*, he told her. "Watch the news tonight," he said. "We did something big."[12] His request was nondescript. With very little access to the outside world, Anne got in touch with her mom who checked in on her in the hospital, telling her to bring a newspaper when she visited next. When she finally received the headlines, the lead story in nearly every outlet was the massacre at Brown's. She saved the newspaper clippings and also recounted the call in a journal.[13]

Weeks went by and Anne was focusing on recovery. She concentrated on her detox program, attended therapy, and tried to take care of her physical and emotional needs. Finally, on January 25, she was discharged and began adjusting to everyday life.[14] A few days after her release, Jim called her and asked her to come to his house, their usual hangout spot where he lived with his brother, sister, and mother.

When she arrived at Jim's house, Juan Luna was there with him tinkering in the garage. To them, it was "the shop." The three of them moved their hangout to Jim's basement bedroom, the same bedroom where he grew up.[15]

Jim's basement bedroom was a retreat for him and his friends, a place where they'd spend hours. He guarded it closely, valuing his privacy. It was the spot where when Jim got his hands on drugs, they'd try them out, from cocaine and pot to more potent contraband. The room was small. There was a punching bag that they knocked around. Music was often blaring in the background—typically heavy metal like Metallica. He had a switchblade and a hunting knife. Next to his bed he used to keep a .38 revolver with six bullets in the chamber. He was proud of the gun, showing it off to Anne a few months earlier.

Sitting on Jim's bed, the three of them were chatting. About Anne's time in the hospital. About work. About school. Finally, Jim asked Anne a question. *Do you want to know what Juan and me did at Brown's that night?* Anne agreed. *Eileen already knows this*, he said, explaining that they had used their friend as an alibi.

Juan and Jim launched into an extended explanation about that night. *That's right, we drove to the parking lot of Brown's*, he explained, describing how they arrived in Juan's Ford Tempo and parked north of the restaurant's snowy parking lot. They brought rubber gloves, his .38 snub-nosed revolver with wooden grips and bullets, and a knife with a brass knuckle handle. Knowing they'd toss them in the trash afterward, the two of them wore old clothes.

Before entering, they placed a wooden wedge in the back employee door, ensuring it was locked.[16] As a former employee of the restaurant, Juan was helpful in understanding the layout and routine. The two men attempted to change their walking pattern in hopes of throwing off anyone watching in the parking lot. It was a different kind of gait than what people would associate with them and one that would obscure their footprints in the snow. Leave no trace.

When they arrived at the main entrance, Juan covered his hand with a sweater to open the door to ensure no fingerprints were left behind. The two were unmasked. As a past worker, Juan was certain to recognize some of the faces, including the Ehlenfeldts. It was just after 9:00 p.m. All around, the employees were cleaning up. More people were present than Juan had expected for that time of night.

Nerves set in. Juan approached the counter and did something unplanned: he ordered a meal. He recognized Lynn Ehlenfeldt, who served him, taking his $10 bill then handing him change for a $6.69 meal.[17] *Hi, how are you?*, she asked, unclear if she could recall his name.[18] Juan also noticed a young boy that he used to work with named Mike.

Lynn reopened the register at 9:08 p.m.[19] The employees hastily put together Juan's meal on a green tray. It was a four-piece chicken dinner, which Juan grabbed and met Jim at a booth near some windows in the restaurant. He took a few bites of the greasy chicken. *What the fuck are you doing?* Jim quietly whispered to Juan as they waited at the booth.[20] After a few bites, Juan wiped his hand with a napkin and took the tray to a swing-top garbage can near the booth. The two of them headed to the bathroom, putting gloves on inside.[21] Jim gripped the gun and handed off the knife to Juan.[22] It was time.

Jim approached the counter, firing a shot into the ceiling. "Everyone get down on the floor and no one will get hurt," he yelled.[23] One of the young employees, a tall skinny Asian-looking kid, was mopping up. He pulled out a wad of cash from his pocket and offered it to him, pleading for peace. "Put your fuckin' money away and go to the back of the store," Jim commanded him.

As madness ensued, one of the adult employees ran toward the counter and tried to escape, but the door was wedged from the outside. As he ran back to the counter, Jim shot him and ordered him into a walk-in cooler of the restaurant. When he spotted the male owner, Jim commanded him into the cooler as well. As the other employees were laying on the ground petrified, Jim fired several shots into the cooler, killing the two men. He was methodical, picking up shell casings after he fired and putting them in his pocket so as to leave no trace behind. The two men then quickly emptied the registers.

In a moment of fight or flight, another one of the adult male employees made a run for the exit. The door was jammed from the outside. Juan approached him in a karate stance and socked him in the face. Jim approached, hitting him on the skull with the butt of his revolver. Wobbly and bleeding, they led the employee back to the others near the walk-in freezer. Juan and Jim then took the youngest employees into the freezer and huddled a Latino man, the cook, inside.

Outside was Lynn, the owner, with the key to the safe still wrapped around her arm on a plastic coil. Jim was clutching his revolver and Juan had a knife. She was huddled near the safe, just outside the kitchen. *Open the safe*, he instructed her. She was shaking as Juan dangled a knife over her. When she wasn't quick enough, Juan got angry. *Let's go, bitch!* he said, proceeding to slit her throat slightly after the two-chamber safe was opened. Jim then handed Juan the gun and proceeded to mop up some of the blood on the floor near the safe[24]

Jim took the money and placed it into a canvas bag used for carrying cash, then dragged Lynn to the freezer with the remaining five employees. The people inside begged them not to shoot. *You don't have to do this!* they exclaimed. Juan fired one bullet, then Degorski took the gun and fired multiple shots into the crowded freezer. The restaurant fell silent, with only Jim and Juan remaining. Outside, cars passed by completely unaware of the viciousness that had just taken place.

Jim continued collecting the bullet shells. Hastily, the men took a mop used for cleaning the restaurant floors and poked the bodies to ensure they were dead, then used it to clean up some of the footprints they had made in the blood.[25]

The five employees and two owners of Brown's had been interrupted during closing. Now, Jim and Juan started a closing routine of their own. They locked the exterior doors. Juan cut the power to the restaurant on a circuit breaker. With that, the clock stopped at 9:48 p.m. Juan left first, followed by Jim, who tossed some plastic tops to soft drinks near the garbage.

The two of them had a gun, knife, and dirty clothes to dispose of. They drove away, tossing their outfits in a dumpster. To dispose of the gun, they headed to the forest preserve in nearby Carpentersville. They were familiar with the dark woods there,

SOMETHING BIG

having fished or smoked pot often at a nearby dam. When they arrived at the flowing Fox River, they tossed the gun, casings, and knife in the dark water. After covering their tracks, they met up with Eileen Bakalla in a nearby grocery store parking lot. Jim called her for a ride at Jake's Pizza.

Sitting on the bed in Jim's room, the two of them finished their story. Anne's suspicions from the phone call and newspaper clippings were confirmed. Her boyfriend ended with a warning, another way to assert control with fear.

"If you ever tell anyone about this, we'll kill you."[26]

****

They'd anticipated it. Having worked at the restaurant, it was almost certain that Juan Luna would be called in for questioning just like all the others. The task force was checking alibis of every Brown's Chicken employee over the past few years. They were making sure nobody held obvious grudges, no disgruntled former employees or axes to grind. So when he finally received the call in February a few weeks after the murders, Juan ran it up to Jim. *They want me to come in, what should we do?* he asked him while Jim was on the phone sitting in his basement. They hatched a plan.[27]

Sitting next to Jim while he talked on the phone with Juan was Anne Lockett. They were hanging out like any other typical occasion. But this time was different. Jim had a proposition for his girlfriend. More of an order, really. Anne would accompany Juan Luna to the headquarters of the police task force investigating the murders and pretend to be his girlfriend. She couldn't be his alibi given she had been in the hospital at that time, but it would help with appearances, and she could nevertheless back up his story. *And you'd both better dress up*, he demanded. Juan and Anne needed to look presentable. Like the kind of people no one would ever suspect for the slaughter of seven innocent individuals.

Anne and Juan donned business attire for his February 17 interview, with Juan wearing a black tie, white shirt, and sharp trench coat. His Sunday best. The two of them drove to the task force building in Palatine on Quentin Road, and when they entered, there was a large lobby that the police had made into a waiting room. It was empty, and Anne sat down while Juan was guided to the back by a police officer from the task force.

The task force building was cubicle city. As the temporary headquarters for the investigation, nothing fancy was needed. Back at the officer's desk, there was a small table, a chair, and a typewriter used for recording responses from interviewees. Juan sat down.

The officer began with the basics—address, date of birth. Then, some additional probing, but nothing that suggested any lingering suspicion from the police. *What was your job at Brown's?* Juan was a breader and cook, hired by the previous owners then leaving in June of 1992 just after the Ehlenfeldts purchased the restaurant.[28] *Why'd you leave?* For a better-paying job, he explained. *Who did you get along with? Who did you dislike?* Juan talked about his other employees. Some were his pals, others were just okay, but he had no beef with anybody.

Finally, the moment he'd prepared for arrived. A crucial question. *Who were you with that night?* Juan told the officer that he spent the whole evening with his ex-girlfriend, a girl named Eileen. *What's Eileen's last name?* the officer followed up. Juan paused. He couldn't remember. The two were acquaintances, but not incredibly close. *Uhh, I don't remember her last name*, Juan told him. The officer was unfazed. He continued completing the two-page form of standard questions.

Juan was led through cube city to a separate room in the building for finger and palm printing. His hand was placed on a flat surface and rolled in ink, then placed on a blank card to capture the outline. A double-sided card was used for the palm prints, and the officer placed Juan's right palm on the card to capture the print. Inadvertently, he left the other side blank. Juan Luna's left palm print was not taken. With a Polaroid camera, the officer took a picture of Juan.[29] And with that, after an hour and a half, Juan Luna was let go. He had passed the test.

For each of the employees and other key interviewees, investigators at the task force took a photo and printed them out. Eventually, those pictures were placed on a wall, all portraits of people connected in any way to the massacre at Brown's.

The pictures were indistinguishable. Each individual had some connection to the restaurant. They all had alibis. And there were no obvious motives. If you stood back and stared at them, the collage of photos was a blur, a performative exercise akin to the clichéd corkboard in a detective novel with thumbtacks connected by string in search of a pattern. Here, there was no obvious pattern.

But on closer inspection, one Polaroid stood out from the rest. Among the sea of faces, only one person pictured was wearing a tie and dress clothes. Only Juan Luna had prepared for his close-up.[30]

CHAPTER 11

JERRY

Palatine, Illinois was a quiet suburb. But it would be inaccurate to say there was *never* any violent crime. In Palatine, people killed people, just like everywhere else in America. Murder happens in the city, the country, and even places that dub themselves *A Real Hometown*.

There was the mysterious disappearance of Stephanie Lyng, who vanished one October morning. Her body was never located, but prosecutors were able to garner a conviction nevertheless, a rare occurrence under those circumstances. Then there was Elizabeth Ehlert, who allegedly placed her newborn baby in a creek in 1990, leaving the child to die shortly after giving birth secretly in her home and was also suspected of killing her mother.[1] Or the case of Dr. Lee Robin, who bludgeoned his wife to death in 1989 by hitting her with an axe twenty times and drowning their two-and-a-half-month-old daughter in their bathtub.[2]

To say that the Palatine police were not ready for a case of this sort would be a true statement. It's also a statement that, in many ways, is meaningless. Handed the same set of facts, no police department of Palatine's size could have possibly been prepared to solve this case alone. Chief Jerry Bratcher recognized this almost immediately.

The department which Bratcher oversaw kept the streets safe for a village that was generically suburban. Palatine was a place people moved to for good schools and safe neighborhoods. The department's day-to-day entailed what one might expect. Traffic stops for speeding motorists and the occasional drunk driver. Retail theft in the village's downtown area or in various strip malls was common but certainly not pervasive. A residential burglary happened here and there.

When Chief Jerry Bratcher came to Palatine in 1974, he inherited a department that was suffering from low morale and a city council that blamed his predecessor for poor leadership and eventually forced him to resign. Bratcher came with a diverse swath of experience that benefitted the department. At seventeen, he had joined the Marine Corps and served in the Korean War, eventually attaining the rank of sergeant and working as a drill instructor. Because of this, he knew how to motivate people. After leaving the Navy, he found his way into law enforcement, starting off at the bottom rung of the DeKalb police department, a city about an hour west of Chicago that housed the campus of Northern Illinois University.

After a brief stint in the private sector as a salesman for Regency Life Insurance Company in Springfield, Illinois, Bratcher's first opportunity to serve as a chief came in the small town of Rochelle, a place even farther west surrounded by farms and canning factories.[3] There, he learned the ropes of managing a department, from dealing with the city council to handling the discipline of an officer who acted out of line.

Bratcher believed in the importance of education, both formal and informal. A man with two master's degrees, he was well read. When new officers came onto the force in Palatine after the police academy, he'd make them do case briefs, an exercise found in every first-year law-school classroom of summarizing court cases to better understand the law. It was key for his officers to know how to act by the book so their work was not for naught.[4] What good is a sloppy arrest if the person is quickly let go?

Under his leadership, the department innovated. He created a dual-ladder career program where officers could gain extra money for being efficient and productive members of the force. His private-sector experience helped him understand the value of creating incentives to perform.[5]

The Palatine police became accredited by a national group called the Commission on Accreditation for Law Enforcement, the second department to do so in the state of Illinois and one of the first in the nation.[6] They rolled out a DARE program to crack down on drug use among teens in the community. Palatine implemented neighborhood-based policing which required officers to be out in the community, presenting themselves as familiar faces rather than a burden. Law enforcement see people in their worst moments, and this was an opportunity to have a more wholistic view of the area they were sworn to protect.

Now fifty-nine, Bratcher was at the top of his game. In 1993, the force counted more than one hundred among its ranks, two deputy chiefs under him, sergeants for various beats, and commanders who handled investigations and research.

On the day after the murders, Chief Bratcher quickly called for help from other departments and agencies such as the Cook County sheriff's police, Northern Illinois Police Crime Lab, and the FBI. Because of his strong rapport with other chiefs in the area, departments from other suburbs and the city of Chicago willingly sent investigators to assist.

The police station was housed in the basement of the Palatine Community Center, a building that served as the village's nerve center, with the mayor's office and departments like public works on other floors. A former high school, there were still empty classrooms upstairs in the building which were quickly turned into a makeshift press conference room. The station was buzzing.

To outsiders, the fact that the police department in Palatine didn't even have its own building was evidence that they were ill-equipped to handle the case. But while the Palatine police were certainly running the investigation, Jerry Bratcher was not overly territorial or unwilling to ask for help. In fact, he asked for help from anyone who would give it.

With outside help flooding in, it became clear the station's basement facilities would be insufficient to house new team members, so Chief Bratcher's team gained access to an unused administrative building owned by the local school district on Quentin Road.[7] The building was already well equipped with phones, copy machines, and other office materials. There were conference rooms, cubicles, and a lobby. When the village electrician finally called to get the building set up with power, he was informed it would be at least two weeks before the job could be done. When the team explained the urgency, the building was turned back on in just a few hours. All of Chicagoland was watching.

Jobs were divvied up to different task force members, like who would continue helping with the crime scene, and who would interview suspects, who would communicate with the victims' families. Those coming from jurisdictions other than

Palatine were paired with a hometown officer to guide them.[8] Inside the break room, a pot of hot coffee was constantly simmering, with snacks and donuts nearby. A communal "pop fund" of loose change was set up for the vending machines or office supplies.[9] Near the back door of the office, a grill was set up for cooking hot dogs by the dozens. Back at the Palatine Community Center, evidence from the crime scene filled up an old classroom, including doors and countertops from the restaurant.[10] The phones continued ringing nonstop.

When the Martin Blake lead fell through hours after the murders, the task force continued to be overwhelmed with tips. Every robbery provided a false sense of hope, like that of a nearby Mexican grocery store or Taco Bell. Psychics reported their visions with certainty, even contacting the families to share their thoughts. Crossed lovers called to report their exes. Others reported dreams.

"Earl states that he is the last surviving member of the Palatine murders," said one such tip from a local resident with a particularly vivid imagination. "Earl is a federal marshal answering only to the president," the officer wrote, copying the words conveyed to them by the caller. Clearly, only in his head was Earl a secret agent reporting directly to the most powerful man on earth. And unfortunately for the police, a great deal of their time was spent sorting through messages like these.

Ten days after the killings, a body was found just five miles from the scene of the crime in the nearby suburb of Barrington. Discovered near some train tracks, the corpse was dismembered, with its head missing entirely.[11] A tipster alleged they saw someone matching the description of Paul Modrowski, a nineteen-year-old, at Brown's that night. Police arrested him and his friend Robert Faraci after investigating. Having experienced the chaos of the Martin Blake questioning, police were more tight-lipped. They interrogated Modrowski and Faraci, but their alibis checked out. Eventually, the body was identified as that of Dean Fawcett. The crimes—both horrendous—had no relation. The men might have killed someone, but it wasn't the seven people at Brown's Chicken that night.

There was no honeymoon period for the Palatine police, and criticism came immediately from some of the families, people in the community, and the media. Some of the family members said the police ignored their concerns when they reported their loved ones missing. They could have found them still alive, they said, an argument that tugs on the heartstrings but was inaccurate. Others said their concerns were ignored because of racism, citing their accents or status as immigrants in a community that was mostly homogenous and white, a claim to which police responded strongly. When the police finally announced the names of the victims after sixteen hours, the department was criticized for waiting too long.[12]

Reporters trawled Palatine armed with cameras and microphones interviewing anyone who would talk. Local coffee shops and the Palatine Inn, a nearby diner and mainstay of the community, became crowded with newsies looking for a scoop. Nearby business owners who claimed to have information said they'd never been contacted. "The police have not been here," the owner of a beauty shop that closed that night at 10:00 p.m. told a camera crew from ABC-7, with her blonde hair well-coifed, purple eyeshadow darkened under her eyes, and flashy hoop earrings dangling from her ears. "They've not been here at all?" the reporter asked credulously. "Nope." She then smiled. "Just reporters," she said, hinting that this was far from her first visit from a member of the media.[13] Residents who lived nearby Brown's said they heard gunshots that night but had not been asked for information, an assertion that police tested by firing gun shots inside and stationing officers nearby to listen. Newspapers narrowed in on the failure to obtain footage from the security cameras of a nearby 24/7 gas station that might have caught a glimpse of the killers.[14]

The criticism was loud and unceasing, with nuanced answers from police a weak response to quell the fears. Required to keep the investigation under wraps and not reveal more information than necessary, the Palatine police were restrained by a muzzle preventing them from responding to certain allegations.

Help was sent to the task force by more than twenty-one different police departments and law enforcement organizations.[15] Palatine police were more than grateful for the assistance, but bringing in outsiders also meant opening themselves up to internal criticism of their handling of the investigation. No one questioned that the police borrowed from Chicago had more experience solving complex cases and homicides. And that's why Chief Bratcher brought them into the fold seeking to learn from their experience. But he would come to resent the meddling from outsiders.

***

Richard Zuley's reputation preceded him. A longtime member of the Chicago police force, Detective Zuley specialized in investigating homicides. If he walked into a room, you wouldn't associate his bookish demeanor, large square glasses, and business attire with being one of Chicago's shrewdest murder investigators. But Richard Zuley was the real deal, the kind of detective who took matters into his own hands and didn't wait for instructions. If he found a hot lead, he'd pursue it solo. When a theory seemed right to him, he'd investigate accordingly. Armed with this know-how, Detective Zuley was one of many officers borrowed from the Chicago police to assist the Palatine task force in their investigation.

Jailhouse snitches had been a fruitful source of information for homicide investigators in the city of Chicago like Zuley, but a source that many also approached with caution. There were incentives for someone already in prison to lie. But Detective Zuley was used to navigating these tricky sources. When he obtained information from a jailhouse informant named Renaldo Aviles pointing to a member of a Puerto Rican street gang named Jose Morales Cruz as a suspect for the murders in Palatine, he acted fast. Both men were members of the Puerto Rican Stones. Zuley dug into the lead, speaking with informants in Cook County Jail and attempting to corroborate the story.

The task force met for daily briefings and roll calls to share information and regroup. Which potential suspects fell through? What new leads merited more attention? What were people hearing on the ground? One afternoon, Detective Zuley revealed what he'd discovered about the Puerto Rican Stones members to others on the task force. He said a woman overheard two guys speaking Spanish with a Puerto Rican accent, saying they alluded to the murders. Zuley had rock-solid evidence too: a customer who was allegedly turned away from the restaurant that night described a figure that matched a fellow gang member. The lead—Lead 80—seemed promising.

Open to pursuing any possible avenue, police questioned Jose Morales Cruz at Cook County jail. But Detective Zuley was left out of the process, and he was furious.[16] "This is bullshit, cutting us out," he vented.[17] It was his lead and his hard work that got police to this point. It was also true that the rest of the Palatine team had far less experience questioning gang members or depraved criminals, and Detective Zuley made sure to let them know just how far superior his investigative skills were when he confronted them about it. "What did you do?" Zuley said to Commander John Koziol of the Palatine police. "You've only worked on two murders in your life! How many gang-banging, murdering, robbing Puerto Ricans have you ever interviewed in Palatine?" he yelled.[18] But Koziol and the rest of the Palatine police persisted.

To Koziol and investigators like Detective Bill King, it became clear after interviewing Cruz that their information was not accurate, and no pot shots taken at their level of experience could take away that fact. The customer who allegedly saw a person turn them away at the restaurant that night had made the story up. The woman who came forward originally was revealed to have a long history of duping others. She'd swindled friends for money. She'd even faced charges for pretending to be a nurse at a previous job. Jose Morales Cruz, the informant, was found dead in his cell in an apparent suicide from an asthma medication called theophylline. Others suspected foul play. Either way, for the time being, Lead 80 faded. Unsurprisingly, Detective Zuley did not take kindly to this development. He'd seen this kind of pattern before, and as one of Chicago's lead homicide detectives, he felt there was more to be discovered. He persisted, and unwilling to let the lead go and cooperate with the direction of the task force, Zuley was quietly disappeared from the team and forced to return to his regular job with the homicide division of the Chicago police. The disagreements between him and the Palatine police became unworkable.

SOMETHING BIG

As an investigator on high-profile cases, Zuley had developed sources in the press over the years. Occasionally the media was useful for drawing public attention to a matter. So after leaving the task force, he turned to Chuck Goudie of ABC-7, perhaps the task force's most hated journalist for his unceasing coverage and withering criticism of police. In September, a few months into the investigation, a confidential report revealing the dispute over Lead 80 aired on the 10:00 p.m. news that caught Chief Bratcher completely off guard.

One afternoon, the pagers of the officers working the task force began buzzing as they were called into a meeting with Chief Bratcher. *Maybe there's a break in the case?* some wondered with hope. Gathered together at the task force headquarters, the crowded room of officers waited patiently. Then, hushed silence fell upon the room as Bratcher approached the podium. "Good afternoon, *gentlemen*," he said sternly, purposefully enunciating the last word for dramatic effect. He paused for an uncomfortable amount of time and stared forward, then addressed the reason for their gathering. "Someone in this room has made a career decision."[19] He told the task force members that he would find out who leaked the information to the media, and it would be dealt with accordingly. The broadcast not only threatened to jeopardize the secrecy of the investigation and much of the information shared in the latest report was false. Eventually, an investigation by the Chicago police department traced the leak back to Detective Zuley, and he was suspended for a single day. It was a symbolic slap on the wrist.

Instructed by his superiors at the Chicago police to let go of the investigation, Detective Zuley still persisted. He continued digging. He kept making phone calls. He chased down that irresistible lead. One day, Zuley visited Manny Castro's silk-screen printing business in the city seeking to speak with the father of Michael Castro. He left his business card and a pager number, and the two eventually talked on the phone. Detective Zuley asked Castro about his son and any potential gang connections he might have had. *Had you or your son had any contact with any Puerto Rican gangs through your store?*, he asked. The line of questioning fueled by a belief among task force members that Michael may have known his attacker because of the wounds he sustained. It appeared he might have fought back at the time. Not to mention, Manny Castro had sold guns at his store in Chicago, something Zuley thought may have attracted unsavory characters. On the phone, Manny Castro learned intimate details about how his son was murdered for the first time from an investigator no longer working the case.[20]

Early on in the investigation, the Palatine police had assigned one specific officer, Detective Jack Byrnes, to serve as the liaison for the families. It was a way of ensuring only quality information reached them and there was no confusion about who they could go to for questions. Manny Castro gave Byrnes a call to inform him of the contact he'd had with Richard Zuley. Byrnes was furious. And after another investigation into his conduct, Detective Zuley was again suspended for five days in June of 1994 by his superiors at the Chicago police. Detective Richard Zuley's meddling into the Palatine police's investigation was over. For now.

***

"Tomorrow marks a grim anniversary," said CBS 2 Chicago's Lester Holt on that evening's broadcast. "It'll be one year since seven people were shot in the Brown's Chicken restaurant in the quiet northwest suburb of Palatine." Reporters again descended upon Palatine for coverage of memorial services and interviews with families.

"Does this case keep you up at night?" a reporter asked Chief Jerry Bratcher during an exclusive interview outside the shuttered restaurant in January of 1994. "It's usually the last thing I think about when I go to sleep and the first thing I think about when I wake up in the morning," Bratcher said after a long pause, dressed in a black trench coat and tie with his breath visible in the cold. "It's with you all the time."

The memory of their loved ones was also with the families all the time. The Brown's Chicken sign was removed from the restaurant a few days before the first anniversary. It was one less reminder of the tragedy that had struck that dull strip mall corner. The Castros continued praying, with a framed picture of Michael draped in a rosary and surrounded by prayer cards, candles, and colorful pictures of Jesus and the Virgin Mary with their hands clasped sitting atop a piano in their living room. The Ehlenfeldts' daughters began a routine of checking in with one another despite having spread out across the country. Marcus Nellsen's mother, Diane Clayton, penned him a letter. "It has been one year since your life came to such a tragic end," she wrote. "I will never understand how such a horrible thing could have happened, but I have finally accepted it, for I have no other choice."[21] Evelyn Urgena, Rico Solis's mother, welcomed reporters into her home to talk about her son. "You can still smell him," she said, hugging his old work shirts kept in a wooden cabinet in the house and putting them to her face to demonstrate a routine she'd done to remember her son.[22]

With the investigation having slowed, the outside help dispatched to Palatine began rolling off the investigation, the temporary task force office closed, and police moved back into the Palatine police department in the basement of the village's community center.[23] About ten officers were working the case.

Just two months after the first anniversary in March, two fingerprint examiners from the Chicago Police department matched a fingerprint found on the inside window of the restaurant to a thirty-five-year-old man living on the west side of Chicago named Terry McGee.[24] It was done using a state-of-the-art computer identification system called the Automated Fingerprint Identification System. [25]They brought him in for questioning along with his half-brother. A warrant was obtained, and his house was searched for guns, ammunition, and anything that could link him to the crime.

McGee had a record, and he made for an unsympathetic suspect. He'd served a prison sentence for armed robbery in 1983.[26] He was convicted of theft in 1975. He served another six months in prison for unlawful possession of a weapon.[27] Plus, experts had matched a fingerprint to the scene. It had to be. The science doesn't lie. But McGee begged to differ.[28] His family was hounded by the press at home and at the station, with some covering their faces with jackets to avoid the paparazzi-like atmosphere. "This is just another tragedy that happens every day in the Black community. You get one record, and every time something happens, they come for you," his half-brother told the press when questioned.[29] In the end, the fingerprint was a mismatch. It was an anomaly, something that rarely occurs in criminal inquiries. Yet another indication that this was not your average murder investigation.

CHAPTER 12

RITA

Knickknacks. Tchotchkes. Collectables. Rita Mullins loved them all. Having run an antique shop from the first floor of her home in Palatine for many years, she never passed up on the chance to browse through a new shop when the opportunity presented itself.

As she scanned the shelves of a gift shop in Washington, DC, in January of 1993, Rita Mullins sensed hubbub around her. "You know who that is, right?" whispered someone next to her in amazement. In the distance, she recognized the man. It was James Earl Jones, one of the most famous actors on the planet.

No wallflower, Rita decided to walk toward him and introduce herself. She readied one of her business cards and approached the superstar made internationally famous for his role as Darth Vader in *Star Wars*. "Hello, Mr. Jones, my name is Rita Mullins and I'm the mayor of Palatine, Illinois," she said, handing him the card. Jones looked down at it, then back up. "Oh," he said in his low, baritone voice, "I'm so sorry."

***

Rita Mullins had never really been *from* anywhere. That is, until she moved to Palatine in her teens. Born to a military family, her parents had crisscrossed the nation to Massachusetts, then California and Hawaii for a time, back to Massachusetts, North Carolina, and eventually settled down in Illinois where they had roots in Palatine. She attended Palatine High School, went off to college and eventually married her husband in 1965, then had kids and decided to raise them in the village.

Politics had always been a side project for her as she was raising her three kids and working stints in insurance, banking, real estate, and as a small-business owner. She helped out with local candidates who she knew by knocking on doors and hanging leaflets on front doors. For her, the work was always behind the scenes, making calls and knocking on doors while, in her view, the men at the top of the ticket took all the credit. So instead of continuing to play second fiddle, she decided to run for office in the early 1980s for the position of city clerk of Palatine. It was a thankless, mostly nonpolitical position that paid a pittance and was almost always held by women. She underwent the proper certification, learned correct minute taking for meetings, mastered *Robert's Rules*, and kept things in order. It was the perfect avenue for learning more about municipal government. Technically a village, people referred to it interchangeably as a city. The mayor, previously named the village president, led the government.

While in her second term as village clerk, the new first-term mayor continued battling with the village council. Frank Munch was a flamboyant personality. His approach to government was atypical, and he had a knack for picking fights.

SOMETHING BIG

One day, Rita Mullins was in the copy room at village hall. The mayor was conspicuously making photocopies of checks, made out to him from a development company with which the city council had recently approved new business. The mayor had broken the tied vote. Now, he was being paid. Rita was stunned at his gall, and when she informed the village council of what she'd seen, they appointed her to investigate. This was something you expected in Chicago, not Palatine. When her report was released, it made some headlines, but it mostly faded. So the village council decided the matter must be dealt with politically. With the support of her colleagues, Rita ran in 1989, and stressing her experience and belief in the power of good government, she won by a two-to-one margin.[1]

Mayor Rita Mullins focused on the basics: fire, police, water, sewer, and roads. She annexed unincorporated parts of the city to expand the taxbase. She advocated for redevelopment of the area's downtown business district. Rita Mullins poured her heart into being mayor of Palatine, treating the role as a full-time gig despite only being paid a small stipend.

Being the children of Palatine's chief sometimes got on the nerves of her children. "My basement is flooding!" one constituent called during a heavy rain when Rita's daughter picked up the phone. "What's she gonna do about this?" he yelled. Her daughter was unimpressed. "Do you want her to come over with a bucket?" she replied, peeved at the suggestion that somehow every problem that materialized in Palatine was her mother's fault, even the weather. Such is the life of a small-town mayor.

Early in her tenure, Rita became heavily involved with the US Conference of Mayors, an advocacy group focused on bolstering the needs of American cities before the federal government. Rita Mullins was a triple minority for the group—female,

Republican, and the head of a small city. It gave her access to resources and new ideas, and it was also a forum to hobnob with big-city mayors when she became part of the group's leadership. On the dais at big annual conferences or on the White House lawn after meetings with the president would be the leaders of places like New York, Chicago, and Los Angeles—plus Rita Mullins, the mayor of Palatine, Illinois (population: 50,000). Critics back home criticized her for her involvement, claiming she was too distracted building a national profile. But Rita recognized the value.

On January 9, 1993, Rita Mullins had been driving home when she called her husband from her car phone. "Do you want me to pick up something from Brown's Chicken?" she asked him, just blocks away. They decided against it, opting for leftovers instead. Like so many others, Rita Mullins went to bed that night only to be woken up by the terrible news at Brown's. What followed was work she never signed up for as mayor—but work that would prove to be the most important of her career.

For those not involved in the investigation itself, there was an awkward feeling of the need to help but not quite knowing what to do. Rita Mullins started by lowering the flags to half-mast across the village. At the first press conference at the Palatine Community Center alongside police and other community leaders, she addressed the impact on the community in front of reporters. But press conferences and flags were distant. Serving as the village's griever-in-chief was an entirely different task.

Word came from Frank Portillo that the company had received checks from its insurance company in the amount of $4,200 to pay for the burials of each individual.[2] A check that put a value on the invaluable. So Rita Mullins and the deputy city manager, Michael Cassady, accompanied Portillo to deliver the checks to each of the victims' families. Children still processing the loss of their parents. Mothers and fathers coming to grips with the fact that they'd outlived their kid. *Please let us know however we can help you*, Rita would try and calm them, knowing no words from a person from the government could truly soothe their pain. They sat on living room couches, listening, witnessing the tears and pain.[3]

Most people after the death of a loved one have the chance to grieve in private. But the families' suffering would be out in the open, with each funeral a public event. Just hours earlier, a member of each family had been forced to identify their loved ones' bodies at the morgue.[4] Now, they were saying goodbye to their family member surrounded by cameras and crowds, more people around them than ever before yet among the loneliest days of their lives. Not to mention, the lack of closure that came with holding a funeral but still wondering with each passing moment when the murders would be solved.

Lynn and Dick Ehlenfeldt's funeral took place at the Kingswood United Methodist Church where they'd been pillars of the congregation. Inside, nearly seven hundred people gathered, the altar filled with flowers and an easel in the front with a collage of family photos providing a snapshot of their lives.[5] The celebration of Lupe Maldonado's life happened at Santa Teresita's Palatine, the crowd half Latino and half white and the ceremony given in Spanish and English.[6] His casket was then sent back to his home in Celaya, Mexico.[7] Thomas Mennes's brother Larry delivered the eulogy at St. Thomas of Villanova in Palatine, with his family still in shock. "Tom was a simple guy," he said of his brother. "You could probably fit all of his belongings in the trunk of a car."[8] Marcus Nellsen's casket was draped in a flag at Willow Creek Community Church, a photo of his daughter sitting inside. Only a child, she tried to wake her father up, too young to understand what was happening.[9] He received a full twenty-one-gun salute upon his burial at Memory Gardens in Arlington Heights, and his parents were handed the folded American flag from the casket.[10]

As the youngest of the group, the ceremonies for Michael Castro and Rico Solis were even more heart-wrenching. The boys' age was a stark reminder of the hideous nature of the tragedy. Both the Castro and Solis families held joint wakes for the two high-school friends where the two families actually discovered a distant relation to one another through relatives in the Philippines. It was a realization that brought them even closer in this darkest hour. Hundreds of classmates, family members, and even strangers poured in to mourn the loss of the two high schoolers. Rico Solis would be buried in the clothes he purchased with his first paycheck just three months earlier.[11] His final mass took place at St. Edna Catholic Church in Palatine.

As always, the press was never far, always seeking a compelling visual. Sometimes they got too close, peering into the open casket of Michael Castro with TV cameras running as his mother wept in sorrow. They were eventually asked to leave.[12] Flowers abounded, a white crucifix hung from the door of the casket, and a little plush puppy could be seen inside, with the deceased wearing a red shirt with the words "U.S. Marines," an ode to his life goal.[13] At Michael Castro's funeral, friends carried the caskets into St. Theresa's Catholic church and hundreds of cars followed in the procession.[14] He was the final victim to be laid to rest.

For Rita Mullins, the public grieving continued in Palatine. At Cutting Hall, a local performing arts center, she led the city in a memorial service five days after the murders. Normally the mayor wore hats. Rita Mullins had a hat for every season and a hat for every reason. Hats for holidays, weddings, or a day at the racetrack. But today her strawberry-blonde hair was uncovered, and she dressed plainly in a gray shawl, pearls, and a cross around her neck. A dozen microphones were tied together at the wooden podium. When she spoke, her voice was gentle. "The Bible's shortest verse is 'Jesus wept,'" she told the crowd, quoting John 11:35. "Tonight, Palatine wept."[15]

"At this time I would like everyone to stand and join me in holding hands in a moment of silent prayer."[16] Standing back, Rita grabbed those on stage before an audience of around 250, leading them in prayer and reading the names of the seven victims. Guadalupe Maldonado. Michael Castro. Lynn Ehlenfeldt. Richard Ehlenfeldt. Marcus Nellsen. Tom Mennes. Rico Solis. What else was there to say with so much uncertainty in the air? In the auditorium, some of the families watched and embraced. Attendees teared up.

Pastors from across the community shared their thoughts. "And they say that kind of thing doesn't happen here because we don't have that kind of neighborhood around us," a Lutheran minister observed somberly. "And they say it can't happen here because we don't have those kind of streets. But it did."[17] Rita Mullins heard variations of the same line over and over. *It's not supposed to happen here.* The refrain came to annoy her. It was a thoughtless line. Where exactly *is* the murder of seven innocent people supposed to happen?

The audience said prayers and sang hymns, like "How Great Thou Art." To some, the tragedy at Brown's was proof of God's absence. How great Thou art? If God is everywhere, was He in the restaurant that day? Or the bullets that took their loved ones? Stale declarations from religious leaders—*it's in His plan, they're in a better place*—were cold comfort.

But for others, the display of faith was a source of strength. Left to deal with unspeakable tragedy, those suffering turned to God for comfort and understanding. Sometimes it's better not to try and comprehend the incomprehensible.

In this process—the grieving, the media, the investigation—so little was in the families' control. Surrendering themselves to a higher power was perhaps the only thing over which they truly had agency.

***

Neighborhood watch meetings were typically sparsely attended in Palatine. In a safe community, getting residents to care more about public safety was like selling water to fish. But the events of January 8 changed that. People started locking their doors. Business owners escorted their employees to their cars. Firearm sales soared. Fortunately, the Palatine police already had a crime prevention unit. It ran neighborhood watches, did security surveys of people's homes and businesses, and built relationships so people would be more willing to share information with law enforcement.

Officer Brad Grossman entered a house in Palatine one afternoon for a neighborhood watch meeting and headed down to the basement. It was a normal community gathering like dozens he'd held before, but as he made it down the steps he was shocked to find more than eighty residents gathered. They were packed together, squished on couches, crouched on the floor, and seated on the stairs. People were hungry for more information. It was the physical embodiment of the unease in the community. There was a hunger for information.

Officer Grossman greeted the residents and spoke about the steps the department was taking. He gave them information about how to protect themselves at night and simple precautions to harden their homes from criminals. *What's happening with the Brown's investigation?*, one resident asked, addressing the proverbial elephant in the room. *We've got dozens of officers working day and night to solve this crime, and Chief Bratcher has brought in the best help from across the country to assist*, he explained, taking them through the expansive efforts. When he finished, the residents gave a standing ovation for the work the department was doing, a message of appreciation he took back to those laboring around the clock back at the task force.

To draw in more tips, an award fund called "Palatine Cares" was set up by Palatine alderman Jack Wagner. The owner of a chemical disinfectant company, his business was left with the unenviable task of cleaning up the crime scene at Brown's when no other cleaning service would take the job.[18] The fund started with a $1,000 investment from Wagner.[19]

First just a few dollars, the fund ballooned to over $100,000 by the end of January. Frank Portillo pledged a hefty sum, fundraisers and events were held, and students at Palatine High School chipped in. When the announcement of the fund was first made, a paper bag was passed around among the press corps gathered, and they were among the first to contribute.[20] The Filipino community in Chicago came out and helped fundraise for the Solis and Castro families. A billboard was erected urging people to call a hotline and report new information. The village of Palatine came together.

Before the murders, Rita Mullins was set to attend the annual winter meetings of the US Conference of Mayors in Washington, DC, and she decided to continue as planned. Throughout the event, the massacre at Brown's was still fresh in her mind. As she sat on the edge of her bed in the Capitol Hilton in downtown Washington, she scribbled notes on a yellow legal pad, trying to express her pressing thoughts. "Wake up, America," she wrote. "Heed the sound of the shots that rang out in my city, and were heard around the world." She sent the piece off to the *Daily Herald*, the main paper in the northwest suburbs, which printed it on the front page the next day.

Gun control had always been an issue for which Rita Mullins advocated, even before the shootings. She'd accompanied James Brady, namesake of the Brady Bill, onto Wrigley Field when he threw out the opening pitch at a Cubs game years earlier. She'd studied the issue. Rita grew up quail hunting with her father and knew about guns.[21] She respected the Second Amendment. But the tragedy at Brown's brought things closer to home. It also elevated her visibility on the issue.

At the winter meeting, gathered before hundreds of the nation's most prominent mayors, she echoed her calls for a change in gun policy. "Seven good members of our community, our collective family, lost their lives," she said. "Their deaths must not be forgotten, their deaths must move us forward, into an America where handgun violence has no place."[22]

Rita Mullins continued to use her platform to call for stricter gun control in Washington, even visiting the White House on multiple occasions to lobby for the issue and use the story of Palatine as evidence of the pressing need for reform. At home, the agony in her community grew. Six months passed, and little progress was made in the investigation.

SOMETHING BIG

At the Brown's Chicken, some of the victims' families displayed their deep frustration for everyone to see. Printed on computer paper, they plastered a message on the now-vacant storefront for all the passersby to see: "Who Killed—7 People—6 Months Ago?"

***

It was summer, and Anne Lockett was trying to lose weight. She wanted to look fit. At least, that's what she told her friends about her newfound exercise-and-diet craze. With summer nights providing a relief from the insufferable heat, the recent high-school grad would go on long walks, strolling through neighborhoods, down busy streets, and traversing the green public parks of Palatine. Sometimes three miles, sometimes four. For company, she'd often invite a friend to tag along.

Anne and her friend would trot across Palatine and catch up. The routes sometimes changed, but they'd always end up at the corner of Smith and Northwest Highway. There, the Brown's Chicken building stood lifeless in its lonely spot in the strip-mall parking lot with an unmanned squad car in the lot to deter bystanders from investigating themselves. Cars whizzed by, and the faint sounds of summer—cicadas and crickets—could be heard in the distance. The village's water tower loomed in the distance.

Let's sit for a bit, Anne would say, proceeding to plop down on the concrete outside the restaurant. They'd stare at the building's white painted bricks and slanted green roof. Nearly half a year had passed, but fresh flowers were still ever-present. Mourners left pictures of their friends and loved ones. Teddy bears. Colorful balloons. The kind of scene you pass on the highway and think, *I wonder what happened there?* Except no one who passed the corner of Smith and Northwest Highway wondered. Everyone knew what had happened on January 8, 1993.

Anne sat outside the restaurant. She was anxious but tried playing it cool. It was time to broach the subject. "How do you think their parents feel now?" she'd ask shyly, referring to the deaths of everyone found that day. "Probably still horrible," her friend would reply, the kind of response everyone in Palatine shared. "Do you think they were scared when it happened?" she'd ask. "I imagine they were horrified," her friend would say. Nearly everyone in the village thought about what had happened, but in the months that followed it was not a subject they dwelled on. Life moved on for those disconnected to the victims.

Anne's questions were banal. The kinds of things anyone would wonder upon seeing the site.[23] Yet with each question, Anne was attempting to elicit some kind of response. She sought an opening, a reply that would help her work up the courage to say what she really knew about what happened at Brown's Chicken that night. Then she'd remember the ominous warning she'd received from Jim Degorski and Juan Luna. It gave her pause.

They'd killed seven people that day. Why not one more?

SOMETHING BIG

The front page of the *Daily Herald* the day after the bodies were found in the Brown's Chicken restaurant in Palatine, Illinois. Photo courtesy of the *Daily Herald*.

Palatine police climb onto the roof of the Brown's Chicken & Pasta restaurant to search for clues.

Palatine police climb the snowy roof of the Brown's Chicken restaurant on January 9, 1993 in the aftermath of the killings. Photo courtesy of the *Daily Herald*.

SOMETHING BIG

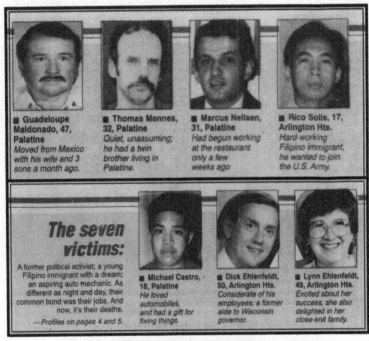

Photos of the seven victims.
Photo courtesy of the *Daily Herald*.

Early Saturday evening, Palatine police bring out the first of the seven bodies found in two walk-in coolers at the Brown's Chicken & Pasta, 168 W. Northwest Hwy. *Daily Herald Photo/Mark Welsh*

In the early evening of Saturday, January 9, 1993, Palatine police bring the first seven bodies out of the building as a crowd looks on. Photo courtesy of the *Daily Herald*.

SOMETHING BIG

The Brown's Chicken restaurant in Palatine at the corner of Smith and Northwest Highway is blocked off by police cars in the aftermath of the killings. Photo courtesy of the *Daily Herald*.

Palatine Mayor Rita Mullins and Brown's Chicken owner and co-founder Frank Portillo address the media at a press conference. Photo courtesy of the *Daily Herald*.

The new task force headquarters are in the old district offices of Palatine Elementary District 15.

Daily Herald Photo/Vincent Pierri

A sign blocks the entrance to the temporary headquarters of the police task force. In the aftermath of the killings, more than a hundred uniformed officers and civilians worked the case full time. Photo courtesy of the *Daily Herald*.

SOMETHING BIG

Despite the sudden, violent deaths of their parents, the daughters of Richard and Lynn Ehlenfeldt said Thursday they were not raised to live in fear or live in the past. Joy, Jennifer and Dana Ehlenfelt, left to right, also said they were overwhelmed by the outpouring of support they've received. *Daily Herald Photo/Vincent Pierri*

In an effort to get ahead of the media frenzy, the daughters of Lynn and Richard Ehlenfeldt—Jennifer, Dana, and Joy—give a press conference talking about their parents' lives. Photo courtesy of the *Daily Herald*.

Palatine Police Chief Jerry Bratcher gives an update on the case. Photo courtesy of the *Daily Herald*.

Frank Portillo gives an interview in the Brown's Chicken corporate headquarters. Photo courtesy of the *Daily Herald*.

SOMETHING BIG

J. Terrence Brunner, executive director of the Better Government Association, criticizes Palatine police for their investigation of the 1993 Brown's murders. *Daily Herald Photo/Joe Lewnard*

Terry Brunner, head of the Better Government Association, gives a press conference in 1997 presenting the release of his group's report criticizing Palatine police for their investigation of then-unsolved murders. Photo courtesy of the *Daily Herald*.

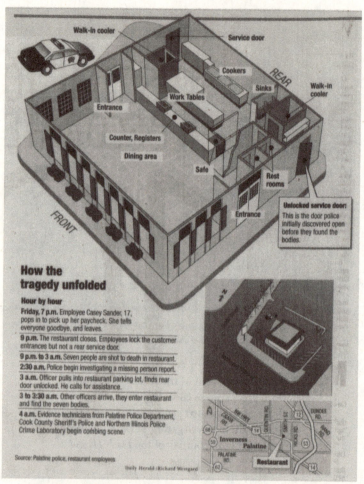

This sketch from the *Daily Herald*, the main newspaper in the northwest suburbs of Chicago, illustrates the layout of the restaurant. Photo courtesy of the *Daily Herald*.

SOMETHING BIG

Juan A. Luna, middle, and James Eric Degorski appear before Cook County Judge Margaret Mary Brosnahan during their bond hearing Saturday.

Juan Luna, left, and James Degorski, right, appear for their first hearing in court following their arrest for the murder of seven people. Photo courtesy of the *Daily Herald*.

Eileen Bakalla identifies Juan Luna in the courtroom during his trial for murder. In her testimony, Bakalla describes how Luna and Degorski met up with her the night of the killings and described what happened. Photo courtesy of the *Daily Herald*.

Relatives of Guadalupe Maldonado walk out of Courtroom 500 at the Cook County courthouse during the 2007 trial of Juan Luna. Photo courtesy of the *Daily Herald*.

The jury box in Courtroom 500 sits empty awaiting the jurors who would decide whether or not to sentence Jim Degorski to death. Photo courtesy of the *Daily Herald*.

Mary Jane Crow, sister of Brown's Chicken murder victim Michael Castro, leaves the Cook County Criminal Court building at 26th and California in Chicago Tuesday with husband Steve after defendant James Degorski was found guilty of seven murders.

Mary Jane Crow, sister of Michael Castro, leaves the Cook County courthouse during the trial of James Degorski. Photo courtesy of the *Daily Herald*.

CHAPTER 13

CHUCK

From Harpo Studios in Chicago, *The Oprah Winfrey Show* attempted to tackle a story the nation was following with both fascination and disgust. When David and Sharon Schoo first decided to set off on a beach vacation, they'd made the usual preparations for a trip of the sort, packing their suitcases for their nine-day relaxation tour in Acapulco, Mexico. They purchased the cheapest plane tickets they could find from Continental Airlines. But the regularity of the trip mostly ended there.

Instead of bringing their children or hiring a babysitter, they decided instead to leave their four- and nine-year-old daughters home alone in northwest suburban St. Charles. They left strict instructions outlining the two meals a day the children were to eat consisting of dry cereal and TV dinners. The parents put together an inventory of everything in the house. And they warned their daughters that they would be disciplined if they did not behave.

Home alone, the children were left to fend for themselves. But when a fire alarm went off in the house, they called 911 and were told by the operator to go outside for safety. *Where are your parents?* neighbors and authorities asked when they found the children in the cold. Their answer quickly made their parents an overnight international sensation. When they returned to O'Hare Airport from the trip in late December, the Schoos were greeted by a horde of TV cameras and promptly arrested.

Filming an episode set to air in the second week of January, Oprah questioned guests about the real-life *Home Alone* parents. "On the phone right from WLS-TV here in Chicago is Chuck Goudie who's down in Acapulco," the host said. "I understand you're the only reporter down there. What've you learned?" Goudie walked Winfrey through what he and the ABC-7 investigative team had discovered, with the audience listening intently to every detail. The Schoos planned the trip for a month. They found a room at the Versailles Hotel off the beaten path away from the tourist areas for just thirty dollars a night. They checked out abruptly at 7:00 a.m. and never phoned the children from the hotel to see if they were okay.[1] When the episode aired the next week, it broke records for *The Oprah Winfrey Show*.

Chuck Goudie and his team were sent to Acapulco to investigate a story making headlines across the country for an entire week. When they were finished, Goudie and the team boarded a plane for O'Hare. It had been a whirlwind trip, and when he landed back in the cold of Chicago on Saturday, January 9, he was ready to head home and relax. But those plans were dashed when upon arrival, Goudie and his team learned of the murders at Brown's Chicken. Their post-voyage rest would have to wait.[2]

When Chuck Goudie came to Chicago in 1980 at the age of twenty-four, the station that became his home was undergoing rapid change. New talent faced skepticism for their inexperience and a lack of understanding of the city. And as the youngest of a new crop of cub reporters, Goudie took the brunt of much of it.

Journalism called Chuck Goudie from a young age. In college, he helped put himself through school at Michigan State after his father died by working for radio stations in the area and freelancing for a Detroit TV station covering the state capitol in Lansing. Following graduation the next year, he headed to North Carolina to work at a TV station for three years. He spent time as a sportscaster, but the arrangement would not last, as he was tasked with the impossible assignment of filling the shoes of a longtime, beloved hometown newscaster. When he received the opportunity to head back north to for a job at WLS-TV, also known as ABC-7, he jumped at the chance to work in one of the country's largest TV markets.

In 1980, Chuck Goudie worked as a general-assignment reporter, covering everything from festivals and parades to murder and government corruption. It was baptism by fire. And within a decade, he was heading up the station's investigative unit, which afforded him ample time to take on stories, digging deep for new scoops instead of being beholden to daily deadlines and filling airspace.

Working in a new city required developing new sources. That meant knocking on doors and making phone calls. He had to get to know people, like politicians and politicos for segments about that year's election or everyday police officers who could serve as sources on high-profile investigations. Being good with people helped, but so too did the heft and credibility of working for a station like ABC-7. The channel had eyeballs all across Chicagoland.

Along with dozens of print reporters and TV journalists, Goudie covered the Brown's Chicken story on a daily basis in the weeks that followed. He stood outside bundled up in a jacket and gloves while reporting live from outside the restaurant's parking lot in Palatine in the freezing cold. He covered the funerals at a distance while throngs of mourners filed into the pews of churches across the northwest suburbs.

But Goudie dug deeper too. He wanted to know what was actually happening in the investigation behind the scenes, not just regurgitate talking points printed in news releases or thrown out like chum to the press corps at news conferences. He'd done this kind of thing before on cases like the Tylenol murders, which killed dozens from cyanide poisoning and remained unsolved. He spoke with police working the task force on the record and off. He worked sources he knew from previous cases. He knocked on doors of people connected to suspects.[3]

To some, particularly the police task force, the deep digging of investigative reporters was a nuisance. They were like vultures, feeding off detritus to fuel a predatory lifestyle. It was all about entertainment, and any destruction along the way was just collateral damage. To others, they were fearless defenders of the truth, always protecting the little guy in David-versus-Goliath-type fights—corrupt politicians against good government types, big corporations against powerless employees, the police against those who are policed.

Tips poured into ABC-7's investigative unit about the case. Some were less credible than others, like the psychics who had visions. Others merited a further look. One such tip came from two informants three weeks after the murders in late January of 1993. Two men contacted Goudie with information about the killers. *It's four guys in Schaumburg who killed those seven people*, they said on a three-way call. *We tried contacting the Palatine police but nobody's gotten back to us*, they stressed urgently.

SOMETHING BIG

Goudie was intrigued, and he shared the view that the task force wasn't moving quickly enough. On Thursday, January 14, he sat down with the two men. Their faces were entirely blacked out, and only silhouettes would be visible for viewers at home. The source, his only distinguishing mark a dark outline of a baseball cap on his head, told Goudie that three men went to the restaurant that night with a fourth driving a getaway car. "It was just a robbery and that was it, just to get some money because they needed money," he told Goudie. The story was compelling. Why weren't the police acting quicker?

Armed with this information, Goudie and the ABC-7 team knew they had a story. It was Martin Blake all over again, with police hiding in unmarked vans and storming the suspects when they least suspect it. Made for TV. So that night, the crew from ABC-7 staked out the two-story apartment complex in Schaumburg in the winter cold. They waited for a dramatic scene. And waited. But no police raid came. No one was taken away in handcuffs. No drama for the cameras.

The next day, Chuck Goudie called up the task force to inform them of what he'd learned. He told them he was going to run the story unless he received information from them contradicting it. In that sense, he was asking them to break the tight veil of secrecy surrounding the investigation. The police declined. *We can run one of two headlines tomorrow*, Goudie explained forcefully in response. *Either it's "suspects in custody" or "dithering cops fail yet again to act in a timely manner."*[4] He was playing hard ball.

On that evening's broadcast, Chuck Goudie and his team got their wish. Palatine police went to the scene to take three men to the station to question them. There was no drama for the cameras, just police officers calmly walking the men to their squad cars. The sideshow infuriated the Palatine task force. What Goudie didn't know, and police hadn't shared, were the many red flags in the informants' stories. They'd supplied information that was inconsistent with the crime, and it tended to show they were probably making the story up. Not to mention, by this time, thousands of tips had poured in to the task force, and if they immediately acted on each one with a shred of credibility, they'd have gotten nowhere. Like jogging in place.

When twenty-four-year-old Rob Starling, twenty-seven-year-old Steve Brown, and seventeen-year-old Rashad Brooks were brought in for questioning, their names were run through the ringer on the news. The men had been watching a soap opera on TV along with three women and another man when police arrived that afternoon at around 1:00 p.m. Only one was kept later for an outstanding warrant for armed robbery in a different city.

The decision to air a report like this had not been made without careful deliberations. Placing an anonymous source with his voice distorted and face obscured had its risks. It meant that a person was not tied to their word. Lying to the media, after all, was not a crime. So the work of the investigative team was discussed in the station's daily meetings and with the managers that made editorial decisions.[5] They decided that while the Palatine police felt they were meddling, the report was worth airing. One man's meddling is another man's investigative journalism.

When the story aired, the focus was on the police waiting too long to investigate. "It took almost one day for police to question those named by the informants," Goudie declared, clutching a microphone in a trench coat in front of the Palatine Community Center. They showed images of police walking to the apartment and avoiding the cameras. Packaged neatly, the leads seemed logical to viewers. It was yet another knock against the Palatine police.

The report that night then ended with interviews of the three men who'd been taken into custody. "On our way down, I looked at Rob in the car and I said, Rob, look at the way we're being treated," the man said to the cameras in a Chicago Blackhawks jersey seated at his kitchen table. "We're here for one reason only: we're being accused." His friend Robert Starling continued. "I was scared, and I didn't know what was going on," he said. They proceeded to describe what they alleged was mistreatment from the police. The task force was desperate, they argued. "They need somebody," he noted. "They're scared like I'm scared today. They're scared because they have got to answer. Somebody's got to answer for this."

The next day, Eric Zorn, a columnist for the *Chicago Tribune*, asked the question that was on everyone's mind. "Who's running this murder case?" he posed rhetorically. Was it the task force or the media? He criticized ABC-7 for being "the station that wanted to play the role of Sam Spade but ended up playing Barney Fife," alluding to bumbling TV cops.[6] The media were the ones who looked foolish to the *Tribune* columnist, not the police.

First, reporters forced the task force's hands with a lead that investigators knew wasn't entirely credible or worth their immediate attention but for which they'd be crucified in the press if they did not pursue. It was a cool-headed judgement made by the people who actually had access to all the information. Then, when they looked into the matter after being hounded, they were criticized for doing so.

The Palatine police were often faced with decisions like this. Choose *X* and you're berated. Choose *Y* and you're accused of being too slow. When your options are lose-lose, it's easy for people to point fingers from the outside when they don't have all the facts.

The capricious nature of the investigation, with leads like this bubbling up then popping in spectacular fashion, was disappointing. It frustrated police. It annoyed the press. And most of all, it agonized the families who were left wondering just what exactly was happening. Were the police bungling it? Maybe critics were correct?

Leads like this continued. That week, there were reports that the Palatine police were pursuing another three suspects. The lead sounded almost comical. One of the men allegedly played with a butterfly knife while he spoke. Another man was an extraordinary 6'8" and three hundred pounds with a penchant for leather jackets and slicked-back hair.[7] Another was described in a confidential communication to other police stations as "Italian looking," a narrative that did not sit well with the Joint Civic Committee of Italian Americans when leaked. "What's to prevent them from picking up every Italian walking down the street?" the group asked without the slightest hint of sarcasm.[8] Chief Jerry Bratcher apologized for the description, noting that the police use the words that are given to them by witnesses. In the end, the man who provided the information was arrested for providing false information.[9]

Damned if you do, damned if you don't.

CHAPTER 14

FRANK

Most street corners in the bustling Chicago Loop in the 1990s were alike. At each angle was another skyscraper towering stories above and blocking any view of the sky. Along the sidewalks were busy businesspeople clutching briefcases and walking hurriedly toward their next meeting. Yellow taxis could be heard honking as they weaved in and out of the hectic traffic rushing by.

The corner of Clark and Monroe, home to the headquarters of the Chicago Crime Commission, stood out. Tourists and natives alike craned their necks upwards each time they passed the fifteen-story neoclassical red brick office building decorated with the "Weather Bell," a two-foot-wide, three-foot-tall device installed in the 1950s suspended above the sidewalk that changed colors based on the weather forecast.[1] Neon red warned pedestrians of an impending heatwave, yellow connoted colder weather, and green alerted passersby that the forecast would be consistent.

On Wednesday, November 29, 1995, the bell attached to 79 W Monroe shined green as temperatures remained steady in the low twenties. A few stories above on the sixth floor,

Brown's Chicken cofounder Frank Portillo sat in a conference room overlooking the street in the offices of the Chicago Crime Commission.[2] In his early sixties, Portillo had large aviator glasses and wore his hair in a ponytail, a mane of hair that distracted from the front half of his head, which was completely bald.

All around the office staffed by about a dozen employees were green file cabinets filled with records the non-profit organization used to track crime in the city of Chicago, with a particular focus on gangs. Books and spiral-bound reports put together by the commission filled shelves throughout the office. Displayed throughout the workplace was the organization's logo—a black-and-white fingerprint with the loops, whorls, and arches that resembled an ink print taken after processing a criminal.

Portillo was anxious. As head of Brown's Chicken corporate, he'd seen incredible highs and disheartening lows. He was used to the boom-and-bust cycle of business. But the killings at the Palatine franchise left him shaken. As CEO of the company, Portillo was used to managing his way out of problems. Where an issue came up with a franchisee, he could help train a person falling behind. When KFC launched an ad blitz in the Chicagoland market, he focused hard on new marketing tactics to garner attention. The investigation into what happened in Palatine, however, was completely out of his control. For a Type A personality, letting others take the wheel proved agonizing.

"You've got a problem in Palatine," one of his operations managers told him the morning the bodies had been found in the restaurant.[3] Since then, Portillo had done all that he could to make things right. Along with Mayor Rita Mullins, he went door to door visiting the families of the victims. He'd gotten to know the Ehlenfeldts during the nine months they operated the

Palatine franchise. When the community put together a reward to help catch the killer, Portillo pitched in $25,000 of his own money.[4] To help raise funds for the families, he put donation boxes in each of the Chicagoland Brown's Chicken stores.[5] He beefed up security in the franchises, installing cameras and panic buttons.[6] Compared to other fast food restaurants in the area, each Brown's Chicken franchise became a bona fide Fort Knox.

Despite his best efforts, each and every decision he made to boost the business was overshadowed by the rotten stench of the Brown's Chicken Massacre. The name was repeated over and over on radio, TV, and in print. Thousands of stories for years had associated his business with the worst killings in Illinois history. The name stuck. Within two and a half years, nearly sixty of the one hundred restaurants had closed. Sales declined 35 percent in the months after the killings. Many repeat customers just never returned.[7] Their fried chicken may have, as the slogan proclaimed, tasted better, but was it good enough to risk your life?

If any publicity is good publicity, then Frank Portillo had a banner year in 1993. But this publicity seemed to prove that old adage false, a fact that would soon become even more clear as the company's revenues continued to tumble.

Perhaps naively, Portillo tried appealing to the better angels of Chicagoland TV news producers. He picked up the phone and called around to the media suggesting they stop referring to the restaurant with each mention of the killings. He pleaded with them to stop using the word "massacre." *Perhaps "tragedy" or the "Palatine tragedy" might be a better fit*, he proposed. Unsurprisingly, his calls went mostly unheeded.

In May of 1995, Portillo met with Chief Jerry Bratcher, task force head Jim Bell who'd recently been brought in from the

FBI, Commander John Koziol, and others to get information about the investigation to calm his nerves. He prepared for the meeting by studying up with fellow members of the Chicago Crime Commission who knew what questions to ask an officer. "I don't mean to be disrespectful, but can I ask you how many homicides you've handled?" he asked one of the FBI agents assisting Bell. The mood in the room shifted. Indeed, that particular agent had only worked three in his career.[8] Frank turned to Koziol. "This is a small town," he said. "I don't mean to be disrespectful, but how many murders have you investigated?" The question did not go over well. "I'm no country bumpkin!" Koziol shot back, offended, throwing his pencil in the air in response. The police would never speak to a civilian about an active investigation, but they'd made an exception for Portillo and did not like how he was responding to their good will gesture. Frank Portillo later asked to set up a follow-up meeting where Chicago Detective Richard Zuley, the perpetual thorn in the side of the Palatine police, could join. "I hate that fucking son of a bitch, but I'll set up a meeting with Zuley," Chief Bratcher conceded.[9] It never materialized.

Portillo had been patient. In the days after the killings, he appeared at press conferences alongside police and community leaders. He tried to be helpful where he could. But the investigation had reached a logjam, and he'd gradually lost confidence in the Palatine police. Frank Portillo had seen enough.

Over the years, Portillo and his attorney began hearing rumblings of dissension among the task force. He learned about Richard Zuley, the ace Chicago detective, being asked to leave the task force by Chief Bratcher and the Palatine police. Drips and drabs reached him from Zuley about the allegedly botched Lead 80, Zuley's prized silver bullet.[10] He couldn't fathom why one of Chicago's most experienced, shrewd homicide investigators was being ignored by the Palatine police. *These guys simply don't have the gravitas to handle this kind of investigation*, he started saying publicly. A few days before Thanksgiving, he called up Terry Brunner, the head of a watchdog group called the Better Government Association, searching for a way to shake up the Brown's investigation from the outside.

In November of 1995, more than two years after the murders, Portillo was making the case to the leaders of the Chicago Crime Commission and the Better Government Association to launch an outside inquiry into the Palatine police's handling of the investigation. These suburban cops had bungled things, he thought, and it was time to expose their failures.

The Chicago Crime Commission had a storied past. Founded in 1919 during prohibition, the group's purpose was to shine a light on mafia-linked crime and was funded by business and civic leaders fed up with corruption. Many politicians in Chicago during that time chose to take bribes rather than enforce the law, so this citizens' group took it upon themselves to put out a list of "public enemies"—a phrase they coined—and put Al Capone at the very top. The group was successful in pressuring officials to act and played a central role in helping finally put Chicago's most notorious gangster behind bars.[11] By the 1990s, however, the group had largely lost its focus. It had no vision. No reach.

Frank Portillo had been appointed vice president of the commission following the killings and took a very public role traveling to other businesses to talk about safety.[12] He recruited new dues-paying members. With his vision, the group found a clearer focus. He used his platform to lobby the speaker of the state House for mandatory sentencing for crimes committed with a gun in a retail store, which they dubbed "safe retail zones." He plastered bulletin boards in small businesses like Brown's and Jiffy Lube about how to contact legislators, rating them on their record on crime. He gave speeches. "If we citizens don't get involved in our government, then we have no one to blame when our government goes bad," he implored groups. "We must have swift sentencing and swift punishments." Frank Portillo was tough on crime.

Summoned by Portillo, leaders of the commission heard his argument for why they should get involved. The BGA also had its early roots in prohibition and was founded by teetotalers again fed up with those turning a blind eye to corruption in Chicago. As time went on, the watchdog group concentrated more on investigative journalism, and corruption at all levels of government became its core purpose. They were goo-goos. Good government guys.

For two hours at the commission headquarters, Portillo laid out the case for why the two groups should get involved, and those gathered discussed potential steps forward.[13] Early mistakes were made. In his view, police weren't following up on one of the most promising leads, the one from Richard Zuley. These suburban cops were simply over their head. Personality clashes on the task force were hindering any progress. More cooperation among investigators was needed. *This is exactly the kind of thing our two organizations were created to pursue*, he implored them.

The BGA was led by Terry Brunner, a man who was a true believer in the mission of his organization. The silver-haired investigator was fearless, somewhat eccentric, and he didn't care what critics said if it meant getting to the right answer. Before committing, Brunner called around to his media connections

SOMETHING BIG

to see what they knew about the case and if it was worth their time. *What's the deal with this Brown's Chicken case?* he asked his sources. The BGA knew how to operate with the media. They had arrangements with TV stations in Chicago to work on stories, and each year, they hosted big fundraisers for the organization that were attended by all the top journalists in town dressed in formal attire and ready to rub elbows at the storied Drake Hotel.[14]

Terry Brunner was no hack. A former prosecutor, he had an understanding for how police operated. Since taking the helm of the BGA, he'd expanded its reach, landing major new funding to open an additional office in Washington, DC, and worked on major investigations with the likes of Mike Wallace on *60 Minutes* and Geraldo Rivera.[15] In the past, he'd uncovered lewd sex scandals involving county politicians, poked at corruption on the state level, and developed a knack for investigating large-scale controversies.

Aside from the press, Brunner set up a meeting with Zuley at the Swissôtel, a swanky hotel overlooking the Chicago River. He was accompanied by the BGA's chief investigator, Mike Lyons. The two men were surprised when they met the man people raved about as Chicago's ace homicide detective. They expected someone rough and wrinkled, the kind of guy cast in police shows. Zuley, to them, looked more like a physics professor than someone you'd fear in the interrogation room.

For years, Richard Zuley had been trying to draw attention to Lead 80. Before having his hands slapped by superiors and the Palatine task force, he made the case internally that there was a gang connection to the case. He leaked information to media sources who aired the dissension to the public. Zuley remained totally convinced that this was the avenue to pursue, and the Palatine police, these suburban cops, had mismanaged the inquiry. Cooperating with the BGA was another way to advance this belief. *They've got no idea what they're doing*, he told Lyons and Brunner.

The BGA team had heard enough. They agreed to launch an investigation into the case in April of 1996, quickly forming a panel that gave it the stamp of legitimacy.[16] Former FBI agents, a newspaper editor, a retired Chicago police detective, a former prosecutor, and even a former United States attorney general, the highest law enforcement officer in the land, were appointed.

Reaction from the Palatine police was defensive. "Anyone who doesn't think we'd do back flips to solve this is out of their minds," Chief Jerry Bratcher insisted to press when asked for comment. "It's been blood, sweat and tears. We are committed to solving this."[17] Police were not interested in allowing an outside group to meddle. Some criticized Portillo's motives, arguing that a recent lawsuit from the Castro and Solis families alleging he had not done enough to create a safe work environment made him biased.[18] Those allegations questioning his motives, as well as the lawsuit itself, were a gut punch to Portillo.

With no cooperation from the Palatine police, the panel had little access to up-to-date, accurate information.[19] Brunner criticized the lack of cooperation. "You can't talk about it because it's an ongoing investigation?" he asked sarcastically. "Well this is now year four," he said, drawing attention to the lack of progress.[20] The panel had no subpoena power nor could they make arrests. They'd have to rely on convincing people who'd been involved in the task force effort to sit down for an interview.

The work of the investigation mainly fell to the staff at the BGA, and Mike Lyons, their chief investigator, led the effort.

They began interviewing everyone who would sit down. Former cops on the task force who were no longer working the case. Members of the media. People who'd provided tips. Anyone who would talk.

Informed by his military service in Vietnam and time as a reporter, Lyons had a unique manner interviewing. He almost never took notes. He preferred just to listen. Lyons was messy but not unorganized, the kind of person who kept a completely disheveled desk with stacks of papers but could tell you exactly where the transcript from the interview he conducted six months ago sat in the pile.

Aside from his professional experience, Lyons relied on another social lubricant to get people talking: alcohol. "You gotta use Jack Daniels," he'd say when preparing to question someone. Sure, developing a rapport and the trust of a source was key, but sometimes it was easier to just get them drunk. "I'm going to get some people to share their deepest, darkest secrets with me," he'd tell others at the BGA.[21] Sometimes it was a bar. Other times a restaurant. Often, it was a diner like Denny's. For some inexplicable reason, he would come to find that people loved spilling their secrets at Denny's.

Mike Lyons and Terry Brunner interviewed more than sixty sources for the investigation, including former members of the task force.[22] It took nine months of digging. After analyzing everything, they put together a report on their assessment. It was a direct parallel to Richard Zuley's longtime concerns about Lead 80 involving the Puerto Rican Stones. The lead that never died.

When the board put together by the two organizations saw the report, there was infighting. It was too inflammatory for many. Too opinionated. They decided not to approve it and opted to release a separate, watered down report. Brunner was upset, and he blamed the group of esteemed individuals' own worries about reputation and ego for the reticence. They didn't want their name on something that would impact their careers and status as vaunted pillars of the community. Instead of putting up a fight, Brunner released the report as that of the BGA staff. If others wouldn't put their name on it, he would.

The language of the report was indeed incendiary. "Bratcher's troops were like the Argentine Army—generals with chests full of medals who had never seen combat and suddenly, the Falklands, and it all began to crumble against the battle-tested British," the report said. It harped on about Chief Bratcher's salary and supposed conflicts of interest saying he'd "created his own feudal kingdom in Palatine." Even the title was salacious. "Patent Malarky: Public Dishonesty and Deception," it was called, borrowing a phrase Bratcher had used to defend the integrity of his investigation in earlier interviews about the task force's work. "I think Bratcher would give you the hard sell that the sun rises in the west," Bratcher told the press of what he thought of Palatine's police chief.[23]

In terms of substance, the report itself did not assert that members of a gang in Chicago committed the murders, but rather focused on alleged mistakes that police had made. The goal was simply to criticize the investigation and its methods, not to solve the case. It was released in November of 1997 to much media fanfare and a closely watched press conference, centering on allegations of sloppy handling of evidence and Lead 80.

Bratcher defended his own actions publicly. "There's no perfection in the world in anything any of us do," he explained. "But generally speaking, the steps we took, we did the right thing."[24] Mayor Rita Mullins had sharp words for Brunner. "Is

Brunner more of an expert than the guy from the FBI whose job it is to go in and help with these majors crimes?" she asked rhetorically.[25] The mayor later asked the Illinois State Crime Commission on which she sat to review the report and release their own take on the issue.[26] They defended the police, saying the report was totally biased and "95% baseless."[27]

While the Palatine police were uninterested in cooperating with the BGA and Chicago Crime Commission, they did agree to enlist other help in 1997 to jolt the investigation. The task force contacted producers from *America's Most Wanted* to see if they'd be interested in doing a segment to spotlight clues that might lead someone to come forward with information. They wanted to highlight tidbits such as the type of shoe prints found at the scene, the caliber of gun, and the timeframe in which they believed the killings occurred.

Episode ten of the 1997 season of *America's Most Wanted* aired on a Saturday night at 8:00 p.m. in May.[28] *Now, from our Washington Crime Center: John Walsh*, the program began. The host walked out to his usual studio with a wall of TV screens displaying missing persons and cases that the program had helped solve. In the background, operators worked phones, flipping through papers and looking busy. By that time, the show had helped put an end to nearly five hundred cases.[29] They agreed to take tips from callers and pass them along to police.

America's Most Wanted was incredibly popular. It had a viewership that spanned to all fifty states. Anne Lockett was one of those viewers. She saw the evidence presented and interviews from families. She saw their agony. She saw the leads police presented as glimmers of hope but knew they led nowhere, distractions back to the abyss of uncertainty that perpetuated the pain for everyone involved.

Watching the program stirred something in Anne Lockett. She remained terrified of the threat from her ex-boyfriend Jim Degorski and Juan Luna years ago. Jim still tried to get ahold of her here and there. *If anyone calls asking where I am, please, don't tell them*, she'd instruct her mother and close friends. A profound fear weighed on her. But so too did the burden of keeping in this dark secret.

After watching the show that aired that May, Anne Lockett sat down and wrote a letter. It was a long, anonymous note. And just as the show implored its viewers, she popped it in a mailbox and sent it off to Washington.[30] It was just one among thousands of tips over the years. A needle in a haystack—destined never to be found.

CHAPTER 15

CASEY, TODD & JOHN

The weight of Casey Sander's survivor's guilt was crushing. It was a suffocating feeling that was hard for her to shake. And even though she knew she'd done nothing wrong, it burdened her constantly.

Rico Solis had wanted more hours at Brown's Chicken. So Casey had been happy to switch shifts that fateful night after picking up her paycheck. Instead of working that evening, she went to the Fremd-Palatine crosstown basketball game with her boyfriend, Todd Wakefield.

Casey Sander was your average, occasionally dorky teenager.[1] Somewhat reserved, she took time to warm up to people and kept her social circle small, participating in stage crew helping plays behind the scenes and working on Palatine High School's *Cutlass* newspaper staff. She was a brunette who sometimes wore her hair in a ponytail and had a rounded nose. She had glasses that were slightly too big for her face.[2] Her on-and-off boyfriend, Todd Wakefield, could be described in much the same way. A year ahead of her, he was awkward like lots of high schoolers still growing into life. His brown hair was long in the back—a wavy mullet—with bangs that covered his forehead.

Their relationship was innocent. Todd and Casey were really more friends than a serious couple. (Not to mention, Todd was actually gay.) The two would drive around town and get dinner, watch movies at his parents' house, and check out hobby shops in the area which Todd loved as a model plane hobbyist.

Attending the basketball game was a typical activity for Casey and Todd. For them, it was more about the people watching than the game itself. They sat off to themselves in the bleachers, poking fun at their classmates and sharing inside jokes. After the game and a Palatine victory of 50-40, Casey thought about heading back to the restaurant. She wanted to ask the Ehlenfeldts for a raise, but she decided against it. There was no rush. *Forget it, I'll just talk to them tomorrow*, she told Todd in the car.

Michael Castro and Rico Solis were both classmates of Casey and she worked nights with them at the restaurant. The employees there could be split into two groups—the teens and adults. Lull times at the restaurant were a chance to bond, and she got to know Rico and Michael, who she both found to be friendly and fun to work with. She appreciated the restaurant owners too. When she started at Brown's and told the Ehlenfeldts she was going on a family trip to Disneyland, they gave her an advance on her pay so she'd have spending money. They were incredibly kind to her. Needless to say, the news of the murders at Brown's Chicken hit closer to home for Casey Sander than most.

Having known the victims personally, she felt an obligation to attend each funeral. For a seventeen-year-old, the emotion of those days was a lot to handle. So too was the constant reminder that she had almost clocked in that night.

SOMETHING BIG

When Casey shut her eyes at night to fall asleep, she was stalked by recurring nightmares. The dream was always consistent. She'd be at work and recognize the familiar interior of the Brown's Chicken restaurant. An armed robber was present. His face was blurred. She and those inside were terrified. The man pointed a gun at her and prepared to pull the trigger. Then, she woke up.[3]

Like so many impacted by the tragedy, she sought help from a counselor. It was a suggestion from her mother, and over time, it helped her cope. Slowly but surely, she began to move on with her life.

Having worked at the restaurant, it came as no surprise that Casey would be interviewed by police. They spoke to all employees past and present. The initial questioning was par for the course. What were your job duties? *I worked as a cashier.* How long did you work there? *About six months.* Who did you know? *I knew everyone.* They took her prints. They took a photo. And at first, that was it.

Over time, members of the task force came back to Casey with additional questions. Their probing became more specific, inquiring about individuals and sharing details with her. They showed her pictures and described their theory of the murders to see if anything stood out. But her story was always the same. *I went to the basketball game with Todd that night*, she'd tell them, proceeding to recount the story of her desire for a raise and decision not to go back. They'd thank her for her cooperation, then move on. Yet the questioning continued well beyond 1993. It went on for years. Casey Sander was interviewed by the police nine times in a span of six years.

By April of 1999, Casey was an adult at twenty-three years old. She'd moved on and gotten married, no longer the dorky teen with big glasses. Late one afternoon, she was driving home around 4:30 p.m. from a nannying job when she pulled into the parking lot of her apartment. Police officers were waiting, and she recognized them from past encounters. "What can I do for you?" she said, barely halfway out of the car. "We'd like to talk to you," one of them responded. She sighed. "I just got home, I haven't eaten anything, can we do this another time?" she asked. They assured her it wouldn't be long, so Casey agreed to accompany them to the Cook County state's attorney's office in nearby Rolling Meadows.

This was her tenth time being interviewed, and the questions began as expected. She recounted her alibi from that night. She told the story about the basketball game. They revisited the dreams. And they brought up Todd. *Todd already told us everything*, they told her.

Hours passed and the questioning continued late into the night. Police went through the motions again, retracing what she'd told investigators. Casey had a glass of water from the water cooler. The interrogators were insistent. *You know more than you're telling us*, they said. They continued recounting the details of that night. *Those dreams you've been having, they're not just dreams, are they?* Exhausted and ready to go home, she finally gave in. "I did it," she confessed.

Casey lethargically described what happened that night, providing much color and detail to the story. She and Todd went in a brown station wagon to the restaurant and he went out of control. It was just the two of them. The bloody shoeprint they've told the public about? That was probably hers, she said.[4] She knew the layout of the restaurant. She knew where the money was. She knew how to help him get in and out. She'd been there.

With the story finally out, Casey Sander was let go around 2:00 a.m. Yet the confession didn't quite add up. Certain details were inaccurate, and police recognized even then that no physical evidence linked her to the crime. Still, she had just admitted to aiding in the murder of seven people. *What the hell did I just do?* she asked herself. The police let her go, perhaps the clearest recognition that they didn't believe what they'd heard. When she got home, she woke her husband up and told him what had happened.

The next day, Casey Sander hired a lawyer. The calls from police stopped.[5]

***

The Palatine police had tried everything to shake up new information. Every three-letter agency, every expert, every witness, every lead. So in the spring of 1995, Chief Jerry Bratcher brought in fresh blood to lead the slimmed-down task force still investigating the Brown's Chicken murders on a daily basis.[6]

At age forty-two, Jim Bell, with his thick brown mustache and bulky glasses, had seen a lot. He'd worked as an FBI major-case specialist, investigating high-profile murders and massacres just like the one at Brown's. When forty-nine women – mostly sex workers and the downtrodden – were killed in the Pacific Northwest, the so-called Green River killings, he was there. He'd done an extensive study on serial killer Ted Bundy. He worked at the FBI Academy in Quantico, for the Salt Lake City police, and was previously chief examiner for the Utah state medical examiner.[7] In the days immediately after the murder at Brown's, he had even been brought in to briefly assist in building a potential profile of the killer, so he was familiar with the case. A civilian, not a sworn law enforcement officer, Bell brought a different skillset.[8] He'd interviewed more than 125 detectives on high-profile cases across the country, developing a system for looking at complex investigations and creating profiles of potential suspects. Under Bell's watch, the Brown's case would get a new look. Old leads were reviewed for anything that might've been missed. New questions were asked.

Casey Sander's confession brought renewed interest to the possibility that she or people around her knew more about the case. In June of 1998, police interviewed Todd Wakefield in Denver, Colorado, where he was working as a flight attendant. He provided them information that he was allegedly the last person at the restaurant that night, and he paid for his meal with a $10 bill. That recounting matched what investigators believed. He told them a dollar amount for the meal that roughly matched the change left behind in the register. He went into detail about what went down that night, mentioning his friend John Simonek. There was no mention of his old high school girlfriend Casey Sander. Her role and what she'd told police seemed to just fade from the arc of the story.

John Simonek became the principal focus for Jim Bell. The next month, in July of 1998, investigators sat down with Simonek for a first interview. *Todd was my best friend*, he told them. But he had an alibi, telling police he was at a buddy's house that night. Police returned to question him a second time, and he changed his story slightly. He and Todd had hung out that night, actually. The shifting narrative aroused suspicion.[9] During a third interview, more details came to mind. *Todd really loved guns*, he explained, noting that his old friend was an avid reader of the magazine *Guns & Ammo*. They continued gathering more information, but nothing critical had been elicited.

Am I a suspect? he asked. Police informed him that he wasn't and were ready to finish up the interview. Then something unusual happened. "I just had a vision," he told them. "It just popped into my head."[10]

Simonek recounted his revelation. That night, Todd Wakefield came to his parents' house where he'd been living. He knocked on the basement window of his bedroom, and his friend Todd was covered in blood. *I cut myself on accident*, he told his buddy. They tried to wash up but threw out the clothes instead. His memory was fuzzy on the vision. It was a strange turn of events, but far from the first time someone had convincingly told police about a dream or a vision. Still, his story continued to evolve.

For the fourth interview, investigators went to Simonek's house in the suburbs to talk. The TV was blaring in the background. His phone was ringing. There were too many distractions, so he was brought to the state's attorney's office where things would be quiet.[11] His answers were even more vivid. That vision? It was reality. He and Todd drove to the restaurant that night where Todd ordered a meal, then shouted for everyone to get on the ground. He had a gun, and John shared a detail about a bullet hole in a metal hood of the kitchen. After the robbery, the two men drove home and threw out their clothes. With many details matching reality, it seemed like a huge break to Jim Bell.

The John Simonek and Todd Wakefield stories had Bell convinced they'd found the killers. But others on the task force had serious doubts. There were too many holes. Too many inconsistencies. Detective Bill King of the Palatine police had worked the case since day one. He knew more about it than anyone, and while he was open to considering all options, this didn't seem like the right avenue. His boss, Commander John Koziol, agreed. They pushed back on Bell, and the task force held off on pursuing the two men.

But in August of 1999, Detective Bill King headed to a summer vacation and was halfway to New York while Commander John Koziol was relaxing in Wisconsin. They were taking a much deserved break. With the two main critics of the Simonek and Wakefield story gone, Jim Bell decided to move forward. On August 5, 1999, he had John Simonek arrested during a traffic stop. *Place your hands on the hood!* they told him.

In an interview room at the courthouse in suburban Rolling Meadows, Jim Bell and Officer Jack Byrnes, another longtime task force member, conducted the questioning. They then asked another detective to interview him alone. *Where's Bill? Where's Koziol*, Detective Frank Medrys asked. *They're not available right now*, Bell told him. Just keep moving.

Medrys entered the room as Bell looked on through a two-way mirror. "What we're going to do this evening is we're going to have Mr. Simonek describe to us as he has done several times previously this evening the event of January 8, 1993, at the Brown's Chicken located at Smith and Northwest Highway Road in Palatine. Is that correct, John?" Simonek walked him through the events in detail while a camera was rolling. "Could you please indicate on that drawing of the interior of the Brown's Chicken and Pasta where the freezer, as you recall, was located?" Simonek made a mark on a diagram, one of many. The detective used it to help illustrate the story of that night.

> <u>Detective Medrys</u>: How did those individuals get from the number 7 to the number 8 location in the second freezer?

> Simonek: Todd had me escort them over there.
> Detective Medrys: Okay.
> Simonek: After we got over there, he told me to close the door on them. So I shut the door. As I was turning around to walk back to where he was, I heard him start shooting.
> Detective Medrys: What did you do then?
> Simonek: I started freaking out. I didn't know what was going on. I ended up getting finished as I was getting over there and I just saw bodies in the cooler—or the freezer. Sorry.[12]

The details were convincing. Police knew the kind of gun that was used, and so did Simonek. They hadn't found leftover shell casings at the scene of the crime, and Simonek alluded to picking up the evidence as the crime was committed. He talked about shooting into the cooler and hitting the plastic strips that kept cold air inside.

> Detective Medrys: Okay, you say it's a revolver. How are you sure that it was a revolver?
> Simonek: The side dropped down, and it was a little wheel.
> Detective Medrys: Okay, thank you. Perfect.
> Simonek: And he unloaded it, put some of them in his hand, and put some in his pocket and a few fell on the floor.
> Detective Medrys: Okay.
> Simonek: He proceeded to reload the gun and made me—told me to go kill those other

two people. And I argued with him and told him, "No, do it yourself. I don't want any part in this."

Detective Medrys: Okay.

Simonek: I recall shooting somebody outside the freezer. I don't remember how they got out there though.

Detective Medrys: Okay, and you did that how?

Simonek: I shot through the plastic slits or strips that they use to keep the air cool in when the door was open.

Detective Medrys: Okay, and then what did you do?

Simonek: I handed him back the gun, shaking, extremely upset. He made me help him carry one of the bodies that I had shot outside the door.

Detective Medrys: Okay. Thank you. Could you explain to us how the body was moved?

Simonek: He had picked the arms up and I got the feet and we carried it in. He went in first and we laid it on its right side facing east.

Plain as day, John Simonek admitted to murder. Skepticism of the confession defied common sense. Why on earth would someone admit to killing seven people if they hadn't done so? And in such detail.

Simonek continued his story. He told the detective how Todd Wakefield stabbed two people. Or maybe three, he wasn't sure. He talked about his nerves that night and pleading with his friend to stop. He tried to just block this all out of his memory, a logical explanation for why this confession had taken more than five years to materialize.

> <u>Detective Medrys</u>: Are those the facts of the case and your voluntary statement that you wish recorded at this time?
> <u>Simonek</u>: Yes.
> <u>Detective Medrys</u>: Okay. John, if you desire to, now would be an excellent moment to express your feelings during this and subsequently afterwards.
> <u>Simonek</u>: I'm very sorry it happened. I am very, very sorry I got caught up with him—with Todd. I wish now I would've never met him, would've never have become friends with him. And I just want this to be over. I hope he gets locked up. I don't want any more to do with him.

With a taped confession now acquired, Jim Bell became certain he'd cracked the case. Todd Wakefield and John Simonek were responsible for the Brown's Chicken murders. End of story. When they heard what Bell had done, John Koziol and Bill King, both of whom had been on vacation, were furious.

But in a murder investigation, police are only half of this process. It's prosecutors who determine whether or not to charge him with a crime. Bell eventually brought this evidence to an assistant state's attorney who'd been working the case. *We've got the confession, we've got these unique details that nobody else could possibly know, and it's all on tape*, he said. *This is the guy*. Prosecutors agreed that the evidence was persuasive.

Why would someone confess to a crime they didn't commit? Especially one that was eligible for the death penalty. And yet, there simply wasn't enough there. No DNA evidence. No prints matching those at the scene. To be sure, the task force had sent an officer undercover to pose as a co-worker of Simonek who worked as a semi-truck driver, but he made no incriminating statements.[13] It appeared perhaps the men were merely regurgitating the information they'd been told by investigators. They'd parroted information learned in the interrogation – with bits filled in from news they'd heard about the story over the years – then spewed out a completely fabricated tale. That, or they were just plain nuts. The state's attorney filed no charges against John Simonek or Todd Wakefield. Having spent countless months on this lead, Jim Bell was furious.

Every member of the task force in Palatine, now made up of half a dozen men, had spent years of their lives on this case. It was all they thought about. As the head of the department, Chief Bratcher was eager to resolve the case. He'd been in law enforcement for over forty years, and he knew this was the thing for which he'd be remembered.

On August 15, 1999, Jerry Bratcher retired as chief of the Palatine police.[14] The next year, Jim Bell resigned as head of the task force.

CHAPTER 16

JENGIFER, DANA & JOY

Signature Cleaners was welcomed to Palatine in October of 1994 with much fanfare. The grand opening had the usual trappings of a ribbon-cutting. There were sticky buns and other morning treats for attendees. Local leaders were present and ready to deliver canned remarks. Reporters—an unusually high number—gathered to snap pictures and ask questions.

The owners of the dry cleaners had spent three months on renovations that cost them nearly $500,000.[1] They redesigned the interior, knocking down old counters and commercial kitchen fixtures and replacing them with cleaning equipment. They coated the walls with fresh paint and turned the green slanted roof brown. For the convenience of customers, a full-service drive-through was added.[2]

It seemed like a complete transformation. But just feet away tied around a utility pole was a memorial ribbon that flapped in the wind visible to the cars passing by, an enduring reminder of the building's sullied past. "I don't think it should be a major issue," one of the business's owners told reporters gathered when asked about the dry cleaners occupying the old site of Brown's Chicken. "We're trying to create a whole new business."[3]

Twenty-one months had passed since the killings. Yet no matter how much the new owners of the building wanted to convert it into something new, that dry cleaners would always be known for that one ill-fated night. It was a place that people would point to when they passed or strike up a conversation wondering when the killers would be caught. For this reason, perhaps, it was clear from the beginning the arrangement wouldn't last. It didn't help either when on day one a delivery man refused to enter the building.

The question of what to do with the site of the empty Brown's Chicken building was the source of much disagreement among those in the community and the families of each victim. Some pondered a memorial, an idea to which village officials were sympathetic but wary. Others thought the building should be torn down entirely. Frank Portillo insisted that the restaurant reopen. It was about principle. Not letting the bad guys—whoever they were—win.

With their parents gone in the aftermath of the killings, the Ehlenfeldt daughters already had enough to deal with. The days and weeks that followed had been a blur. Jennifer, the oldest, went back to Wisconsin to try to resume her new job as an aide to a state legislator in Madison. Dana, the middle child, returned to college. Joy, the youngest, drove down to Champaign to start her first semester at the University of Illinois. Instead of her parents dropping her off as planned, she drove alone, trailing her sister in a car packed with all her dorm room belongings on the busy highways outside Chicago and past the barren cornfields and painted barns of central Illinois.[4] It was the kind of drive that leaves you time to think.

The Thursday after the murders and after their parents had been laid to rest, it was decided that the three Ehlenfeldt daughters would hold a press conference. It was a recommendation from the Palatine police partly aimed at warding off the media, who'd been searching the area for an exclusive since the news broke. If they came out and spoke in a controlled environment, the hope was that they'd be left alone. They agreed.

Jennifer, Dana, and Joy all sat in the chambers of the village council at a long table. To their backs were the plaques marking the spot on the dais for each city council member and the Palatine seal hanging from the white wall behind them.

Wires from microphones snaked across the table, and reporters scattered nearly a dozen tape recorders to capture the audio. Spare bundles of Kleenex were not far. Around each of their necks was a gold cross gifted to them by Fred Brown, the son of the founder of Brown's Chicken.[5] Their lapels bore the light blue ribbons that were being handed out at Palatine High School. In the middle sat Jennifer with her curly brown hair and a collared blouse and sweater. Her sisters flanked her, with Dana in a purple sweater to her left and Joy wearing a black-and-white flannel to her right.

The event was quick but not painless. Their shoulders were slightly slouched, an obvious sign of the uncomfortable nature of the ordeal. Jennifer opened the press conference by reading a statement for the media. Journalists then asked them questions about their parents and the restaurant. They talked about calling each of the families who were also in grief. "I can't begin to say enough for the people who worked there," Dana said. "My parents viewed it as a family."[6] There was initial talk of re-opening the restaurant, but they also expressed an early desire to move on. "Our parents would want us to fulfill the goals that we have set out to accomplish and the goals that they wanted us to accomplish," Joy noted, recognizing that their parents would not want their lives to stand still because of the tragedy. "And we will get through this because of our parents," Jennifer interjected. The photographers continued flashing pictures as she continued. "They taught us how to cope, they taught us how to survive, and they taught us how to be strong." After fifteen minutes, the press conference ended. And for the most part, the media left them alone.

While the daughters tried to resume their lives, aunts and uncles stepped in to help manage the affairs that remained. There was the house in Arlington Heights that had to be sold. And of course, a decision needed to be made on what to do with the restaurant in which Dick and Lynn had invested so much time and energy. Despite the hope, re-opening it seemed impractical for so many reasons. It would tie the daughters down to something they'd never signed up for, a burden their parents would have never wished upon them. The emotional toll would have been unfathomable working in the site where they were killed. Not to mention, succeeding would have been nearly impossible with the stigma of the restaurant always lingering.

Manny Castro made himself pass by the restaurant location on numerous occasions after his son's death. It was his own way of dealing with the haunting reminder of that day that stood at a prominent intersection that anyone in Palatine would have to go out of their way to avoid. It was his very own psychological inoculation. But no matter how many times he passed, seeing that building still stung. "Whenever I look at that building, it dissolves my soul," he told a journalist when asked about what to do with the location.[7] Not one to wait around for other people's help, he took matters into his own hands, gathering signatures on a petition to have the establishment torn down.

SOMETHING BIG

It was something he'd done years before also hoping to turn it into a memorial.[8]

Frank Portillo responded to the petition drive with a press conference of his own.[9] "Knocking down the store would just destroy the Ehlenfeldts' dream, which I don't think would be right," Portillo told reporters. He suggested instead starting a scholarship fund at Palatine High School and encouraging legislators to pass tougher crime laws for retail theft.[10] In his view, whether the building stood or not, that intersection would always still be there, and passing it wouldn't feel any better for the families or himself if it was a razed parking lot, a new business, or a somber memorial.[11]

No one had anticipated dealing with a lawsuit as a result of the Ehlenfeldts' murder. But for the owner of the building their parents had leased, it was the only option. He filed a lawsuit in August of 1993 for back rent. Eventually, the daughters officially decided not to reopen that December in a statement they released through an attorney.[12] The decision was made. They'd eventually settle for $57,000.[13]

Frank Portillo was disappointed by the decision not to reopen, but he let it go. He still wanted a presence in Palatine. It was a way of showing that his business would not be defeated by this tragedy. And in 1995, he had his wish when a new location opened in another strip mall just a few blocks away.[14] The new location, coupled with the dry cleaners at the old site of the Palatine franchise, made him feel that his business's reputation was on the mend.

But by 1998, the dry cleaners failed and a "For Lease" sign was posted out front.[15] The owners blamed the building for being too big and nearby competition. Still, there was no question a stigma remained. The site again sat eerily vacant.

The events of life continued for the families. There were marriages and daughters without a father to walk them down the aisle. Babies were born without grandparents to dote on them. Sons and daughters graduated from high school and college. Careers took new turns in directions for which the seven victims would have been immensely proud. Family members moved away from Illinois. Each time a new break in the case came, they held their breath, only to be disappointed when things fell through. In time, many of those praying for a resolution resigned themselves to the possibility that it might never be solved.

In April of 2001, the decision was made to finally raze the Brown's Chicken restaurant at 168 W. Northwest Highway.[16] The village of Palatine was so ready to move on from the site's past that they covered the $25,000 cost for the demolition crew.[17] Many of the victims' family members showed up to watch the building be destroyed. An *X* marked each window of the restaurant.[18] Two news helicopters hovered above the site as a demolition crew readied themselves.[19] TV news cameras and newspaper reporters walked around the site searching for quotes and compelling visuals. Strangers gathered at the site to watch, an oddly similar scene to the weeks of January 1993 when people sat in the cold parking lot for any sign of the seven victims.

Today, instead of yellow police tape, a chain-link fence was erected around the site. The normally busy intersection hugging the location was slow as cars braked passing by. Some people took pictures. Others exchanged stories about where they were when they heard the news that day.[20] "It should have come down a long time ago," said the owner of a nearby deli when asked by reporters for her thoughts. "It is time to move on. Hopefully this brings some closure to it."

SOMETHING BIG

Before beginning, the wrecking crew observed a moment of silence for the victims. "God bless their souls," the general contractor uttered.[21] The decision was made to start the demolition in the back of the restaurant where the victims had been killed. It was a symbolic gesture.

A large yellow backhoe with a shovel arm was put into position to start the process. The machine began taking slow but forceful hits to the building which crumbled the walls. It made holes in the frame exposing the interior of the structure for everyone gathered.

As the demolition continued, Mary Jane Castro, Michael's sister, watched from behind the fence. She'd come thinking it would be cathartic to see the building come down. But being there brought her back to that dark morning in the parking lot of Brown's Chicken wandered aimlessly. It brought her back to waiting hopelessly at the police station for good news. It brought her back to the memory of her brother, and she became overwhelmed with emotion. Raw emotion.

Mary Jane started running around the fenced enclosure, calling for the crew's attention. *Stop! Please stop!* she yelled in desperation. The men paused and the machine shut down. She approached the building. From a pile of wreckage, she picked up a dusty red brick. Clasping it in her hand, she walked around to another part of the half-wrecked structure where a window was still intact, launching it straight into the glass. It shattered. She let out a scream. Around her, those gathered—the reporters, passersby, the crew—were silent. They understood, even if they couldn't *really* ever understand.

Mary Jane reached to the ground for other pieces to throw at the building one after the other. It was a release of years of tension and torment. Finally, she broke down in tears. The crew embraced her with a hug and her husband carried her away.

The work resumed. The backhoe took more strikes at the building, and after thirteen whacks, the job was done. Eight years had passed since the murders, and the Brown's Chicken building at Smith and Northwest Highway was finally erased from Palatine's landscape.

PART 3

A Hare was making fun of the Tortoise one day for being so slow. "Do you ever get anywhere?" he asked with a mocking laugh.

"Yes," replied the Tortoise, "and I get there sooner than you think."

The Tortoise and the Hare
Aesop's Fables

CHAPTER 17

JUAN & JIM

Time heals all wounds. But what happens when life appears to stand still? For the Mennes, Castro, Ehlenfeldt, Solis, Nellsen, and Maldonado families, the years went by because they had to. Without closure, however, that time was agonizing. One minute, you're waiting for your loved one to come home, merely wondering why they're late. The next, your entire life has changed. The funerals attended by hundreds. Constant calls from reporters. Suspects that came and went. A steady stream of info from police and news reports that were impossible to avoid and then...nothing. Deafening silence. Waiting for years. A proverbial purgatory.

January 8 became a somber anniversary that was marked each year by the families. It was a painful reminder of what happened that day. But for others, moving on was easier. Life did not stand still for Juan Luna and James Degorski.

Juan Luna was born in 1974 in Zacatecas, a mid-sized city in Central Mexico known as a silver mining hub in a state of the same name. The region had a robust agricultural industry, with ranches and farms growing chili peppers, guava, sugar cane, grapes, and beans. His father, Juan Sr., worked as a farmhand. His mother, Alicia, sold tortillas and raised their children.

At the age of nine, Juan Luna's family decided to leave Mexico. It was the typical immigrant story of people in search of more opportunity, better education, and a chance at the American Dream. At that time, they had three children: Juan Jr., Jorge, and Brenda. The family settled on moving to Chicago, with its large and vibrant community of Mexican immigrants, as their home. And they soon expanded their family, giving birth to their daughter Elizia in the United States.[1] After their move in 1979, the Lunas eventually went west and ditched the city for the suburbs.

The family learned to adapt in their new country, finding jobs, a new place to live, and learning English. When he got older, Juan attended Fremd High School in Palatine. It was a change from the city. Juan was quiet. And yet, in a way, everyone knew him. Not because he was a star athlete or academic standout, but because he was one of the only Latino kids in school. Fremd was suburbia, and of the two high schools in Palatine, it was the one that tended to be whiter and wealthier.

Teenage life was normal. Juan and his friends would get drunk around town, sometimes hanging out in a ditch behind a local strip mall for privacy. He smoked pot and experimented with other drugs with friends. While he was shy on the outside, he could have a temper. In school, he struggled with a learning disability and was placed in special education courses, but he was just your average teen. He held down jobs like at Brown's Chicken.

After graduating high school in 1992, Juan continued working jobs like one gig at a nearby pie restaurant. But Juan was ready for a change in his life. A big change. He decided to head back to Mexico, uprooting his life to live in the place where hadn't resided since he was a child.

During a two-year stay, he met a woman name Imelda in his hometown of Zacatecas.[2] There was a spark, and in 1994, the couple married, eventually returning to the United States. Initially they lived with Luna's parents who'd remained in suburban Crystal Lake. In 1995, Juan Luna became a naturalized American citizen, and two years later in 1997, their son was born.[3]

Juan Luna lived a perfectly ordinary life. Imelda settled into a routine in Illinois, and the two raised their young boy. He was a loving father, picking him up from school. He was a supportive husband, shopping for groceries, sorting through bills, and facing the everyday ups and downs of any marriage. The family resided in a subsidized complex called Meadowdale in suburban Carpentersville not far from where he went to high school. It wasn't glamorous, with dark hallways, drab carpet, and thin walls that barely muffled the noise of neighbors' blaring TVs, but the family made it work.[4] Juan was employed at an appliance store called Gulgren Appliance six days a week installing fridges, dishwashers, and other equipment.[5] He earned eleven dollars an hour.

The paths of Juan Luna and Jim Degorski crossed occasionally through mutual friends, but as a father with a young child, their lives were on separate paths. And while the difficulties associated with immigrating to a new country were no doubt a challenge, they paled in comparison to Jim's early life.

With his friends off having kids, going to college, or building careers, Jim Degorski was still behind. He'd put his studies on hold at Fremd and didn't graduate on time. He eventually mustered up the drive to get a GED and put school behind him, finishing in 1994 with a D average.[6]

Jim had plenty to blame for his outbursts, his lack of concentration, and his academic struggles. Growing up in suburban Hoffman Estates, he was surrounded by the prototypical American family living out their days in homes with two-car garages, tidy yards, and the stability of suburbia. Jim's family life provided only anguish.

The Degorski house was dysfunctional—and then some. Jim was the second oldest of five kids: Kathy, the oldest, born in 1979, then Jim in '72, Brian in '74, Kevin in '76, and Megan in '79. His father was probably never ready to have one child, let alone five. With work consuming much of his father's time, Jim often stepped in to help with the younger kids, cooking mac and cheese dinners and taking them out on adventures in the suburbs.[7]

William Degorski had nicknames for all the children. Kevin was "the favorite." Brian was "the mouth" for his tendency to argue back. Kathy was "the princess." Jim had a few names. "Devil worshiper" was used to mock his love of heavy metal and how he dressed. "Druggy" made fun of his need for ADHD medication. And his father called him "the retard" after he was held back in school.[8]

Diagnosed with schizophrenia, problems arose for William Degorski.[9] A Vietnam veteran, he developed depression and had nightmares. He struggled to hold down a job. In the parking lot at his office at Motorola, he threatened colleagues one day during an outburst where he brought a gun and was forced to see a counselor.[10] When he refused to get proper help, he was terminated. The joblessness only caused more issues.

SOMETHING BIG

Jim's father was sex crazed. He was constantly asking his wife for more and never satisfied. He talked about sex openly with his children, occasionally pleasuring himself in front of them. He encouraged his sons to masturbate, talking dirty about their mother and sisters. He put peepholes in the walls of the house so he could monitor his children. When he entered what he referred to as his "Indian phase," he walked around the house naked, only a loincloth covering his crotch. He drank, and he sometimes carried a gun around the house.[11]

Jim's mother, Pat, tried to stop the endless need for sex and physical abuse in a unique way. She gorged herself. Pat decided the only way to protect herself was to become so obese that her husband would no longer be sexually attracted to her. No longer able to throw her around. She reached over 370 pounds, giving herself diabetes, hypertension, and chronic pain as a result.[12] Pat suffered from depression and attempted suicide at various points. She became totally convinced that her husband would try to poison her, so when she made family meals she baked only casseroles in a single dish. She knew her husband would never kill the kids.

A sign on the wall at the Degorski home denoted a family code: "loose lips sink ships." Placed there by their father, it was a reminder to keep quiet about what goes on in the family. But in November of 1989, tensions reached their peak when Pat accused her husband of molesting one of their daughters. He blamed his actions on his service in Vietnam, his past as an adopted child, and childhood sexual abuse from a priest. She obtained a protective order, and he was ordered to leave the house. The Degorskis were finally free of their father.

But Jim's father left little hints that he was watching. He tracked the mileage on his kids' cars. He put tape on the doors to see if they'd been opened. He placed candy on their pillows when they weren't home.[13]

As a teenager and young adult, Jim Degorski tried his best to avoid the chaos at home. And despite the drama, he was generally a happy kid. Still, he drank to excess, numbing himself to those problems. When he and his brother injured themselves while inebriated, Jim was ordered to a drug treatment center with his brother. He tried to get better, attending Alcoholic Anonymous meetings half-heartedly.[14]

After high school, Jim worked wherever he could find a paycheck. He tried his hand at washing and polishing cars. He worked construction. He cleaned offices. He worked as a janitorial assistant at a suburban country club. And for the most part, people found Jim Degorski to be a hardworking employee.

Jim continued dating too. He was always looking for a girl. In the fall of 1994, he broke up with his girlfriend Anne Lockett.[15] He dated on and off. And eventually, he met Jennifer Peters, a friend of his sister's who'd remained close with the family.[16] She was kind to him and always encouraging. She told him he could be more, pushing him to start a handyman business of his own. Jim was inspired, and he decided to give it a try. "Jim of All Trades," he called it. It was a great way of employing the skills he'd learned in other jobs. He did basic remodeling work, cleaned offices, repaired boats, and other tasks.[17]

Jim moved into a house in Wauconda, Illinois that was older and painted yellow, situated on a nice block with kind neighbors who he came to appreciate. The house was split into two units, and he rented the bottom half. He talked with people, got to know their kids, and became a part of their lives. They sat outside at the picnic table with guests and by the bonfire pit in the yard. Jim had a place to play his music loudly with no one to tell him to turn it down. Finally, he felt free.[18]

Jennifer moved in with Jim at the home in Wauconda. But their relationship was volatile—not because of any violence, but because of her own immaturity. She was constantly threatening to break up with him over trivial fights. Small matters resulted in full-on blowups. But Jim was patient with Jennifer.[19]

Jennifer decided to move to Arizona in August of 2000 when the two were not dating. As a teacher, she believed she'd have better luck finding work there. Plus, it was a nice change of pace from the winters of Chicago. They stayed in touch, talking on the phone. There was an intense attraction that remained, and she yearned to see him.

Why don't you come with me? she asked him. It was a big leap for Jim. He'd finally started building a stable business in Illinois that supported him. But he loved Jennifer. So Jim gave it all up, heading southwest to give the desert a try.[20] The change was difficult for him, and he had trouble finding work. It was tough to recreate a word-of-mouth, referral-based handyman business in a state where he knew no one. So in 2001, he decided to head back to the Midwest.[21]

The Degorski children by this time had moved to different parts of Chicagoland and different parts of the country. He decided to try Indiana on for size, moving to Indianapolis where his brother Kevin had an apartment. *I'm sick of the crime in Chicago, that shithole*, he told friends.[22]

Jim and his brother eventually moved into a brick ranch home in December of 2000.[23] For work, Jim found a job with Associated Services Inc., a company that managed a number of condominium complexes in the area. He made repairs in the units, took care of the exterior, and cleaned when necessary.

It was easy for Jim to keep in touch with friends from high school. He'd call them up wherever they were in the country to check in. His old high school friend Eileen Bakalla was one of those people. *We're taking a trip down to Florida*, she told him that year, referring to her and her new fiancé. *Do you want to come with?* she asked. Jim agreed to play third wheel, driving down to the Sunshine State with the two of them in April of 2002. They fished, rode bikes and rollerbladed, and went on head-clearing nature hikes.[24]

In Indianapolis through his maintenance job, Jim made a friend named Walter Hanger. A devout Baptist and father of five, Walter was open about his faith. He read his Bible, and he attended services with regularity. He went on mission trips to places like Peru, Russia, and an Indian reservation in the United States. He always prayed before meals.[25]

His friend's outward Christianity intrigued Jim, and he started asking questions. One day at work, the two men were outside taking out trash at a condo complex when Jim began to inquire. He was curious. "If somebody killed somebody, will God let them into heaven?"[26]

CHAPTER 18

MELISSA

Spring had always been a busy time for twenty-eight-year-old Melissa Benz. Things picked up for her and her husband's landscaping business as the grass grew green from winter and flowers began to bloom from the frozen earth. In the spring of 2002, Melissa sat in her basement office where the couple ran the operation in Fox Lake, a suburb northwest of Chicago. She was catching up on office work. When the phone rang, it was yet another distraction from the materials piling up on her desk—bills, invoices, upcoming requests and customers to deal with.

Hey, it's Anne, she heard on the other end of the line. Anne Lockett and Melissa had been close in high school ever since they were assigned to share a locker during their freshman year at Fremd High School, and the two friends had been diligent about keeping up with one another and sharing life updates. Some good, some bad. Graduations and marriages. Moves across the country. Gossip about old high-school friends. But no matter the news, the two supported one another.

The two women chatted as any normal catchup began. Anne's tone, however, lacked the casual nature of their typical chats. There was a sense of hesitation in her voice. Anne began asking questions about their past, reminding Melissa of otherwise unremarkable moments.

"Do you remember all the phone calls we've had over the years where I told you never to give out my address?" she said, alluding to a nearly decade-long request she'd had of friends and family. *Just play dumb*, she'd ask. *You don't know where I am, you don't keep in touch, and you've got no idea.* Melissa had always found her friend's requests strange, but she hardly thought twice about it. Her friends just assumed it was because of the drinking.

Their conversation continued and was equally vague. Then, Anne had another request of her friend. Just a simple favor. "So, I have a letter, and I need you to forward it for me."[1] Anne didn't want it coming from the post office where she lived, and she didn't want to be associated with the contents. Melissa needed more information. This was a strange demand. She started prying. "Well, what's the letter? Why can't you do it? And why do you need it to be postmarked from here?"[2] Anne gave excuses. She deflected. *The details aren't important*, she explained. *Please just do this for me.* Melissa continued giving noncommittal responses.

"Do you remember when Jim used to be mean to me?" she said, alluding to her abusive ex-boyfriend, their mutual high school classmate who Melissa loathed. "Or when I was in the hospital?" It all seemed like a random collection of unrelated statements. To her friend, it was still entirely unclear what Anne Lockett was getting at.

"I know who...who killed all those people," she said nervously, a remarkable assertion that begged for follow-up. "What people?" Melissa exclaimed. She was dragging it out of her.

Finally, Anne opened up. "I know who killed all those people at Brown's." Melissa coaxed more information out of her friend. She couldn't possibly let her stop there.

It was Jim Degorski, Anne explained. That made sense to Melissa, even if the entire thing still seemed unbelievable. He was a bully, had a temper, and was always nasty to women. *And Juan Luna*, Anne said. Knowing him to be shy, a wallflower, someone you barely knew was around, Melissa was astonished.

The news simply didn't register. It was like a doctor informing a patient of a tough diagnosis, with their face going numb and ears ringing with silence. She needed to hear it again to process. With hindsight, a lot made sense to Melissa. The walks around Palatine, always ending up at Brown's, where her friend wondered aloud about the impact the killings had. Bringing up the massacre at parties unprompted around friends. Asking friends if anyone had an update on the case anytime she heard a familiar name like Martin Blake. Anne Lockett had been dropping clues—in her own roundabout way—for years.

After nearly a decade, Anne Lockett was ready to come forward. Melissa rejected the letter idea, but she had another suggestion. It was time to tell the police. But Anne had concerns. The threats from Jim and Juan years ago still lingered, but she was willing to press ahead. She worried about her own liability having waited so long. Was she in legal jeopardy? She had, after all, accompanied Juan to the task force building for his interview in February of 1993 when investigators questioned all past employees of Brown's. Yet she'd never lied to anyone. She never told authorities false information or misled them. Nobody ever asked.

The two old friends spent about an hour on the phone when Melissa decided to determine her friend's level of liability.

She needed to convince Anne that her actions would be heroic, not criminal.

Years before running the landscaping business with her husband, Melissa had worked at a gas station in Palatine. The establishment was 24/7, an arrangement that caused plenty of excitement for anyone working the night shift. Like Melissa when she was working, the Palatine police had irregular hours, and the gas station was the perfect spot to kill time and grab a cup of coffee or a late-night snack. Because of this, Melissa had gotten to know quite a few Palatine police officers over the years. She felt close enough to give them a call.

Still seated at her desk in her basement office, Melissa hung up the phone. In between calls, she tried hastily to explain to her husband what was happening. Anne. Murder. Brown's Chicken. *I'll explain later*.

Melissa Benz called the Palatine police number listed and an operator picked up. *How can I help you?* the operator asked. Melissa listed the names of a few officers she knew. None were working that night. She decided to be a little more forceful given the information she'd just been told. This was the biggest case in the history of Palatine, after all. It truly was urgent. "I need to talk to Mike Tulley right now!" she insisted, name-dropping one of the officers she knew. Sensing indifference to the urgency, Melissa revealed her purpose for calling. "I have information about the Brown's Chicken murders." Melissa hung up.

Within a few minutes, Melissa Benz received a call from Officer Mike Tulley. The two talked about Anne's involvement and if she'd put herself in legal risk. *She never lied to the police?* he asked. No, she explained, she'd just held out, worried for her life. They killed seven, why not one more? *She never assisted with the crime?* Again, she explained that Anne was in no way involved.

Tulley assured her that, based on that information, Anne Lockett was in the clear. "Someone needs to call her now," she insisted. "She's finally at a point where she'll talk."[3]

***

Life had not been a straight line for Anne Lockett. After graduating from Fremd High School, she started her associate's degree at Harper College in Palatine in 1995. She then decided to leave Illinois after saving up enough money from working at a pet shop to purchase a mobile home which she decided to take across the country. With her mother in Utah, she headed west to stay with her. She then went back east to North Carolina where she worked seasonal jobs in the Smoky Mountains as a whitewater rafting guide and helping with administrative tasks for the company that hired her. A lover of the outdoors, Anne cherished her time in the peaceful mountains, hiking in the forest, or rocking on the river. In 1996 between summers out east, she lived briefly in Oregon, helping her mother deal with her father's death, enrolling for a quarter again in community college then deciding to pause.[4]

Crisscrossing the country became tiring, so Anne decided to sell her trailer and move in with her sister in Mattoon, Illinois, a small city roughly halfway between St. Louis and Indianapolis. In 1998, she enrolled at Lake Land Community College nearby and received her associate's degree the next year. She found a job working with developmentally disabled adults, helping them with everyday tasks like taking a shower or getting dressed. She thrived in the role, organizing Special Olympics trips and helping coordinate the administration of medicine for residents.

After they broke up in 1994, Anne did her best to excise Jim Degorski from her life. She tried to move on from the abuse. Move on from his controlling behavior and insistence on cutting friends out of her life. Move on from his threat about what would happen if she ever came forward with what she knew. And Jim kept tabs on her, trying to track her down over the years with a phone call here and there. It was a reminder that no matter where she was in the country, she could never really escape her past.

After finishing her associate's degree, Anne Lockett decided to continue her education at Eastern Illinois University studying psychology. By 2002, she'd moved out of her sister's place and settled in nearby Charleston, Illinois. Her apartment was in the quaint town square above a karate studio and across the Coles County courthouse, a Victoria-style building built in 1898.[5]

Melissa Benz was not the first person Anne told about Brown's Chicken. She informed her boyfriend, and the two considered sending a letter. They nixed the idea with worries that, post 9/11 and anthrax scares, it might be considered a hoax. She told her roommate in Charleston, another student at EIU. The news scared him, and the two started locking their doors diligently and obtain firearm-owners' IDs. Anne pulled out her high-school yearbook and showed pictures of Jim and Juan to others so they'd know what they look like if they arrived.[6] They borrowed a gun from her sister, who Anne also told. In an effort to prevent her mother from giving out her contact info to Jim, she finally told her what happened.[7] Anne's secret was no longer so secret.

On March 25, 2002, Officer Bill King sat at his desk in the basement of the Palatine police station. It was the location where he'd spoken to hundreds of people claiming to have information about the murders over the years. He knew more about the case than anyone. Hearing from Melissa Benz, with her frantic insistence that she'd cracked the case, was nothing he hadn't already experienced dozens of times before. He was cautiously optimistic.

Anne walked Bill through the story of what Jim Degorski and Juan Luna had told her in his basement. A few weeks later, after digging deeper, police and prosecutors went to visit Anne at her apartment in Charleston, Illinois. She was nervous, puffing on cigarettes throughout the encounter. Her hair was in a ponytail and on her nose sat wire-rimmed glasses. They went through the story piece by piece—the details she'd been told in Jim's basement that day, how she'd accompanied Juan Luna to the Palatine police station, and how her mother brought news clippings after she received the call in the hospital about them doing "something big." When police asked her if she'd wear a wire, Anne Lockett eventually agreed.[8]

***

Looking in the mirror at the salon, Melissa was beyond pleased with her haircut. She looked great. She felt great. "My hair's never looked so good," she said to her husband when she arrived home. "Let's go out for dinner." Better to be seen while she felt her best. Melissa and her husband readied themselves to leave the house and grab dinner at Moretti's, a local pizza joint. When she stepped on the doorstep of her home, she was greeted by three men in the dark. She was startled.

We'd like to talk to you about the Brown's case, they told her. One of the men had a binder full of papers in his hands. They looked official. "Can we come in?" they asked. Melissa and her husband quickly realized there'd be no date night.

Melissa led her unexpected guests to the kitchen table. The men sat, including Palatine police chief John Koziol who'd recently been elevated as head of the department. She was nervous but glad to finally hear from law enforcement. She and her friend Anne knew how volatile Jim Degorski could be. They worried he might do something irrational if he caught wind of them coming forward, and she felt police weren't sharing enough information with them. But behind the scenes, investigators were methodically preparing to move forward.

"Do you mind if I crack a beer?" she asked, proceeding to offer the men a beverage as well. They declined. As they talked through their questions, Melissa was relieved. Koziol and his team explained to her that they were buttoning up the case and getting things in order. *Just hang tight*, they instructed her.

CHAPTER 19

BILL

Bill King did things by the book. He kept an open mind, but never jumped to conclusions despite the temptation. Being scrupulous often meant moving less speedily than others would like. He was deliberate, not slow, an attitude that developed from having worked the Brown's case since day one. He'd been there on day one helping remove the bodies. He'd tracked down promising leads and seen them fall through to the dismay of what seemed like the entirety of Chicagoland. He'd witnessed the task force balloon to more than one hundred investigators constantly on the cusp of a breakthrough only to see it dwindle to just a handful of investigators holding out hope in the years that followed. Now it was just him and another officer, Robert Bailey, who was on the cusp of retirement.[1] And like many Palatine police officers, Bill King had come to accept that it would take someone coming forward for there to be a true break in the case. Someone, somewhere, someday would talk.

His career began in 1983 with the Palatine police as a patrolman, a role that helped him gain an understanding of the city and its people. He responded to calls of every kind. In 1988, he became a detective and worked investigating crimes for nearly twelve years. Of everything he did, the Brown's Chicken case most consumed him. Just two years earlier in 2000, he had been promoted to sergeant, where he'd supervise other officers and take on additional management responsibilities. His peers and subordinates respected him.[2] Bill King was smart and thoughtful. With square glasses, gray hair on the sides, and a simple mustache, he wasn't flashy. Bill King just did his job, and he did it well.

Hi, Anne, this is Sergeant Bill King with the Palatine police, he told her on the first phone call after hearing the news. *I'll call you tomorrow when I'm back at my desk.* Anne was eager to talk, and Bill King wanted to hear what she had to say. But this was lead number 4,842. With a number that high, it was easy to see why he didn't jump to conclusions immediately. She was hardly the first woman to report an ex-boyfriend. Bill King was patient. He had to be. There was no other way to keep yourself sane working a case like this.

When the two connected the next day, Anne Lockett retold her story, taking King through the suicide attempt that landed her in the hospital, the phone call she'd received from Jim Degorski, and how they recounted the murders in detail to her in Jim's basement a few weeks later. She shared specific details about that night. *Jim and Juan told me that the skinny kid vomited French fries*, she mentioned. That piece of information set off alarm bells in King's mind. Police had never made that detail public. Anne Lockett was telling the truth.

Bill King began digging into Jim Degorski and Juan Luna. Where were they from? Had we spoken to them? Who might have more information? The new lead was a closely guarded secret even within the police force. Only those on a need-to-know basis were told. Even the slightest hint of renewed interest in the case would prompt the media to start digging.

The most clear-cut way of verifying Anne Lockett's story was to find a connection from the two men to the scene. Given Juan Luna had been interviewed in the past by police as a former employee, King had an easy excuse for paying him another visit. In late March 2002, Sergeant King and Officer Robert Bailey drove to suburban Carpentersville to Juan Luna's apartment. They knocked on the door. When there was no answer, they left a business card with contact information and received a call back the next day. *We're interviewing all past employees of Brown's just trying to collect more information*, he explained to him. *Can we come talk to you?* he asked. *Sure*, Juan Luna told them, *I just need to find someone to watch my son.*[3]

On April 3, 2002, Sergeant Bill King, recently promoted, and Officer Bailey returned to the apartment at 11:00 a.m. They knocked, and the man who greeted them at the door was slightly stocky, with short black hair, a mustache, and wire-rimmed glasses.[4] *Please come in*, Juan Luna said to the officers. Inside, Bailey remained by the door, concerned that Luna might bolt. They walked through their usual questions—alibi, past work at Brown's, rapport with the victims.

As they neared the end of the conversation, Sergeant King casually asked him a pivotal question. *Do you mind if we take a buccal swab of your mouth?* he told him. "What do you need that for?" asked Luna skeptically. "To eliminate you as a suspect," he explained. This was for his own good, actually. They were just trying to help him out. "Lots of people have given us buccal swabs," he says. "We won't have to bug you again." Luna agreed. "Okay."

Sergeant King pulled out an envelope from his coat pocket containing a stick with a cotton swab. He handed it to Luna, who rubbed it on the inside of his cheeks then handed it back to King, who sealed it for safe keeping then wrote Juan Luna's name and the time on it. "Can we talk to you again if we have any other questions?" he asked. "Sure," replied Luna.[5]

For Jim Degorski, the process was more complicated. He was not a former employee, nor had he ever been interviewed by police other than knocking on his front door to confirm Juan's alibi in 1995 when Jim Bell and his team were taking a fresh look at the case. Police asked Jim Degorski to stop by the Palatine police station when he was in town running an errand. In an interview room, Sergeant King and Officer Bailey questioned him about where he was that night, about who he hung out with, his past girlfriends, then asked him for fingerprints and a buccal swab. He agreed.[6]

In the days that followed, both men were surveilled by police, with officers sent to Indianapolis to monitor Degorski during the day. "Don't get caught," they were told. In plain clothes, they monitored his movements by day in a pickup truck, seeing if he did anything suspicious or tried to skip town unexpectedly. They'd retire for the night at a hotel then pick up again in the morning.[7]

Sergeant Bill King sent both DNA samples to the Northern Illinois Police Crime Lab for testing.

***

Huddled in a hotel room, Anne Lockett was terrified about what she was being asked to do. She'd avoided speaking with Jim Degorski despite his constant attempts to track her down over the years. The prospect of doing so while recording the conversation was even more terrifying. But police had received a court order to tape a phone call between the two, and she'd agreed to go along.

The police coached her along with scenarios. It was a maze of responses she was supposed to track, each one crafted to elicit a different, incriminating response from her ex. They put together a plan for Anne in case Jim started asking questions. She dialed up Jim, and the recording began.

> <u>Anne</u>: What do I tell them when they ask me about what you have done?
> <u>Jim</u>: I don't know what you're talking about.
> <u>Anne</u>: I'm talking about Brown's Chicken.
> <u>Jim</u>: What about Brown's Chicken?
> <u>Anne</u>: You know what I mean.
> <u>Jim</u>: No, I really don't.[8]

With two officers listening on the line, Jim Degorski offered up very little. But she continued pressing him for more information. She put on the best theatrical performance she could muster, knowing the case depended on it.

> <u>Anne</u>: Well, how about you tell me something about the murders so I can help you. Just something.
> <u>Jim</u>: I don't know.
> <u>Anne</u>: Well, exactly. I mean, are you basically throwing your cards in and saying fuck it, I'm going to go to jail for multiple murder? That's what you want to do?[9]

Jim Degorski did not deny this assertion outright, but his responses were also not all that convincing. The call was a dud. In a court of law, police knew it wasn't enough. Most of the conversation was unusable.

For years, Anne Lockett had feared for her safety. Now, she'd been thrust into the middle of what she feared the most, with her cooperation and her word the lynchpin of the police's case. Silence from law enforcement did not help, with weeks going by without hearing much of anything. She began to worry about her safety once again, unsure if Jim Degorski or someone else might make an attempt at revenge once learning she'd come forward.

Police moved to stitch up the case, but Anne Lockett and Melissa Benz, unaware of the action behind the scenes, were concerned with the lack of progress. Why weren't police moving quicker? Through family friends in Palatine, Wilma and Cyril Plazak, they conveyed their frustration. The elderly couple decided to take matters into their own hands.

Sitting in her office in the Palatine village hall one day, Rita Mullins's phone rang. It was her friends, the Plazaks. They explained the unbelievable information they'd learned—the girlfriend coming forward, the two men who committed the murders. Located in the same building as the police, Rita Mullins went down the hall to speak to Sergeant Bill King, who she knew was the expert on the case, one of the only remaining officers on the task force. *I just received a call about a lead from Brown's Chicken, they say they've got news of a suspect's girlfriend*, she told him. Playing it cool, King thanked the mayor, pretending as if it was news to them. *We'll follow up*, he assured her. He kept quiet about just how much they already knew. There was no room for error.

SOMETHING BIG

On the morning of May 15, police approached Eileen Bakalla, the friend who'd met Jim and Juan just after the murders and brought them to her apartment to count the money, in her driveway as she headed out to work.[10] *We'd like you to accompany us back to the station*, they asked. She was coy but headed into one of the unmarked cars that surrounded her.[11]

Eileen Bakalla had bought a pair of shoes with money she knew was stolen from the restaurant after the murders. She'd lied to investigators for Juan, agreeing to be his alibi in November of 1995.[12] She knew everything about what happened that night. After being given time to speak to a lawyer, she obtained a letter from police assuring they would not attempt to prosecute her. Then, she talked.[13]

***

When police discovered the four-piece chicken dinner in a garbage can at Brown's, it was unclear what use they'd have at the time. But Jane Homeyer, the forensic scientist present on day one, knew even then where the science was likely headed. In 1993, DNA technology employed restriction fragment length polymorphism analysis, or RFLP. Put simply, a large amount of a DNA sample of decent quality was required to find a match. Saliva from a chicken bone was not enough. But by 1998, just four years later, the technology had advanced greatly, allowing far less material to be used through polymerase chain reaction, or PCR, analysis. When this technology became available, the saliva from the DNA was retested. A profile was successfully obtained from the sample, but there were no matches against people police had questioned or in any relevant criminal databases.

On the afternoon of May 7, 2002, Sergeant Bill King received a call from the Illinois State Police Crime Lab. "I'm sending you a written report of the tests on the most recent DNA samples you sent us," the tech said. "What does it say," King asked. "One sample matches." King could feel the anticipation. "Which one?" he asked. "The one belonging to someone named Luna...Juan Luna. It's identical to the DNA that came from the two chicken bones."[14]

CHAPTER 20

ALESIA

Jim Degorski was still groggy from the night before. He'd been drinking with friends and his sister, who was visiting Indianapolis. His seasonal allergies didn't help.[1] It was just after 3:00 p.m. on May 16, 2002, in Carmel, Indiana, a suburb outside Indianapolis. Temperature hovered just below sixty degrees and there were a few light drizzles. Degorski pulled into a gravel parking lot at the construction site where he was working and got out of his truck. He was preparing for his next task, taking tools from his personal car and loading them into his company-issued vehicle. He started filling out the paperwork he completed before every job, and his friend Walter Hanger stood nearby.

From across busy Route 421 sitting in a gas station parking lot, Sergeant Bill King and Detective Dan Briscoe had been waiting for nearly an hour for Jim to arrive. Dressed in plain clothes, they approached Degorski's truck as he was transferring his tools. Having been interviewed by him a few weeks earlier, Jim Degorski recognized King.

"I'm here to talk to you about the Brown's Chicken case," King told him. Jim paused. "What do you want to know?" he asked, keeping his cool. "We're here to ask you to return to

Chicago with us," King said. "We want to ask you some questions about the case." Degorski obliged but was concerned about his work. "What should I do with my truck?" King pointed to another local law enforcement officer who'd accompanied them. "That officer over there is from the Indianapolis police department. He'll take care of it."[2] Degorski handed him the keys and Briscoe then patted him down. He then signed a form agreeing that he was willingly accompanying the officers back to Illinois. *I, Jim Degorski....*

Briscoe drove the unmarked Palatine police car home while King sat with Degorski in the back. *I'm surprised it took you this long*, he told them, readily admitting to his involvement in the murders. Slightly lost, they had to ask one of the local officers for directions for the three-and-a-half-hour ride back to the northwest suburbs. In the car, the men talked about Indy 500 racing and if Jim followed the sport or ever attended races. They discussed his childhood in Hoffman Estates and how Jim went to night school to finish up his GED.[3] He offered up information and was chatty. He knew he'd been caught.

Degorski downplayed his role from the beginning. "I helped control the people inside," he said, placing the blame on his friend Juan Luna. "I shot a couple people Luna wouldn't kill."[4] They stopped at a rest stop. *Do you want anything to eat?* they asked him. *I'll take an iced tea*, he said.

The officers received word from deputy police chief John Koziol to head to the Streamwood police station instead of Palatine to avoid the media.[5] With more officers brought back to work the case, there was no guarantee their progress wouldn't leak. Briscoe stopped again later for gas, and Degorski used the restroom without handcuffs.[6] The men continued talking about the murders. "Don't worry," Jim told them. "I'll make it easy on you."[7]

SOMETHING BIG

***

Two unmarked police cars monitored Juan Luna from outside his apartment complex. The next twenty-four hours had to go exactly as planned for police. Taking the two men into custody at once was a logistical feat, but it was necessary to avoid either man potentially learning of the other's arrest and skipping town. It was Thursday, May 16, 2002. Wearing blue jeans and a white T-shirt, Juan Luna left his apartment shortly before 3:00 p.m., hopped in the car, and drove away. In the back seat sat his four-year-old son, Brian. Officers followed.[8]

Luna pulled into the Shell gas station at Hazard Road and Route 25 in Carpentersville, Illinois. He got out of the car, then approached a gas pump to fill up his tank. Suddenly, police officers surrounded him. Officer Robert Bailey made the arrest. "Mr. Luna, you're under arrest for the Brown's Chicken murders," he said. "Put your hands behind your back."[9] Still buckled into the back seat of the car, his son Brian began to cry, unaware of what was happening to his dad. Another officer took Luna's son out of the car and into a police vehicle. Luna looked back as officers whisked him away. *Where are you taking him?!* he asked worried. To avoid the press, Luna was driven to nearby Hoffman Estates instead of the Palatine police station.

***

The interrogation of Juan Luna took place in a barren ten-by-fifteen-foot room. His fingerprints were taken, and he was continually advised of his Miranda rights.[10] *You have the right to remain silent, do you understand?* Luna agreed. *Anything you say can be used against you in court, do you understand?* Yes. *You have a right to have an attorney before or during questioning.* Understood. *If you cannot afford one, an attorney will be provided for you.* Got it. *Do you still wish to speak to me about that night?* Juan Luna, after more than nine years, was ready to talk.[11]

For nineteen hours, Luna told police everything that had happened on the night of January 8, 1993.[12] He talked about knowing the ins and outs of the restaurant as a former employee and knowing that around 9:00 p.m. the restaurant would be mostly empty. He knew there were no cameras or alarms. He talked about ordering the meal and demonstrated the karate stance he took to prevent one person from escaping the restaurant. He answered questions in detail and, by his own admission, willingly.

> Interrogator: Did Jim shoot him in the back as far as you could tell?
>
> Luna: Yes.
>
> Interrogator: Now, what happened to that guy after he said, "Oh, I've been shot."
>
> Luna: Well, he was kind of like this, drowsy a little bit. Jim grabbed him, pulled him back, and he told him to go into a west side cooler.
>
> Interrogator: From where you were, could you see the west side cooler?
>
> Luna: Inside?
>
> Interrogator: Inside.
>
> Luna: No, I couldn't.
>
> Interrogator: Could you see the door of the cooler?
>
> Luna: I could see the door.
>
> Interrogator: Did you see the guy in the west side cooler with Jim?
>
> Luna: Yes, I did.

<u>Interrogator</u>: Okay. Now, what did you see next?
<u>Luna</u>: Well, what I saw next was there was someone else laying on the floor in the west side cooler, and he told him to get up and I also heard some more shots. They were kind of like a little rapid, a pause, and then again some more shots.
<u>Interrogator</u>: Now, the second guy that went there, had you ever seen that guy before? The second guy that Jim took into the cooler?
<u>Luna</u>: Yes, he's one of the owners.
<u>Interrogator</u>: Married to the lady that you identified in exhibit number three?
<u>Luna</u>: Yes.

Luna talked about how he became animated that night. How things went from silence to total pandemonium. "As everything got wild and crazy, I guess I got caught up in the moment and cut her throat."[13] He talked about shooting the gun. "The people inside were yelling, 'Don't shoot us!'" he said. "Their hands were shaking."[14] He blamed Jim Degorski as the main instigator, saying he hatched the plan mostly by himself.[15] He expressed remorse. "If I could do this all again, there's no way in hell I'd do this at all," he said. "I feel very sorry deep in my heart."[16] The confession was all captured on tape.

At the police station in Streamwood, a nearby suburb, Degorski was also interrogated by police. Sergeant Bill King informed Jim of his rights, using a little yellow card he carried in his pocket. On one side was the language for the five points he'd read to interviewees, the other was for conducting line-ups.[17] Always methodical, King read each point one by one.

That evening, Degorski again confessed to the crimes of January 8, 1993, when interviewed by King, Briscoe, and others. Michael McHale, a prosecutor with the Cook County state's attorney, went in at 3:00 a.m. to question Degorski on tape. "I told you I'd make it easy on you," he said. "I just want to tell it once, that's all."[18] Throughout, he was emotional. "I'm having a hard time," he told investigators with his head bobbing down.[19]

The cameras rolled. McHale again informed Jim Degorski of his rights and asked him to recount the story he'd told police over the past few hours. He talked for about four minutes, then stopped. *I don't like being filmed*, he explained. Jim Degorski was camera shy.

***

Across Chicagoland, TV programming was interrupted that afternoon with special reports of the arrest of the Brown's Chicken killers. Javier and Pablo Maldonado heard from a cousin that the men who killed their father had been captured. "Turn on the TV!" he exclaimed over the phone. "They caught the guys who did the murders!"[20] They called their mother in Celaya, Mexico, to inform her of the news. The families were used to the false sense of optimism, but it was clear this arrest was different. "This one is legit," an officer told Diane Mennes, Thomas Mennes's sister-in-law that afternoon.[21]

"Where's the Puerto Rican gang members?" said a member of law enforcement when asked for comment. "I'm waiting for the apologies to come in."[22] Families tried coming to terms with the lack of a concrete motive. "It's sort of ironic," said the Ehlenfeldts' middle daughter, Dana. "They're the kind of people my parents always tried to help."[23]

SOMETHING BIG

Palatine police announced the arrests at a press conference led by John Koziol. That year, 2002, Koziol had been elevated to chief of police of the department with more than a hundred officers and thirty civilians.[24] His father had been a police officer, and it had always been his calling. When the murders happened in 1993, he had been a detective sergeant involved in investigating. The investigation gave him perspective in life and in his career. Compared to the Brown's Chicken murders, other cases seemed small.

A former bouncer at a bar when he was in college, Koziol had broad shoulders and was fit.[25] He stood at the podium alongside other members of law enforcement and the mayor. Jerry Bratcher was nearby along with the Cook County state's attorney, Richard Devine, and members of his team. They announced the murder charges and explained how they found the two men. "It galls me that these two individuals, who are void of human conscience, took the lives of seven decent, law-abiding Americans," Koziol said clearly and forcefully for the TV cameras. In the audience, family members applauded each person who came forward to speak. Some wept, their tears mixed with relief and sadness. Those gathered hugged one another.

The conversation immediately turned to discussion of the death penalty, which prosecutors indicated early on they would pursue. Many of the family members were understandably supportive. "They killed my son, that's what they deserve," said Manny Castro. "If they're going to the electric chair, I'll pull the switch. If they're given an injection, I'll give the injection. If they're given a firing squad, I'll pull the trigger."[26]

Koziol avoided using the press conference to address past critiques of the police. "It's time to move on," he told those gathered. "It was never about the police versus the media, it was about seven innocent victims and their families."[27] He spoke about the motive, which still confounded. "They never really gave us one," he said. "They just did it to do something big. They are people without a soul and that's all we know about them." He spoke directly to Luna and Degorski. "I'm confident you will receive the death sentence you so justly deserve."[28]

Police quickly dispelled any rumors that Eileen Bakalla might be charged. It angered some, but it made logical sense, because prosecutors needed her cooperation. Others turned their dismay toward Anne Lockett. Should she be charged? "If we were to prosecute every balky, reluctant or recalcitrant witness, we'd have to build a jail the size of Rhode Island," said a spokesman for the state's attorney's office.[29] It would have a chilling effect on prosecutions. "The public should understand that witnesses have real fear about testifying against criminals who kill people, especially ones with multiple victims."

Perhaps more importantly, people wondered why she'd waited so long. But for some of the relieved family members, the case broke exactly how it should have. "God works in mysterious ways," declared Diane Mennes, Tom Mennes's sister-in-law.[30] "If she would have come forward at first, they probably would have thought she was loony toons," she said, alluding to Anne Lockett. "A lot of people were coming forward at the time accusing their exes." Richard Ehlenfeldt's sister Ann agreed. "In my mind, I'm glad it happened now because I think there's more likely to be a conviction with DNA evidence."[31] And indeed, had Anne Lockett come forward years ago, it would have been her word versus theirs without any DNA evidence to back her up. "She is the hero who caused this case to be solved. It took courage for her to come forward," Linas Kelecius, a Cook County assistant state's attorney working the case told reporters.[32]

One particular revelation did not sit well with many: the realization that people in their own community had committed this heinous act. By all accounts, Juan Luna and James Degorski were like anyone else in the suburbs living their normal lives. They went to the same high schools, attended the same churches, shopped at the same grocery stores, lived in the same neighborhoods, and had even encountered one another at various points in life. "These people came from Palatine. These people came from Fremd," explained Mary Jane Crow, Michael Castro's sister. "I'm completely baffled. To think these people are that evil, I'm baffled."[33]

The media gathered at the press conference asked to hear from the man who'd help put the final pieces of the story together, so Sergeant Bill King approached the podium. King was someone used to working behind the scenes, not facing the flashing lights of the press corps. He was reserved, eschewing the flare of his boss and other speakers. "Can you tell us what you're feeling today?" a TV reporter asked. "I'm feeling very happy for the families. I was pretty convinced when I heard some of the statements the lady made that we were looking at the right guys," he informed them in his quiet voice. "What toll has this taken on you personally?" another journalist inquired, alluding to the nearly decade King had spent working daily on the case. "I don't know yet," he told them. He paused. "It's my job and it's what I did."[34]

By this time, police had spent more than nine years on the investigations. More than 150 investigators had been involved at some point. It cost the city nearly $1 million.[35] Past criticism of the Palatine police dissolved. "I know Chief Bratcher wanted to solve the crime just like anyone else. I feel bad I was a critic, and if I could do it all again, I'd take it back," Frank Portillo said upon the announcement.[36] "They should feel fully exonerated," said Mary Jane Castro's husband about the police.[37] The Castro family then purchased three banners with the words "Thank You Palatine Police" and hung them across the village.[38]

***

The Cook County jail was a veritable dungeon. Housing thousands of pre-trial detainees, the gray-and-white ninety-six-acre complex next to the county courthouse at 26th and California Avenue had long been under federal oversight for poor conditions. Over the years, it had housed such criminals as Al Capone, John Wayne Gacy, and Richard Speck. Some Chicagoans referred to it ironically as "Hotel California." Unlike the song, it was not such a lovely place.

Violent fights among inmates and against correctional officers were not uncommon at 26th and Cal. Suicides took place with an alarming regularity.[39] Some inmates threw feces and urine at officers. Allowed cigarettes, they occasionally started fires. Divisions ranged from maximum security, where inmates were watched closely, to a minimum-security dormitory housing hundreds of inmates in rows and rows of bunks with only a handful of prison staff to monitor. There were rats and mice that crawled into medical facilities and sleeping quarters. It was crowded.

On Saturday, May 18, Jim Degorski and Juan Luna were taken to the Cook County jail, where they would be held pending their next hearing. In his cell, Jim Degorski was emotional. The gravity of what was happening finally hit him. He became erratic and started crying. "My life is over," he said aloud. A guard nearby tried to calm him down, sitting him in a chair in a holding room.[40] Another approached him and began arguing. "Are you the Brown's Chicken guy? What are you doing here?" Jim was not wearing any handcuffs or shackles. "Fuck you," he responded.[41]

Jim Degorski had only known the outside world and the freedom that comes with it. In Cook County prison, he was no longer in control. Enraged, the prison guard punched Jim in the face twice. His left cheekbone broke. His lips were cut and bleeding. His nose began to swell and the skin around his eye would soon turn purple. *Welcome to the Hotel California.*

Returned to his cell, Jim sat in pain. A shift commander later came to his cell after hearing what had happened during roll call. Jim was still scared. *I fell on the toilet*, he said in an effort to avoid further conflict.

Jim was taken to Division IX, a maximum-security facility that had a dispensary in the basement where first aid was administered. A medical tech named Alesia Hines cleaned the dried blood off his face. *How did this happen to you?* she asked. *I fell*, he told her with a lisp from the cuts. She took his vital signs—blood pressure, pulse, temperature. They made small talk, the kind that's only unremarkable in prison. *What are you in for?* she asked. His response was hard to understand with his lips battered. He repeated himself. *For the Brown's Chicken murders*, he said faintly.

After Alesia Hines finished cleaning him, they moved to a triage area and Jim sat in a chair. As she filled out paperwork, he spotted a newspaper on the desk. Hines glanced at the front page, then back at Jim. "Oh," she said. "That's you." Jim Degorski cracked a joke. "We made front page news."

She was stunned at the man before her. "How can you kill seven people?" she asked, dumfounded. "Were you on drugs? Were you high? Were you drinking?" His reason was much more simple. "Just for fun."[42]

CHAPTER 21

VINCENT

The computer that randomly selected judges at the Cook County Circuit Court either loved or hated Judge Vincent Michael Gaughan. It depended on your view of things. On the one hand, dealing with some of Chicago's most high-profile cases was a great privilege. On the other, it was also an extraordinary pressure.

After being indicted for twenty-one counts of possession of child pornography in 2002, singer R. Kelly landed himself in Gaughan's courtroom.[1] And as if managing the king of R&B's criminal trial wasn't already enough, the murder trials of the so-called Brown's Chicken massacre were assigned to him just a few weeks later.[2]

In Courtroom 500, Judge Gaughan was in control. After a decade on the bench, he had developed a reputation as a tough arbiter. He interrupted. He yelled. He frequently threatened attorneys with contempt. As a decorated Army veteran with a Bronze Star, he simply had no tolerance for nonsense or wasting time. Knowing this, some attorneys were afraid to appear in his courtroom.

SOMETHING BIG

Gaughan had the brains to tussle with the attorneys who appeared before him on the law and the authority to command their respect. He might scold you publicly if you were unprepared or chastise you for showing disrespect in his domain, but no one ever doubted he was fair.

Judge Gaughan strove for evenhandedness. He gave both prosecutors and defense attorneys a hard time. As a former public defender, he understood on a deeper level than many judges the importance of giving defendants a fair shake. Even if they'd later be found guilty—which was usually the case—he wanted their encounter with the justice system to be one that was impartial.

Murder trials were not uncommon on Judge Gaughan's docket, but the amount of evidence that was put forth in this case set it apart from your average gang casualty or revenge from a crossed lover. Police had spent nearly a decade investigating. There were nearly three hundred thousand documents making up the case file. It included police reports, crime-scene photos, telephone records, tip sheets, and summaries of interviews.[3] Prosecutors stored the evidence in a room that was filled with so many boxes it became nearly impossible to walk through it without carefully contorting yourself.[4] It was both a physical and mental maze of information that foreshadowed the Herculean task ahead for each side's lawyers.

Most of what the attorneys would use in arguing their cases could be found in two boxes that prosecutors handed them on the first hearing.[5] Over the next few months, the defense attorneys representing Juan Luna and Jim Degorski began sorting through the information, categorizing each piece, then interviewing or deposing additional witnesses that might be called at trial.

Both men pled not guilty. Despite their willingness to come forward after their arrest, they intended to fight the accusations at all costs. Juan Luna hired a private attorney to represent him, but unable to continue his $11-an-hour job while behind bars and his wife's $7 hourly wage not enough to cover legal fees, the court approved the use of state funds from a pot of money set aside specifically for litigating capital punishment trials. Jim Degorski would be represented by public defenders who had deep experience working on death penalty trials. Unlike other places, Illinois had developed a very robust system for representing capital defendants to ensure even those who couldn't afford representation had access to some of the best legal help available. Being represented by two different sets of attorneys meant the men would not have to worry about conflicts of interest like if either side decided that their legal strategy would be to deflect blame on the other defendant.

Juan Luna's trial was to go first. But it would be months before teams began to develop their strategy and settle on a timeline. There were motions to be filed and arguments to be made. Specific pieces of evidence, like the confession tapes, had to be debated. People had to be tracked down and interviewed. Thousands upon thousands of documents had to be sorted through to ensure nothing was missed, especially a piece of critical evidence that may have been overlooked or a mistake by police that could be attacked. Defending someone with their life on the line was not a process to be rushed.

The strategy for Juan Luna's defense was straightforward. They would attack his confession tape as involuntary and suggest, like the confessions from previous witnesses, police had fed him lines and exhausted him. They would poke holes in how the DNA evidence was handled, sowing doubt in jurors' minds about the trustworthiness of the profile constructed from the chicken bones and palm print lifted from the napkin found at the scene.

The defense of Juan Luna would be led principally by Clarence Burch, a respected private attorney, and Steve Richards, an experienced lawyer with the state appellate defender's office.[6] An evangelical Christian, Burch was known for making passionate arguments in court that were reminiscent of a powerful plea from a preacher's pulpit. He looked the part, wearing well-tailored suits and rising early in the mornings to work out. He would handle the trial phase where jurors would determine guilt or innocence.

Steve Richards was a brilliant attorney. He knew more about the death penalty and its process in Illinois than practically anyone. He was a passionate advocate against the death penalty, and this case was a critical avenue for that work. Able to point to esoteric areas of the law or obscure cases, Richards could also be scatterbrained, constantly losing track of where he parked his car at the courthouse.[7] He had bigger things on his mind. Other attorneys were brought in to assist, including Mark Lyon, Anthony Burch, Dennis Shere, and Allan Sincox, who would focus specifically on DNA evidence.

By 2002, the death penalty was dormant in Illinois. In the 1990s, capital punishment had remained a contentious issue that even politicians in Illinois ran promising to vigorously defend. It was a deterrent to violent crime, they argued, an assertion which opponents saw as entirely unfounded in the data. The punishment was also costly, and trials to determine a person's fate took years to litigate. Using lethal injection, twelve prisoners had been put to death in Illinois in the '90s. It was a resurgence in a practice which had remained unused for nearly three decades before and sparked great controversy.

The root of that revival came from a series of changes the United States Supreme Court had made that completely changed the landscape nationwide with respect to capital punishment. In 1972, the nation's highest court struck down the death penalty nationwide in the case of *Furman v. Georgia*. The majority of justices held that while capital punishment itself did not violate the Constitution, the way it was being applied through state laws could not stand. Just four years later in *Gregg v. Georgia*, the court upheld various state laws that separated the two decisions for jurors—a guilt phase, and a sentencing phase. The court said that as long as jurors had some guardrails and were not provided with boundless discretion, capital punishment statutes were permitted.

Given the green light, states across the country re-enacted death penalty laws. Illinois reinstated it in July of 1977. And the state had plenty of horrendous killers that most Americans would not object to the state doing away with. Using lethal injection, serial killer John Wayne Gacy was put to rest in 1994, garnering little sympathy from the public after murdering thirty-three young men and boys.

At the turn of the century in 2000, Republican governor George Ryan put a moratorium on the practice in Illinois. Three years later, he commuted the sentence of 167 inmates on death row and pardoned another 4, a move that made national news at the time. When Democrat Rod Blagojevich took office in January of 2003, he kept the moratorium. That meant that under the current administration, jurors could still sentence Jim Degorski and Juan Luna to death, but their fate would still be stalled until a more final political resolution was made on the issue.

For prosecutors, this was a case that had the potential to jolt the system and serve as the impetus for reestablishing the death penalty in Illinois.[8] If the senseless murder of seven people didn't merit the harshest punishment available, then what crime would? The defense, principally Steve Richards, viewed this as an opportunity to get rid of the punishment once and for all.[9] And with eleven people on death row by May of 2007, capital punishment remained a live issue.[10]

With this in mind, the teams defending Juan Luna and Jim Degorski had two goals. First, they'd try to get their client off with a not guilty decision from the jurors. But equally important given the high likelihood of conviction was to save their lives from a death sentence.

In December of 2002, Steve Richards had an idea. If he could prove the death penalty in Illinois was being applied arbitrarily, just as the United States Supreme Court had said was unconstitutional, then he could take the issue off the table entirely. Juan Luna's life would be spared, and the law of the land would be forever changed.

Richards proposed to the team defending Juan Luna that they subpoena documents from every state's attorney in Illinois. That meant all 102 prosecutors in every county across the Prairie State, from the places that border Wisconsin to the tip that reaches farther south than Richmond, Virginia. He sought information about every first-degree murder charge brought since 1998, a massive amount of information.[11] In essence, it would result in a court-ordered study of capital punishment in Illinois.

Clarence Burch, his fellow lead attorney representing Luna, thought it was a crazy idea. So too did many of the other people working the case. But they pressed forward anyway, sending subpoenas to all 102 prosecutors, who eventually sent one person to argue on their behalf. It was always a long shot, and Judge Gaughan quashed the motion when it was brought before him. Still, he thought it was a brilliant tactical move.[12]

Trial preparations continued in this manner for many months. New motions were filed by both sides. And eventually, years went by while Juan Luna and Jim Degorski awaited trial. Perhaps one of the most crucial pre-trial arguments centered on whether or not the jury would be allowed to hear the confession tape from Juan Luna. If deemed admissible, it would be a central part of the prosecution's case. The two sides argued over this in June of 2005 in a hearing before Judge Gaughan, with Juan Luna testifying on the stand about his experience. He argued he was coerced and exhausted. The lines had been fed to him. He just wanted to get out of there. "I agreed to this so I could go home to be with my son," Juan told the judge.[13]

Police and prosecutors who had interviewed Juan Luna and taken his video statement after the arrest categorically denied this characterization. They pointed to the tape itself and noted that interrogators had offered him sausage pizza, gave him water to drink, and even a pop to sip on. He chewed on bubble gum the police gave him. Sure, he'd been held a long time by an average person's standards, but this was not a forced confession. Gaughan ruled that the tape was admissible, and jurors would be able to hear it.[14]

In the summer of 2006, the case was moving along at its expected pace when one day, Judge Gaughan was returning from an American Legion event. A proud veteran, he remained active with the organization as time permitted. When he got home, he decided to fix a skylight that needed repair on his home in the Lincoln Park neighborhood of Chicago.[15] He got out a seventeen-foot ladder and put it into place. When he stepped onto it to complete his task, the bottom proceeded to give out. The sixty-five-year-old judge tumbled down, hitting the stairs below him. He broke his left leg, dislocated his right shoulder, and fractured five vertebrae.[16]

There's no good way to fall from a ladder, he'd tell people later. He was right, and it landed him in intensive care to recover. Juan Luna's trial would be delayed again for several months while he convalesced.

For such a high-stakes trial, both the prosecution and defense teams were open to unique tactics to prepare. The Degorski defense team conducted a public poll to see if a fair trial would even be possible in an area where so many residents had followed the story so closely.[17] The Luna defense team conducted a mock trial of their own, hiring a focus group company called Precision Research in suburban Schaumburg to supply them with pretend jurors matching various profiles. They needed to get the most realistic dress rehearsal possible. Clarence Burch and others took it seriously, delivering abbreviated opening statements, questioning fake witnesses, and putting on as realistic as a case as possible. They wanted to understand their weak points. Just like twelve jurors who would soon judge their client, the focus group members deliberated and reached their own decision on whether Juan Luna had committed the murders. Their verdict? Not guilty.

CHAPTER 22

JUAN

The Luna family had no other choice than to adjust to this new life. The arrest had come as a shock, and their new normal meant constant drives to visit Juan at Cook County prison on the west side of Chicago. A member of the family was designated to stay home at all times, waiting by the phone in case Juan called. *You have a collect call from an inmate at Cook County Jail. Do you wish to accept?* the recording went, words that were jarring at first then became rote and unremarkable. Instead of buying gifts for his son on missed birthdays, Juan drew pictures.[1] His son and wife came to visit a few times each month and he spoke on the phone with his son. *Do good in school*, he'd tell him, attempting to parent from afar.[2]

Their son, husband, or father may have been the one awaiting trial, but Juan's imprisonment was a heavy burden on the larger Luna family. Left with one parent to raise him, Juan's parents stepped in to help Imelda with their son Brian. When her husband was arrested for the murders of seven people, Imelda had been completely surprised. With all the media attention centered on the case, their last name was now *infamous*. Like Leopold and Loeb, everyone knew about the duo of Luna and

Degorski. At the playground one day with his grandfather, Juan's son Brian played like any other child, running across the woodchips and slipping down the slide in pure joy. In the distance, his proud grandfather spotted a middle-aged woman pointing directly at his grandson. He smiled, thinking she was admiring how handsome he was. *That's Juan Luna's son*, she mouthed to another friend standing beside her.[3] There was no avoiding the long shadow cast by the murders.

For Juan, life in a small cell in the massive, crowded prison complex was dull. Other than reading a book or taking a nap, there was not much to be done. Just ponder the trial that had taken years to come to fruition. By 2007, the wait was finally over, and *The People of the State of Illinois v. Juan Luna* was set to begin. From jail, Juan penned his parents a letter on a piece of yellow notebook paper.[4]

> *Dear mom and dad,*
>
> *I hope that you have received this Letter in the best of health. Speaking of health I am doing fine. I love you, I miss you and the rest of the family. Tell Imelda and Brian that I love them. Give them hugs and kisses from me. I am finally going to trial. Pray pray pray I will be glad when this case is over so that I can give you all the hugs and kisses when I come home. And stay strong.*
>
> *Love Juan*

Aside from his cell, Juan Luna had only seen Courtroom 500 and worn his tan prison uniform emblazoned with the letters "DOC"—department of corrections—plain white socks, and flip-flops.[5] As he was walked over to the courtroom for the first days of his trial, he would swap his usual uniform for a suit, tie, and dress shoes, escorted by two plain-clothed sheriff's deputies either back at the prison or in a lockup room in the courthouse. *You look good*, a paralegal on his defense team would assure him each time he entered, fixing up his tie to make sure he was presentable for the jurors

Security at 26th and Cal was already tight, but there were extra precautions for the first murder trial of the alleged Brown's Chicken killer. As media and families of both Juan Luna and the victims entered the courthouse each morning, they shuffled through metal detectors and guards with wands, going through an additional round of security outside Courtroom 500. No phones were allowed except for the attorneys—nor were purses, briefcases, or backpacks.

The room itself was stately. The crowd filled the creaky wooden benches without cushions, with the families of the seven victims filling an entire side and then some. The floors were gray linoleum with green squares decorating the high-ceilinged room with marble columns on the walls.[6] As if anyone needed a reminder, the setting itself reinforced the seriousness of the trial ahead.

Jury selection began in late March of 2007. Clarence Burch introduced his client to the crowd of potential selections, and Luna said hello. "Good morning, ladies and gentlemen," he said facing the pool of his peers that would judge him in the gravest sense of the word. He smiled. Then, when Judge Gaughan read the charges against him, he became solemn.[7] More than 150 people were questioned for eight days, with men and women filling the aisles and some sitting on the floor.[8] "God love ya," Judge Gaughan told them over and over, underscoring his appreciation for their service.[9] Juries aren't asked, after all, it's their duty.

The process started with a questionnaire. There were the standard inquiries about past criminal history and views on judicial fairness, but also outside-the-box questions. "Is there a type of high-schooler or teenager you were seen as, such as jock, nerd, burnout or princess, what were you?"[10] It was a search for clues. And because prosecutors announced they'd seek the death penalty, each juror underwent the process of so-called "death qualification" whereby their views on the penalty itself were probed, excluding anyone who opposed capital punishment in all cases regardless of the facts before them. Over the first few days, the attorneys argued over nearly everything and everyone, but time wore them down.[11]

Addressed only by their numbers so as to remain anonymous, nine men and three women were chosen for the case, varying in profession a transit worker and flight attendant to a probation officer and stay-at-home mom. "During the trial, you must not discuss this case among yourselves or have anyone else discuss it in your presence. You must avoid reading newspapers, headlines, and other articles pertaining to this trial or any other source whether it's TV, radio or internet," Judge Gaughan told them on the first day of trial on April 13, 2007.[12] "God love ya."

There would be three phases to the trial. The first involved a decision on guilt or innocence where the jury would decide whether, beyond a reasonable doubt, Juan Luna was culpable for the massacre at Brown's Chicken. The second was technical, and jurors would decide based on various aggravating factors whether he was eligible to be sentenced to death. And during the third, jurors would decide whether to impose that sentence.

"At this time, we're going to have opening statements," Judge Gaughan told the courtroom. Cook County state's attorney Dick Devine rose to deliver his opening salvo. The white-haired top prosecutor was straightlaced and a workhorse more than a show horse.[13] He'd criticized his predecessor for being too involved in the investigative side of things. Now, he was the opening face of the case.

"Ladies and gentlemen of the jury, this case will take us back to the night of January 8, 1993, in Palatine, Illinois," he began. This was the first impression for the jury. "At that time in 1993, there was a Burger King restaurant located in Palatine at Northwest Highway and Smith Road." People looked at one another confused. Devine continued as he walked through an illustration of the Brown's restaurant. "This is the Burger King from an overview. We are looking north. This is the east side." Judge Gaughan interrupted. "Could I have the attorneys over here for a second?"

Summoned for an off-the-record discussion, he realized his mistake. "Excuse me," he told the jury, walking back to the well. "Brown's Chicken. This Brown's Chicken is located at Northwest Highway and Smith Road in Palatine, Illinois."

Framing his case, Dick Devine used dreadful images from the crime scene and the confession tape of Juan Luna. The jurors would not hear from the defendant on the stand, but his words would nevertheless be in the courtroom through the tapes.

The defense's opening argument fell to Clarence Burch, the perfect opportunity for his flair to shine. "You've heard the eloquent and moving dissertation of Mr. Devine," he told the jury. "But he wasn't there. I was not there. The evidence will come from one place and that is the witness stand right there," he told them, pointing to the stand. "You and you alone are the sole judge of the credibility of the witnesses."[14] This was sloppy police work and there was a history of forced confessions. Burch was animated, raising his voice like a pastor in the pulpit and unafraid to gesture his hands.

While Devine opened, the bulk of the case would fall to attorneys Tom Biesty and Linas Kelecius for the day-to-day. Scott Cassidy, head of special prosecutions, was senior in title but deferential to the other lawyers as experts. Michael Ferrara was the junior attorney, helping keep the technology in order and the case files straight.[15]

A victim's family member testified to the last time they saw each of their family members, and instead of having them all speak one after the other, the prosecution spread them out over each day to underscore the loss.

> <u>Scott Cassidy</u>: I would call your attention, Mr. Mennes, to the last time you saw your brother Thomas alive. Do you recall that?
> <u>Robert Mennes</u>: It was January 7th, 1993. He was at my apartment having dinner, which I usually cook for him once in a while. That was the last time I saw him.
> <u>Scott Cassidy</u>: And where did you see him the next time?
> <u>Robert Mennes</u>: At the county morgue.[16]

***

When he first returned to his office after the first few days of the trial, assistant state's attorney Tom Biesty was greeted with cardboard crowns from Burger King on his desk. The team brushed off the mistake because it was indeed minor. They'd prepared for this case for years, and the evidence was largely on their side.

DNA experts explained how a profile of Juan Luna was matched from the chicken bones. And while the story of it all was riveting, the scientific explanations made some of the jurors nod off. "Excuse me," Judge Gaughan interrupted one of the defense attorneys questioning a witness. He looked straight at one of the jurors. "Sit straight up!" he chastised. "There you go. You've got your eyes closed. Don't do that."[17]

For the defense, the handling of the DNA evidence was particularly important. They scrutinized contradictory police reports. The coffee stirrer found in the trash had been thrown out and certain chicken bones destroyed. Certain DNA evidence had been lost and then found on a computer.[18] The bones had been taken to the Field Museum in Chicago and handled on a table with prehistoric birds, school groups, and no gloves. The DNA swabs had also been tossed.[19]

Jane Homeyer walked through the process of pulling prints and analyzing the DNA as part of the Northern Illinois Police Crime Lab. She explained how amino acids leave a person's sweat from fingers or palms and react with chemicals like ninhydrin. Since leaving the lab, she had worked at the FBI in forensic science then in a high-level position with the director of national intelligence. On cross-examination for the defense, Allan Sincox homed in on Homeyer's lack of experience at the time and the process of developing prints from a napkin left at the scene. Importantly, when police interviewed Juan Luna weeks after the murder, they failed to take a left palm print.

> Sincox: So you're saying that someone took Juan Luna's prints and took his right palm

print but not his left palm print, is that what you're saying?

Homeyer: I'm saying that his left palm print was not submitted and was not included on the card. I don't know if it was taken or not, but it was not submitted with what I had my examination of.

Sincox: Did you make a note on anything saying Juan Luna's left palm print is missing, we better go find him and get his left palm print?

Homeyer: Yes.

Sincox: When did you do that?

Homeyer: So that would have been part of my laboratory report on that examination and in my notes as well.

Sincox: Did anybody do that as far as you know?

Homeyer: At some point they probably did, but I did not do a subsequent comparison. I had left the lab by that point.

Sincox: Did you call up the person who took Juan Luna's prints and ask him how come he didn't take the other one?

Homeyer: I don't recall the person's name being recorded on the card who took the prints, but I'm sure I would have reported it out. I know I reported it out, but I'm pretty sure I wouldn't make a personal call to someone.

The error was not one of Homeyer's doing. Nor was it particularly important for the defense's case given police had since obtained a match following Juan Luna's arrest. But for those in the courtroom, especially the family, it highlighted a crushing mistake early on in the police's investigation. Had someone obtained Luna's left palm print in February of 1993, it could have been matched to the napkin just weeks after the murders.

And yet, while it was jarring and easy to criticize police, there was no guarantee a guilty verdict would have come with that evidence. At that time, DNA could not have been extracted from the chicken bones. And even if Anne Lockett had corroborated the story, her credibility would have been easy to attack.

***

As one of the central witnesses for the prosecution, Eileen Bakalla had been hounded for keeping the murders a secret. The media called, wrote letters, and knocked on her door. So when Bakalla came to the courtroom to testify, she was driven in a car with tinted windows and whisked in through a side door to avoid the crowds.[20]

With a glittery white cross around her neck and a floral-print dress, Bakalla corroborated Anne Lockett's story to the jury. She made clear her feelings on Juan Luna. "I just never liked him," she told the courtroom. "He gave me the heebie-jeebies."[21] Yet Bakalla had remained friends with Jim Degorski, and even being accused of the murder of seven people was not going to change that.[22]

On cross-examination, Clarence Burch focused on Bakalla's drug use and her character. The women coming forward were, in his line of the case, untrustworthy drug addicts. She had "reefer" madness, a word he repeated fifteen times. "And when you get high, you begin to see and hear things that are not there?" he asked. "No," Bakalla asserted. Her mind had been clear. "Well, do you become paranoid when you smoke reefer?" he prodded again. "No, it relaxes me. Made me—it relaxes me."

Burch also zeroed in on her failure to come forward. Why now? Why had she waited so long to come forward? Could the jurors trust her after all this? He took her back to the early morning of Saturday, January 9, 1993, driving with Jim Degorski past the restaurant at the corner of Smith and Northwest Highway.

> <u>Burch</u>: And what happened? Tell us. What did you see when you drove past?
>
> <u>Bakalla</u>: I saw ambulances and police cars.
>
> <u>Burch</u>: All right. And I just—this was a horrifying crime, wasn't it?
>
> <u>Bakalla</u>: Yes.
>
> <u>Burch</u>: And you said they had just told you all about the people that had gotten killed, right?
>
> <u>Bakalla</u>: Yes.
>
> <u>Burch</u>: And you did not get out of the car at that point and walk up to a police officer and say, "I have something to say about this!" Did you ever report it to a police officer that night?
>
> <u>Bakalla</u>: No.
>
> <u>Burch</u>: You weren't afraid of Jim Degorski, were you?
>
> <u>Bakalla</u>: Not per se, no.
>
> <u>Burch</u>: And Juan Luna had certainly not threatened you while he was at your house, had he?
>
> <u>Bakalla</u>: Not threatened.

> <u>Burch</u>: He never said one word to you about not telling anybody, did he?
> <u>Bakalla</u>: He said you need to keep your mouth shut about this.

Hearing from someone who'd kept quiet for nearly a decade was difficult for the families. She knew their pain and still did nothing. But more disturbing for the families were the gruesome images of their loved ones displayed at various points in the trial. Juan Luna sat emotionless for most of the trial when the lights dimmed and video played of the crime scene filled with blood or images of the bodies being carried out of the restaurant. Most of the family members, despite words of caution from attorneys and the judge, stayed. Tears flowing, they put their heads down or averred their gaze when it was too much. They held each other's hands for comfort. Strangers bonded closely by their trauma.

"Mom, maybe today's not a good day," Diane Clayton's daughter told her. "They're going to be showing pictures. You don't want to be there," she begged, knowing images of their loved one, Marcus Nellsen, would be shown. But Marcus Nellsen's mother would hear none of it. She wanted to be there for her son, even if it was painful. She'd moved her entire life from Tennessee to Illinois because of the trials.[23] She was going to be there.

Like so many of the families, her presence there was a search for information. For years, the families had heard censored dribs and drabs through a police intermediary or relied on stories in newspapers that often had inaccurate or incomplete information. Now, they could finally hear it for themselves. Their questions about what happened would be answered in a totally unvarnished setting. And while it would be painful, most felt they had no choice but to attend.

When the Cook County medical examiner described in detail how each person died—where they were shot, how they were stabbed, bones that were broken—the emotion in the room was audible. The same could be said of the video of the seven victims, their bodies blackened from the cold of the freezer or cooler where they were killed, taken out on stretchers. Jurors covered their mouths in horror. Family members left the proceedings forever scarred by those images. From beyond the thick wooden doors of the courtroom, their grief could be heard from the hallway.

The trial was not without moments of levity. Perhaps one of the prosecution's strongest witnesses was Dr. Henry Lee, who'd become famous for his testimony at the O. J. Simpson trial and other high-profile cases. Dr. Lee had assisted the Palatine police over the years and knew Chief Jerry Bratcher who he met in Taiwan on a trip abroad for chiefs of police years ago.[24] An expert on DNA evidence, he walked jurors through the process of extracting a profile from the chicken. Raised in Taiwan, he had a thick accent but nevertheless spoke clearly. In a setting filled with unsavory character, Dr. Lee was likeable and gregarious. He ran circles around the defense attorney attempting to shred his credibility. And he provided his own non-expert opinion on other matters. "If a chicken place gave me a piece that small, I'd probably want my money back." The room erupted in laughter.[25]

***

Anne Lockett was pregnant and wore a new maternity outfit her friend Melissa Benz had bought her for the trial. Now thirty-one years old and engaged, she wore a light blue blouse, a skirt, and her hair was neatly pulled away from her face.[26] Since coming forward in 2002, drugs and alcohol had still caused chaos in her life, even leading to an arrest and the loss of jobs. It took those run-ins for Anne Lockett to get serious. She knew if she continued living her life consumed by these vices that she probably would not survive. But by 2004, she was undergoing a detox program. She relapsed, a bump in the struggle. By 2007 at the time of the trial, Anne Lockett was one year sober. Her life was turning a corner.

Brought in surreptitiously like her former friend Eileen, Anne Lockett had similarly been hounded by the press. There were news trucks camped out on her lawn on countless nights.[27] All of Chicagoland wanted the scoop. Prosecutors understood the pressure she was under, and they tried to relieve it. Tom Biesty, one of the prosecutors and a former New York City police officer, approached one of the most aggressive TV journalists in the courtroom hallway one day. "Can I have a word with you?" he asked in his unmistakable New York accent.[28] "Can you lay off Anne Lockett?" he asked. The next day, the reporters were gone.[29]

The prosecution addressed Anne Lockett's weak spots directly—her drug use, her rough childhood, and the fact that she waited more than nine years to come forward. "The guilt I had—that I knew who had done these things—outweighed my fear," she testified. "I felt I owed it to the families."[30] On cross-examination, Clarence Burch again focused on the witness's drug use. He wanted to suggest that perhaps she wasn't in a clear state of mind when she'd received the phone call in the hospital or heard Jim Degorski and Juan Luna recount what they described in his bedroom that day.

"Did you see scary monsters when you were taking LSD?" he pried, alluding to another occasion when she'd used the hallucinogen. "In that flashback, yes," she said. "So in other words, you were hallucinating. You saw things that really weren't there during that time? Is that correct." Anne answered honestly. Yes, she had abused drugs and alcohol in the past, but she was clearheaded about what she heard. Not to mention, both men had admitted as much to police. Her story was consistent, and no personal attack on her past could take that away from her.

On Thursday, April 26, 2007, the defense began its case with Juan Luna's brother testifying about the arrest. DNA experts poked holes in how materials had been handled. A defense expert said that the sample found could match one million other people in the United States while the prosecution's expert said it was a near-perfect match found in only 1 in 2.8 trillion people.[31] Burch and the team pointed to the previous confessions from John Simonek, Casey Sander, and Todd Wakefield to suggest this was a pattern from the police that had repeated itself again with Juan Luna. Steve Bratcher, the son of Chief Jerry Bratcher and a Palatine police officer, was left to defend their actions.

> <u>Burch</u>: So are you suggesting or telling the ladies and gentleman of the jury that a perfectly innocent person in the custody of the Palatine police department who has not been threatened, harassed, intimidated,

or coerced can confess to a crime that he absolutely did not commit?

Cassidy: Objection, judge.

Judge Gaughan: Overruled. I told him I would allow him wide latitude.

Burch: Could you answer the question?

Steve Bratcher: Yes.

Burch: Now, in your history or work as a police officer, how many times has this happened while someone was in custody in Palatine?

Steve Bratcher: That someone has given a false confession?

Burch: Yeah, a false confession.

Steve Bratcher: If I may, I did not realize that he was giving a false confession at the time.

After the police had been peppered with questions from the defense and the prosecution had reinforced its confidence in the DNA evidence, the time came for closing statements. As he entered the courtroom, Juan Luna wore a black suit with a printed tie. He turned around from the defense table and winked at the roughly dozen family members behind him.[32]

"Closing arguments, State," Judge Gaughan instructed. Linas Kelecius, one of the assistant state's attorneys, would lead the close. Kelecius was the details guy.[33] Low-key but nevertheless passionate about his work, he'd been on this case for more than five years and knew every argument that could be raised.[34]

Kelecius distinguished the previous false confessions from the one of Juan Luna that the jury had seen on tape. "The false confession, unlike a true confession, does not and cannot ever lead to additional independent evidence." That additional independent evidence was two things—Anne Lockett's story and the DNA. "Luna's profile matched on all nine loci to a T," he said, reiterating the scientific jargon witnesses had explained to jurors. "Eileen Bakalla completely corroborates Anne Lockett, completely corroborates the confession," he argued. "The evidence in this case of guilt is overwhelming. The evidence of this man's murderous intent to kill is overwhelming. And we ask that you find the defendant guilty of all charges."[35]

After a break, Allan Sincox, the defense's lead attorney on all matters involving DNA, began the team's close. As he started, his cell phone rang. He quickly silenced the call. Then it rang again. "Three times and you're a loser, Allan," Judge Gaughan joked in this high-stakes moment. "Give it to somebody."

After Sincox outlined the defense's concerns about the scientific evidence, Clarence Burch stood for his close. He attacked the credibility of the prosecution's star witness, Anne Lockett. It was the defense's last chance to finish strong.

> "But her mind is so impaired, she said, not only was I on PCP, cocaine, marijuana, speed, I was even doing LSD. When you went into the hospital in '92 and '93, was that your drug of choice? 'Yes, it was. Whenever I could get it, I would get it.' And I said, would it send you on trips? 'Yes, I went on trips, maybe I'd see some Christmas lights and they'd take on some different dimensions and I even saw scary monsters.' That's their star witness."

Burch attacked the confession tape from Luna. It was stilted. Police had fed him the answers. He was merely regurgitating information and used awkward directional phrases like "east side of the building" and "north side." "Would a normal person talk that way? You think Juan talked that way or was he being fed information?"[36] he suggested. "Zero plus zero plus zero equals zero. All the evidence in this case is a zero. It has no cumulative effect. It does not line up."

In their final opportunity to rebut the defense's assertions, the prosecution resuscitated its witnesses. "She may be cold. Her moral compass might not be like yours—I'm sure it's not—her moral values might not be like yours," the prosecutor said of Eileen Bakalla. "But there's no motive, bias, or interest for her to be lying," he asserted. "As a matter of fact, she liked Jim Degorski." Luna and Degorski were just "two losers who found each other, and they wanted to do something big." As the case came to a close, it made no difference what the prosecution or defense thought about Juan Luna. The only assessment that mattered now was that of his twelve peers.

CHAPTER 23

JUROR 56

News of the sequester came as a shock to some jurors. They were told they'd be taken to a hotel and have no contact with family or the outside world. After just two and a half hours of deliberations following closing statements in the afternoon, the group was crammed onto a bus and shuttled to the Best Western overlooking the highway in suburban Hinsdale, Illinois[1] Each double-bed room was stripped of telephones, TVs, and radios. Jurors were not permitted to use cell phones or call home. They entered through a side door and were handed room keys from a sheriff's deputy. Elevators were held for them to avoid contact with other hotel guests. In the halls, the sheriff's deputies kept watch and took orders for food. To keep each other company at the hotel, they sat up and chatted in the lobby.

Over the course of the six-week-long trial, the jurors had grown close. People brought in food to the jury room including in one instance a Crock-Pot filled with savory rib tips that filled the courtroom with barbeque smells.[2] They brought in candy and snacks to munch on during breaks. Some jurors organized a daily raffle to spice things up.

With a view of the Chicago skyline visible from the jury room, the twelve individuals selected to determine Juan Luna's fate started the discussions. An initial poll of the room with raised hands showed about half of the group unwilling to commit to a guilty sentence just yet. They dove into the details of what they'd heard – the gruesome videos, the testimony of Anne Lockett, and the potency of the DNA evidence. *I just don't buy the confession tape*, one of them expressed to the crowd. *It seemed forced, like he was being fed the lines.* Another juror snapped. *Are you kidding me?* The two became heated, arguing back and forth in front of their peers.[3] It was one of many lively disagreements among the twelve chosen ones.

For most in the room, the testimony from Anne Lockett and Eileen Bakalla, coupled with the DNA evidence, was more than enough to overcome any other misgivings. A final vote was taken, and a decision was reached after six hours.

The process resumed in Courtroom 500 with the families and media hustling back to their benches. Twelve sheriff's deputies stood ready to arrest anyone who couldn't control themselves. "I know this has been a long trial," Judge Gaughan told the room. "I know this has been an emotional trial." It certainly had. "I don't want any outbursts in front of the jury. I don't care who you are, you'll go to jail."[4] After a five-minute break, Juan Luna was again brought back into the room. "Bring Mr. Luna out," he said. He sat between his two head attorneys, Steve Richards and Clarence Burch. The jury was then escorted to the jury box.

Fourteen years and four months had passed since seven bodies had been found in the Brown's Chicken in Palatine. The families sat holding hands as they awaited a final answer, and the clerk announced the decision. "We, the jury, find the

SOMETHING BIG

defendant, Juan Luna, guilty of the first-degree murder of Lynn Ehlenfeldt." Juan Luna took his glasses off, cleared his throat, then wiped tears from his face. From behind, his mother sobbed intensely, nearly fainting.[5] Luna's wife put her head down as tears crawled from her face.[6]

That heavy sentence rang out in the courtroom six more times. Guilty—for the murder of Michael Castro, the high school junior with a dream of serving in the Marines. Guilty—for the murder of Richard Ehlenfeldt, one of two loving parents who devoted their lives to helping others. Guilty—for the murder of Thomas Mennes, the quirky guy with a kind heart who wouldn't hurt a fly. Guilty—for the murder of Lupe Maldonado, the father of three who'd only been back in America a matter of days. Guilty—for the murder of Marcus Nellsen, the veteran who served his country honorably. Guilty—for the murder of Rico Solis, the seventeen-year-old who came to the United States in search of opportunity.

***

Clasping votive candles printed with the words "Campaign to End the Death Penalty," a group of somber faces stood behind a podium outside the Cook County courthouse at 26th and Cal.[7] "We're praying for them," said Brenda Sanchez, the sister of Juan Luna, when asked about the families at the event—part rally, part vigil. And indeed, many of the victims' families were returning the favor. "Revenge and justice are two different things," said Mary Jane Crow, Michael Castro's sister, from the podium. At her side were other members of the Castro family, all gathered alongside Luna's kin, the family of the man who killed their son, to oppose a sentence of death. "He did not have mercy on our family, but we will have mercy on his."[8] Manny Castro had changed his position on the matter too.

Standing a few feet away from the press conference, the Ehlenfeldt daughters also reiterated their opposition to reporters. "I am against the death penalty in all situations," Joy Ehlenfeldt noted.[9] It was a belief rooted in what their parents had taught them. No matter how much pain they felt or if they experienced a natural human desire for revenge, the death penalty was not the solution.

The second phase of the trial would determine Juan Luna's eligibility for the death sentence. It was a legal determination based on aggravating factors such as the number of people killed and premeditation.[10] Based on the heinous nature of the killings, the jury quickly determined he was eligible. Now, they were tasked with answering whether or not to sentence him to death.

The rules for what's admissible during the sentencing phase are much looser than the initial trial. The process is filled with emotion as families and friends of both the victims and the person to be sentenced read statements for the jury. As an expert on the death penalty and its processes, Steve Richards led this part of the trial for the defense. Their mission was simply to save their client's life.

Juan Luna's mother testified about her ailing health and how her son offered her a kidney, breaking down in tears on the stand. His brother begged that he not be sentenced to death so he could still see him, even if behind bars. "I just want my brother alive so I can go see him," he told jurors.[11] Old friends testified about threats he'd made in the past, allegations about him torturing animals, and the threatening voicemails he'd left years ago on Kristin Lennstrom's answering machine were played.

The defense team considered putting Luna's ten-year-old son on the stand to testify about their dad, but he rejected the idea. *I can't do that to him.*[12] Instead, a six-minute video was filmed with the child dressed in jeans and a button-down. He reminisced about attending a carnival with his father and winning a goldfish. He talked about going fishing and riding bumper cars. "I want to hug him so badly," the child said to the camera.[13] Luna wept as his son spoke.[14]

Mothers and sons recounted memories of their loved ones. Dads and daughters bemoaned the life events they'd missed as a result. Luna was stoic during most of the statements from family members until Joy Ehlenfeldt, the youngest Ehlenfeldt daughter, spoke. She looked directly at him. "Juan Luna, this is the story of my father and what you took from me."

She talked about her father's love of practical jokes, his passion for politics, and how her nieces and nephews refer to "Grandpa and Grandma Angel."[15] Luna again broke down. "Not only are you responsible for the suffering and grief of six families, you are also responsible for your own family's suffering," she told him. "Your family will join ours in a circle of grief. You owe them an apology. You owe us *all* an apology."[16] The room was silent, filled with fifteen years of pent-up anticipation

When the testimony and victim-impact statements were finished, the jury returned to their room to deliberate. They sat in silence around the twelve-foot-long conference table for a full fifteen minutes soaking in what they'd heard and readying themselves for the heavy decision ahead. "Is everybody ready?" the foreperson finally asked the group.[17]

The twelve men and women raised their hands for a first poll of the room. Looking around, all but one was in the air. Juror 56 was a twenty-eight-year-old stay-at-home mother, Latina, and a devout Catholic. She had worked at a fried chicken restaurant years ago, providing her with a unique vantage point on the crime. The stress of the trial had been enormous. She had stomach cramps throughout and was emotional when the gruesome pictures were presented by attorneys. The grief she saw from the families was moving.

Juror 56's peers asked for an explanation. *I just can't*, she explained somberly. She cited her faith but reiterated that it did not cloud her assessment on the matter. The others were disappointed, and they interrupted her to argue. Then, she shut down. She became silent, staring directly at the foreperson as if to save her from her misery.[18] "Well," he told the room. "That's it." The sense of disappointment among other jurors was palpable. If this was not a cause to impose this punishment, then what kind of crime would suffice? Still, there were no further arguments. The decision was final.

Courtroom 500 filled again, and Judge Gaughan readied the room for the news. At the table with his defense attorneys, Juan Luna made the sign of the cross then took a deep breath.[19] The news was delivered about the jury's failure to reach a unanimous verdict on death. Juan Luna would instead be sentenced to life in prison without the possibility of parole.

Each juror was then asked to confirm that this was their final decision. "Was this then and is this now your verdict?" they were polled.[20] Each agreed, and Juror 56 wept as she confirmed her decision.

CHAPTER 24

JIM

As the name suggested, the prosecutors working *People v. James Degorski* had one client: the state of Illinois. Prosecutors represent "the people," not victims' families. And yet, working a murder case requires them to build a rapport with those affected by the crime. They are the case's most invested stakeholders, and nearly every day, a small crowd of family members would be in the rows behind the prosecutors making the case they'd anticipated for years. They did it in 2007 for Juan Luna's trial, and they would make a second appearance in 2009 for that of his co-conspirator, Jim Degorski.

The families of the seven victims shared a common bond. It was one which so few people could ever understand. When they entered the courthouse at 26th and Cal, the six families entered through the busy security line like everyone else, hobbling through metal detectors and emptying their pockets each morning. They ate together in conference rooms set aside as gathering spots and occasionally alongside strangers in the courthouse cafeteria. They rode the same elevators as the press and attorneys, used the same restrooms, and were surrounded by cameras and microphones at nearly every moment of the most intimate, emotional experiences of their lives.[1]

There was sadness, but it did not prevent moments of joy. They smiled and laughed with one another. They reminisced about the people they'd lost but also got to know one another as individuals, not just fellow mourners. People took shifts bringing in baked goods to share. A recipe book was written for the attorneys with the title of different dishes named after each prosecutor. To lighten the mood one day, the Ehlenfeldt daughters even put together a song and dance to the tune of the "Super Bowl Shuffle," the rap performed by the 1985 Chicago Bears. *We're not talking 'bout Burger King / Whoops! Not a good thing*, they sang to laughs. They belted out a verse for each of the lawyers working the case, then all joined in for the chorus.

> We are the Brown's prosecution crew
> Shufflin' to court, doin' it for you
> We follow the law, we know we're good
> Presenting and objecting like you knew we would
> You know we're here to get a conviction
> Our star witness had a drug addiction
> We're not here to start no trouble
> We're just here to do the prosecution huddle

In the conference rooms, the families gathered each morning for a briefing from one of the prosecutors. *How's everyone feeling today?* attorneys would ask, answering any questions they had about what was to come. The prosecutors would warn the families when graphic videos or pictures would be shown and when they might want to skip the proceedings. Strategic decisions, such as whether or not to call a witness or present a piece of evidence, were explained so they did not worry or second-guess that a mistake was being made. They answered questions and heard the concerns. It was the prosecution's case, but it was their loved ones' lives.

The case against Jim Degorski was similar to that against Juan Luna. The evidence presented would largely be a repeat. Most of the same witnesses would testify. And the tone of the trial would be equally emotional.

There were also big differences. No DNA linked Jim Degorski to the scene of the crime. He had a confession tape, but it was far shorter and not all that helpful. And the prosecution had added new members of the team. Tom Biesty and Linas Kelecius would again lead the case. Lou Longhitano would manage communications with the families in addition to regular trial work. Alan Spellberg was added to ensure appeals issues were taken care of. And Brigid Brown and Maureen McCurry were additional legal help to the team assisting with trial prep and questioning some witnesses.

Jim Degorski was represented by Mark Levitt, a high-energy public defender with short black hair and a passion for long-distance running. He led a team of seven attorneys including Michael Mayfield, Susan Smith, Preston Jones, Brendan Max, Kathleen Moriarty, and Jeff Howard. They were all prepared to fight vigorously for Jim Degorski's innocence and, if need be, his life.

By the time the case began, a tremendous amount of work had been done before the trial. Roughly 130 motions had been filed and argued. There'd been about 180 hearings on the case in court.[2] Now, in 2009, the meat of the trial would begin two years after the Luna verdict.

More than one hundred people were questioned for jury selection, a process that took five days. Six men and six women landed the awesome responsibility of determining Jim Degorski's fate.[3] The mix included a city worker, a stay-at-home father, a Vietnam veteran, and a college student.

Judge Gaughan called in the jurors to the two-level jury box filled with black leather chairs towering above the rest of the room. Jim Degorski was then escorted to the defense table sporting a green shirt and tie, swapping his prison uniform for civilian dress.[4] Jim was serious as opening statements began, hiding any emotion from the outside world.

"The evidence is going to show this was never about the money to Degorski," Lou Longhitano told jurors in the prosecution's opening. "It was all about the thrill. They wanted to do something big. And they made a big splash in the blood of seven innocent victims." They focused on the testimony of Anne Lockett and Eileen Bakalla and the gun which they'd argue was purchased by Degorski from a friend.

The defense focused on the lack of DNA evidence tying Jim Degorski to the scene. Mark Levitt, his lead defense attorney, made clear distinctions between the two cases against Luna and Degorski. "One thing is missing. There is not one single piece of evidence that ties Jim Degorski to this terrible crime," he noted. "Juan Luna is not on trial before you today. Jim Degorski is on trial."

In much the same manner as the 2007 trial against Juan Luna, a family member of each victim was selected to testify to the last time they saw their loved one. Police officers who'd worked the task force were questioned about their work on the scene and the careful nature with which they went about their job. DNA experts laid out the proof they'd uncovered from the chicken bones and palm print from Juan Luna which, while it did not extend to Degorski, linked them together by their confessions. And as with the previous trial, much focus was placed on the false confessions of Casey Sander, John Simonek, and Todd Wakefield.

The prosecution understood that if the jury believed the confessions from Juan Luna and Jim Degorski were all part of a pattern, then they were likely to let him walk free. They needed to distinguish the Sander-Simonek-Wakefield story from Luna and Degorski. Why were these previous confessions false but the ones obtained by police in 2002 to be trusted? For prosecutors, the common link was Jim Bell, the former civilian head of the task force who'd pushed the lead.

"Was this your first interview that you did in the Brown's Chicken case?" Linas Kelecius asked a Palatine police officer. "Yes." The suggestion was that Jim Bell wanted the lead to work so badly that he brought in officers who wouldn't question his direction. "Anything happen between the segments?" Kelecius said, alluding to the breaks during Simonek's interrogation. "Yes. When we'd exit the room, Jim Bell would approach us and he would direct us to ask him about this, ask him that, that sort of thing," the officer explained. "And you were not really up on the facts of the case?" he continued. "No, sir."

> Officer Kirkpatrick: I advised Jim Bell that that was not our protocol, that a state's attorney should be present, and that we should contact a state's attorney.
> Kelecius: What did he say?
> Officer Kirkpatrick: He said that no, we were going to take this statement ourselves.
> Kelecius: Then how did it come to be that this video was taken? How did that come about?

> Officer Kirkpatrick: Same circumstances. Jim Bell directed us to take a video statement. I told him that it was something that we did not do, had never done, and was directed to do so anyways.
>
> Kelecius: To this day, in your entire career as a police officer for how many years?
>
> Officer Kirkpatrick: Twenty years.
>
> Kelecius: Have you ever had that happen again?
>
> Officer Kirkpatrick: No, sir.[5]

On cross-examination, the defense insisted the confession was not forced, and that police were changing their tune. If the officers brought in by Jim Bell thought their actions were so wrong at the time, why did they not object right away? In response, the prosecution zeroed in on the rift between Jim Bell and others on the task force who were on vacation when he decided to arrest Simonek.

> Kelecius: Who did you complain to?
>
> Officer Kirkpatrick: Then commander, now chief, John Koziol.
>
> Kelecius: At the moment you testified that you thought you were acting correctly, but you now today have said that it was improper several times?
>
> Officer Kirkpatrick: Yes, sir.
>
> Kelecius: You no longer thought that everything that was happening that day was correct?
>
> Officer Kirkpatrick: No, sir.

<u>Kelecius</u>: When you complained to your commander, Commander John Koziol, was he surprised that it even happened?
<u>Officer Kirkpatrick</u>: Very surprised, yes.

***

When Eileen Bakalla was called to the stand, her testimony was again central to the prosecution's case. As she settled into her seat, she tried exchanging glances with Jim Degorski. Her testimony there was a betrayal to her friend, and she sniffled and wiped tears from her face.[6] She informed the jury of the phone call she received at Jake's Pizza, how she drove her two friends to Elgin to smoke pot and split the money, and recounted the detailed description they'd given her of the killings at Brown's Chicken.

Anne Lockett was also a central focus of the case, and the defense needled at her drug use to try and destroy her credibility. "Were you sober during your stay at Forest Hospital?" prosecutor Tom Biesty asked, referring to when she first received news of the killings from Jim Degorski. "Yes." He continued. "Were you sober during the basement conversation?" She was clear. "Yes." Anne Lockett cried throughout, dabbing her face with a tissue.[7]

While the gun itself was never located despite an exhaustive search in the Fox River, Jim Degorski was linked to the sale of a .38 caliber snub-nosed Smith & Wesson revolver that he'd bought during the summer of 1992 from a friend of his brother. Then, as Anne Lockett testified, it disappeared.

***

"What is absolutely incorrect in this case, though, is that this was the 'Palatine way' of doing things," Linas Kelecius said in defense of the task force's work during his closing statement. It was a forceful defense of the police work on the case. "This was not the 'Palatine way' of doing things that led to the Simonek statement and the Casey Sander statement. It was the 'Jim Bell way' of doing things. Jim Bell was never a police officer. He wasn't even an FBI agent. He was a civilian employee run amuck." He implored jurors to consider the credibility of the confessions they'd received, the DNA linking his friend to the scene, and the information they'd highlighted about the missing gun. "He wanted to do something big," Kelecius finished. "Give him something big in return."[8]

The defense's central argument was again more simple. "If he was there, they would have linked this evidence to him," Mark Levitt told the jurors. "They did not because they cannot. Because he was not there. Because he did not do this. Because he is not guilty."[9]

After a weeks-long trial, the jury left Courtroom 500 to deliberate in the same place where twelve of their peers had sentenced Juan Luna to life in prison two years earlier. In just two hours, they reached a verdict.

Back in the courtroom, the families held one another and wiped away tears as they waited. Jim Degorski's mother sat silent. "Has the jury determined a verdict?" Judge Gaughan asked the foreperson. "Yes, your honor." It was time. "Madam clerk, will you please publish the verdict." She began. "We, the jury, find the defendant, James Degorski, guilty of the first-degree murder of Rico Solis." She then read through each of the other victims.[10] Guilty on all counts.

With his culpability determined, Jim Degorski was quickly deemed eligible for the death penalty. The next step of the trial would again bring deep emotions to the surface as his family and friends testified as to his character in hopes of garnering enough sympathy from jurors to spare his life.

With her health deteriorating and constrained to a wheelchair, Jim's mother took the stand and told the courtroom about the years of trauma in their family. The abusive husband and father, the rampant substance abuse, and the instability of it all. A social worker and psychologist who'd worked with the Degorski family reinforced his past. "Do you assess families for their level of functionality?" Jim's attorney asked the psychologist. "Sure," she said matter-of-factly. "Can you tell us how this Degorski family rated compared to others in your experience?" he asked. "On a scale of one to ten, it's clearly a ten. It's one of the most dysfunctional families I've ever worked with."[11]

Jennifer Peters, his former girlfriend, told the room of a peaceful man. He was loving. He was caring. He was not who you thought he was. She waved at Jim when she entered the courtroom and he blushed.[12] "Jim Degorski never, ever, ever hit me. Ever," she said forcefully. "I think it's absolutely disgusting the picture they have painted of him. It's not the Jim Degorski I know," she testified. Tisa Morris, one of the prosecutors, dispensed of her credibility quickly. "Now, you told us a couple things about your background," she said to Peters on the stand. "And one of the things that you told us was that you were a theater major?" she asked. "Correct." Morris ended the questioning. "I don't have anything further," she said to Judge Gaughan.

Families again read victim-impact statements that required them to pack in years of pent-up emotion into just a few pages. It was the only chance they'd ever get to acknowledge their loved one's killer. "Do you sleep? Do you have nightmares?" Robert Mennes asked Degorski. "I still see Tom in my dreams as he looked before he died, before he was made to look presentable and decent before he was laid to rest." Jim Degorski had forced Tom Mennes's brother to live with those images, now he too would have to suffer for his actions. Lupe Maldonado's oldest son, Juan, spoke about growing up without a father. "Where's my poppa? Why doesn't he come home?" he said he'd ask as a child, searching for answers. "We would run out of time, paper, and words to explain our pain and how much we miss our dad."

A unanimous verdict was required again to sentence James Degorski to death. But in contrast to the previous trial, those opposed would not stand alone. On an initial vote by the jurors, eight supported it while four were undecided. They discussed the matter further, finally reaching a count of ten to two. Without unanimity, Jim Degorski would remain alive.[13] The trial was over, and Degorski would be sentenced to life in prison by Judge Gaughan. Following years of waiting in agony, the families impacted by the murders finally had answers. And yet, no punishment handed down by a court could bring back their loved ones or alleviate the great pain they'd endured.

After sentencing was complete, Jim Degorski was sent to Stateville Correctional Center, located southwest of Chicago. There, he joined his old friend Juan Luna. More than fifteen years had passed since January 8, 1993, that frigid and dark day the two men decided to rob seven people of their freedom. Now they too would lose all autonomy.

SOMETHING BIG

***

By the time Juan Luna and Jim Degorski were sentenced to life in prison, Brown's Chicken had become synonymous with one of Illinois's worst massacres. New advertising and a push from its founder, Frank Portillo, did little to erase the stigma of being associated with the killings. In 2009, the company filed for Chapter 11 bankruptcy and was eventually acquired by a former executive. Only a handful of restaurants remained.

Many of the Palatine police who worked the case retired, found jobs in other departments, or changed professions entirely. Bill King, Jerry Bratcher, John Koziol, Bryan Opitz, Jack Byrnes, Frank Medrys, Dan Briscoe, Jim Bell, and countless other sworn law enforcement and civilians spent years of their lives trying to solve the case. The task force system used by Palatine eventually became a model for solving other crimes.[14] Rita Mullins served honorably as mayor of Palatine for twenty years.

The reward money raised to catch the killers amounted to nearly $100,000. City officials determined that Anne Lockett and Melissa Benz would split it evenly – $49,064.50 each – for coming forward and finally breaking the case.[15] Lockett was criticized by those who believed she waited too long. She spent about $10,000 on an attorney who represented her during the trials and the rest paying off debts.

The Castro, Ehlenfeldt, Maldonado, Mennes, Nellsen, and Solis families waited fifteen years for answers. But the memory of their loved ones would never fade. There'd forever be signs around, like a sound or a smell that reminded them of what they'd lost to a senseless act of violence. Each new life event marked an occasion a parent had missed. Children grew older, finally surpassing the age at which their mother or father had lived.

The trials in 2007 and 2009 were not a strong source of closure for the families. Despite a decision from a jury of their peers and the overwhelming evidence against them, Juan Luna and James Degorski maintained their innocence after the trials. They never apologized to the families for their actions or for doing what they thought was "something big."

Something big was Michael Castro's goal of joining the military and serving his country. Something big was the story of Rico Solis and his transition to life in America. Something big was Marcus Nellsen's deep love for his daughter. Something big was Tom Mennes's gentleness and adoration for his family. Something big was the dedication Lynn Ehlenfeldt had for helping others. Something big was the chance Dick Ehlenfeldt took on opening a restaurant in hopes of providing financial stability for his family. Something big was Lupe Maldonado's dream of a better life for his children in Chicago.

A few years after the trials, Diane Clayton, the mother of Marcus Nellsen, passed away in her daughter's home. She'd moved to Illinois for the sole purpose of attending the trials. It was important for her to be there for her son when his killers were finally brought to justice. Like so many of the family members, she never missed a day.

After her death, the family began the typical preparations that follow the loss of a loved one. They alerted kith and kin. Funeral arrangements were made. And when they could muster the emotional strength, the family sorted through her belongings. Among her personal items—clothes, pictures, jewelry—were large plastic containers. And when they opened them, the family discovered the boxes were filled with newspaper clippings. For years, she'd been collecting reminders of her son's tragic death.

The six families touched by these murders all dealt with it in their own unique ways. Some clipped newspapers, while others preferred not to revisit the event. But like Marcus's mother, none of them would forget what had happened, even till the end. They'd always dream about hugging, kissing, or telling their loved one just how much they missed them.

And some day, when the time was right, they too would get the chance.

A NOTE ON SOURCES & DIALOGUE

This book is the product of dozens of interviews with police, prosecutors, defense attorneys, victims' families, community members, jurors, and acquaintances of the victims as well as thousands of pages of court documents from the original trials and subsequent appeals. Some sources requested full anonymity—which I obliged—while others were happy to speak fully on the record. In addition to original sources such as trial transcripts and interviews, thousands of contemporary news articles and TV news clips provided a basis for background material.

Memories fade after thirty years, so I sought to corroborate accounts of different anecdotes or details when possible. In some cases, that was either not possible or two accounts may have conflicted with one another, so a decision was made on what to include based on what was most plausible. This is a work of narrative nonfiction, not a history book, but nothing is made up or imagined. This story is as accurate as one can make it without having lived these events personally.

A special thanks to those reporters at the *Daily Herald*, *Chicago Sun-Times*, and *Chicago Tribune* who covered this case so closely over the years. Dennis Shere's *The Last Meal* and Maurice Possley's *The Brown's Chicken Massacre* also proved incredibly helpful as background material. The series "44 Minutes in

January" by *Daily Herald* reporters Sara Burnett, Madeleine Doubek, Diane Dungey, Lee Filas, Christy Gutowski, David Kazak, Joel Reese, Stacy St. Clair, and Shamus Toomey was also a great help.

There is quite a bit of dialogue in this book. Dialogue in quotes is pulled directly from sources such as interviews, news articles, or transcripts. A few quotes were edited ever so slightly for clarity. Dialogue in italics was created by the author and informed by interviews, trial transcripts, or news accounts from the time. When a prosecutor or defense attorney zealously advocates for their client in an opening statement, they paint a picture for jurors of what happened during the commission of a crime based on the information before them. The same can be said of some of the scenes in this book which are informed by all of this information. This is a true story, and nothing is made up, but some color is added where gaps exist that inhibit a cohesive narrative.

There are only a few people who know precisely what happened that night in January 1993. They are either no longer with us or maintain their innocence despite overwhelming evidence against them. May the former rest in peace, and may the latter find peace in finally, once and for all, coming to terms with the decisions they made that night.

NOTES

Chapter 1—Belva & John

1. Fred Leo Brown, interview with author, February 10, 2023.
2. Ibid.
3. Fred Leo Brown, Vietnam War Diary (Combat Ready Publishing, 1998), 11, 34–35.
4. Fred Leo Brown, interview with author, February 10, 2023.
5. Ibid.
6. Fred Leo Brown, "Early Years," https://fredleobrown.wordpress.com/early-years-2/ (accessed January 28, 2023).
7. Fred Leo Brown, interview with author, February 10, 2023.
8. Ibid.
9. Anna Marie Kukec, "Brown's Chicken Files Chap. 11," Daily Herald, December 31, 2009.
10. Dick Portillo & Don Yeager, Out of the Dog House (Triumph Books, 2018), 26; Elaine Poffeldt, "Frank Portillo Had It All—Until a Brutal Murder Drove His Chicago Chain to the Brink of Bankruptcy," CNN Money, October 14, 2002.
11. Dick Portillo & Don Yeager, Out of the Dog House (Triumph Books, 2018), 21–23.
12. Elaine Poffeldt, "Frank Portillo Had It All—Until a Brutal Murder Drove His Chicago Chain to the Brink of Bankruptcy," CNN Money, October 14, 2002.
13. Dick Portillo & Don Yeager, Out of the Dog House (Triumph Books, 2018), 26; Elaine Poffeldt, "Frank Portillo Had It All—Until a Brutal Murder Drove His Chicago Chain to the Brink of Bankruptcy," CNN Money, October 14, 2002.
14. Elaine Poffeldt, "Frank Portillo Had It All—Until a Brutal Murder Drove His Chicago Chain to the Brink of Bankruptcy," CNN Money, October 14, 2002.
15. Anna Marie Kukec, "Brown's Chicken Files Chap. 11," Daily Herald, December 31, 2009.

[16] Elaine Poffeldt, "Frank Portillo Had It All—Until a Brutal Murder Drove His Chicago Chain to the Brink of Bankruptcy," CNN Money, October 14, 2002.
[17] Fred Leo Brown, interview with author, February 10, 2023.
[18] Herb Greenberg, "Brown's Is Spreading Its Wings," Chicago Tribune, March 28, 1984.
[19] Elaine Poffeldt, "Frank Portillo Had It All—Until a Brutal Murder Drove His Chicago Chain to the Brink of Bankruptcy," CNN Money, October 14, 2002.
[20] Herb Greenberg, "Brown's Is Spreading Its Wings," Chicago Tribune, March 28, 1984.
[21] Ibid.
[22] Ron Cohn, interview with author, January 8, 2023.
[23] Ibid.
[24] Ibid.
[25] Fred Leo Brown, "Suicide of a Good Man," https://web.archive.org/web/20190806015214/http://www.angelfire.com/film/fredleobrown/suicide_of_a_good_man/eight.html (accessed via the Wayback Machine/Internet Archive on February 10, 2023).
[26] Fred Leo Brown, interview with author, February 10, 2023; see also Fred Leo Brown, Wall of Blood (Combat Ready Publishing, 1997), 13; supra note 25.

Chapter 2—Lynn & Dick

[1] Ann Ehlenfeldt, interview with author, March 15, 2024.
[2] Stacy St. Clair, "44 Minutes in January: Stolen Lives: Couple Left Legacy of Service, Civic Duty," Daily Herald, January 9, 2003.
[3] Wisconsin Badger Vol. 80, ed. Lindell Carter, (University of Wisconsin, 1965), page 469.
[4] Ann Ehlenfeldt, interview with author, March 15, 2024.
[5] Dana Sampson and Joy Ehlenfeldt, interview with author, June 14, 2024; Ann Ehlenfeldt, interview with author, March 15, 2024.
[6] Dana Sampson and Joy Ehlenfeldt, interview with author, June 14, 2024; Ann Ehlenfeldt, interview with author, March 15, 2024.
[7] Ann Ehlenfeldt, interview with author, March 15, 2024.
[8] Stuart D. Levitan, Madison in the Sixties (Wisconsin Historical Society Press, 2018).
[9] Ann Ehlenfeldt, interview with author, March 15, 2024.
[10] Ibid.
[11] Ibid.
[12] Ibid.
[13] Barbara Wiese, interview with author, September 10, 2024.

14. Robert Becker and Stanley Holmes, "Idealism of the '60s Shapes Restaurant Owners," Chicago Tribune, January 11, 1993.
15. Quiver Yearbook (University of Wisconsin Oshkosh), Class of 1969, https://www.e-yearbook.com/yearbooks/University_Wisconsin_Oshkosh_Quiver_Yearbook/1969/Page_1.html.
16. Ann Ehlenfeldt, interview with author, March 15, 2024, 1 hour and 23 minutes.
17. Quiver Yearbook (University of Wisconsin Oshkosh), Class of 1969, https://www.e-yearbook.com/yearbooks/University_Wisconsin_Oshkosh_Quiver_Yearbook/1969/Page_1.html.
18. "Civil Rights Comes to Oshkosh and Fox Valley," University of Wisconsin Oshkosh, http://www.blackthursday.uwosh.edu/civilfoxvalley.html.
19. Ann Ehlenfeldt, interview with author, March 15, 2024.
20. Barbara Wiese, interview with author, September 10, 2024.
21. Stacy St. Clair, "44 Minutes in January: Stolen Lives: Couple Left Legacy of Service, Civic Duty," Daily Herald, January 9, 2003.
22. Dana Sampson and Joy Ehlenfeldt, interview with author, June 14, 2024.
23. Ann Ehlenfeldt, interview with author, March 15, 2024.
24. Dana Sampson and Joy Ehlenfeldt, interview with author, June 14, 2024.
25. Barbara Vitello, "'A Testament to My Parents': Murders Created Enduring Bond Between Brown's Owners' Daughters," Daily Herald, January 8, 2023.
26. Dana Sampson and Joy Ehlenfeldt, interview with author, June 14, 2024.
27. Ibid.
28. Ann Ehlenfeldt, interview with author, March 15, 2024.
29. Robert Becker and Stanley Holmes, "Idealism of the '60s Shapes Restaurant Owners," Chicago Tribune, January 11, 1993.
30. Ann Ehlenfeldt, interview with author, March 15, 2024.
31. Robert Becker and Stanley Holmes, "Idealism of the '60s Shapes Restaurant Owners," Chicago Tribune, January 11, 1993.
32. Ibid.
33. Dana Sampson and Joy Ehlenfeldt, interview with author, June 14, 2024.
34. Robert Becker and Stanley Holmes, "Idealism of the '60s Shapes Restaurant Owners," Chicago Tribune, January 11, 1993.
35. Dana Sampson and Joy Ehlenfeldt, interview with author, June 14, 2024.
36. Ibid.
37. "Couple's New Beginning Turns into a Tragic End," Associated Press, January 13, 1993.
38. Bill Glauber, "Family Tragedy Didn't Force Jennifer Shilling off Political Path," Milwaukee Journal Sentinel, December 20, 2014.
39. Robert Becker and Stanley Holmes, "Brown's Owner Driven by Passion to Help Out," Chicago Tribune, January 13, 1993.
40. Ibid.
41. Ann Ehlenfeldt, interview with author, March 15, 2024.

[42] Robert Becker and Stanley Holmes, "Idealism of the '60s Shapes Restaurant Owners," Chicago Tribune, January 11, 1993.
[43] Sara Burnett, Madeleine Doubek, Diane Dungey, Lee Filas, Christy Gutowski, David Kazak, Joel Reese, Stacy St. Clair, and Shamus Toomey, "Now, Another Kind of Waiting Begins," Daily Herald, January 8, 2003.
[44] Flynn McRoberts and Michael Lev, "Seven Massacred in Palatine," Chicago Tribune, January 10, 1993
[45] Sara Burnett, Madeleine Doubek, Diane Dungey, Lee Filas, Christy Gutowski, David Kazak, Joel Reese, Stacy St. Clair, and Shamus Toomey, "In the Path of Killers," Daily Herald, January 8, 2003.
[46] Dana Sampson and Joy Ehlenfeldt, interview with author, June 14, 2024.
[47] ABC 7 Chicago, ABC, January 10, 1993.
[48] WBBM CBS 2 Chicago, CBS, January 6, 1994.
[49] Rebecca Carr and Frank Burgos, "7 Joined in One Fatal Night," Chicago Sun-Times, January 10, 1993.
[50] Flynn McRoberts and Michael Lev, "Seven Massacred in Palatine," Chicago Tribune, January 10, 1993; Illinois Minimum Wage Rates, https://labor.illinois.gov/content/dam/soi/en/web/idol/laws-rules/fls/documents/minimumwagehistoricrates.pdf.
[51] CBS Evening News, CBS, January 10, 1993.
[52] People v. Degorski, October 2, 2009, morning transcripts.
[53] Dana Sampson and Joy Ehlenfeldt, interview with author, June 14, 2024.
[54] People v. Degorski, October 1, 2009, afternoon transcripts.
[55] Ibid.
[56] Ibid.

Chapter 3—Kristin

[1] Sara Burnett, Madeleine Doubek, Diane Dungey, Lee Filas, Christy Gutowski, David Kazak, Joel Reese, Stacy St. Clair, and Shamus Toomey, "The Long Wait for One Call," Daily Herald, January 7, 2003.
[2] People v. Degorski, October 5, 2009, afternoon transcripts.
[3] People v. Degorski, October 1, 2009, morning transcripts.
[4] Scott Fornek, "The Loner—James Eric Degorski," Chicago Sun-Times, May 26, 2002.
[5] Steve Warmbir, Dan Rozek, Art Golab, and Dave Newbart, "Flashback to a Violent Past," Chicago Sun-Times, May 18, 2002.
[6] Tom Biesty, Linas Kelecius, Dave Daigle, Palatine Police Department, "Police and Trial Prosecutors' Opposition to James Degorski's Petition for Executive Emergency Clemency," June 30, 2021.
[7] Ibid.
[8] Ibid.
[9] Ibid.

10 Steve Warmbir, Dan Rozek, Art Golab, and Dave Newbart, "Flashback to a Violent Past," Chicago Sun-Times, May 18, 2002.
11 People v. Degorski, October 1, 2009, morning transcripts.
12 Ibid.
13 Tom Biesty, Linas Kelecius, Dave Daigle, Palatine Police Department, "Police and Trial Prosecutors' Opposition to James Degorski's Petition for Executive Emergency Clemency," June 30, 2021.
14 People v. Degorski, September 9, 2009, morning transcripts.
15 Ibid.
16 Ibid.

Chapter 4—Rico & Michael

1 David M., "A Nostalgic Look Back at Growing Up in 1990s Manila," Medium, June 25, 2024, https://medium.com/@tarpmagic/a-nostalgic-look-back-at-growing-up-in-1990s-manila-c5a9a8725ddb#:~:text=The%20 1990s%20in%20Manila%20was,global%20influences%20and%20 enduring%20traditions.
2 Antonio Lopez, "The 1980s and 1990s: The Tale of Two Decades," BizNewsAsia, October 2, 2021, https://biznewsasia.com/the-1980s-and-the-1990s-the-tale-of-two-decades/.
3 Stacy St. Clair, "Move to America Brought Teen's Dreams Within Reach," The Daily Herald, January 9, 2003.
4 Ibid.
5 "Mourners Try to Learn from Teen's Short Life," Chicago Tribune, January 17, 1993 (updated August 9, 2021), https://www.chicagotribune.com/1993/01/17/mourners-try-to-learn-from-teens-short-life/.
6 Rebecca Carr, "High School Mourns—and Waits for News," Chicago Sun-Times, January 12, 1993.
7 Robert Becker and V. Dion Haynes, "Teen Was Always the First One to Offer Help," Chicago Tribune, January 10, 1993.
8 Madeleine Doubek, "Already a Hero to His Friends, Teen Sets Sights on Marines," Daily Herald, January 9, 2003.
9 Rebecca Carr, "Pain, Questions Replace Shock—Healing Eludes Victims' Families," Chicago Sun-Times, January 9, 1994.
10 Ibid.
11 Ted Gregory and V. Dion Haynes, "Friendship Led Teens to Their Jobs, Deaths," Chicago Tribune, January 11, 1993.
12 Casey Sander Haefs, interview with author, June 19, 2024.
13 Ibid.
14 Ibid.
15 Sara Burnett, Madeleine Doubek, Diane Dungey, Lee Filas, Christy Gutowski, David Kazak, Joel Reese, Stacy St. Clair, and Shamus Toomey,

"In the Path of Killers—Twists of Fate Put Workers in Brown's That Night," Daily Herald, January 8, 2003.

16. Stacy St. Clair, "Move to America Brought Teen's Dreams Within Reach," The Daily Herald, January 9, 2003.
17. Sara Burnett, Madeleine Doubek, Diane Dungey, Lee Filas, Christy Gutowski, David Kazak, Joel Reese, Stacy St. Clair, and Shamus Toomey, "In the Path of Killers—Twists of Fate Put Workers in Brown's That Night," Daily Herald, January 8, 2003.
18. Mary Jane Crow, "I Want America to Know Who Michael Was," Chicago Sun-Times, May 19, 2002.
19. Stacy St. Clair, "Move to America Brought Teen's Dreams Within Reach," The Daily Herald, January 9, 2003.
20. Ibid.
21. Ibid.

Chapter 5—Marcus, Lupe & Tom

1. Joel Reese, "Nellsen Was Making a New Start on Management Track," Daily Herald, January 9, 2003.
2. Ibid.
3. Ibid.
4. Mary Nunez and the Nellsen family, correspondence with author, March 29, 2024.
5. Joel Reese, "Nellsen Was Making a New Start on Management Track," Daily Herald, January 9, 2003.
6. Mary Nunez and the Nellsen family, correspondence with author, March 29, 2024.
7. Joel Reese, "Nellsen Was Making a New Start on Management Track," Daily Herald, January 9, 2003.
8. Ibid.
9. Ibid.
10. Mary Nunez and the Nellsen family, correspondence with author, March 29, 2024.
11. Joel Reese, "Nellsen Was Making a New Start on Management Track," Daily Herald, January 9, 2003.
12. Ibid.
13. Janan Hanna and Andrew Gottesman, "Workers' Different Lives, Different Paths Intersect in Tragedy," Chicago Tribune, January 11, 1993.
14. Joel Reese, "Nellsen Was Making a New Start on Management Track," Daily Herald, January 9, 2003.
15. Ibid.
16. Ibid.
17. Ibid.

18   Ibid.
19   Ibid.
20   Ibid.
21   Mary Nunez and the Nellsen family, correspondence with author, March 29, 2024.
22   Joel Reese, "Nellsen Was Making a New Start on Management Track," Daily Herald, January 9, 2003.
23   Ibid.
24   Joel Reese, "Palatine Man Was Seen as Peaceful, Thoughtful Soul," Daily Herald, January 9, 2003.
25   Ibid.
26   Ibid.
27   Ibid.
28   Ibid.
29   Lee Bey and Frank Burgos, "He Tried to Do the Best He Could," Chicago Sun-Times, January 11, 1993.
30   Joel Reese, "Palatine Man Was Seen as Peaceful, Thoughtful Soul," Daily Herald, January 9, 2003.
31   Joel Reese, "Nellsen Was Making a New Start on Management Track," Daily Herald, January 9, 2003.
32   Joel Reese, "Palatine Man Was Seen as Peaceful, Thoughtful Soul," Daily Herald, January 9, 2003.
33   Lee Bey and Frank Burgos, "He Tried to Do the Best He Could," Chicago Sun-Times, January 11, 1993.
34   Joel Reese, "Palatine Man Was Seen as Peaceful, Thoughtful Soul," Daily Herald, January 9, 2003.
35   Joseph Kirby, "Brown's Cook Saw His Job as a Chance for Something Better," Chicago Tribune, January 10, 1993.
36   Sara Burnett, "Hard-Working Father of 3 Began Third U.S. Journey," Daily Herald, January 9, 2003.
37   Ibid.
38   Joseph Kirby, "Brown's Cook Saw His Job as a Chance for Something Better," Chicago Tribune, January 10, 1993.
39   Sara Burnett, "Hard-Working Father of 3 Began Third U.S. Journey," Daily Herald, January 9, 2003.
40   Ibid.
41   Joseph Kirby, "Brown's Cook Saw His Job as a Chance for Something Better," Chicago Tribune, January 10, 1993.
42   Joseph Kirby, "Brown's Cook Saw His Job as a Chance for Something Better," Chicago Tribune, January 10, 1993.
43   Sara Burnett, Madeleine Doubek, Diane Dungey, Lee Filas, Christy Gutowski, David Kazak, Joel Reese, Stacy St. Clair, and Shamus Toomey,

"In the Path of Killers—Twists of Fate Put Workers in Brown's That Night," Daily Herald, January 8, 2003.
44. Lee Bey and Frank Burgos, "2-Job, Blue-Collar Provider," Chicago Sun-Times, January 11, 1993.
45. Stephanie Zimmerman, "Victims' Families Still Wonder: What If?," Chicago Sun-Times, May 19, 2002.
46. Sara Burnett, "Hard-Working Father of 3 Began Third U.S. Journey," Daily Herald, January 9, 2003.
47. Sara Burnett, Madeleine Doubek, Diane Dungey, Lee Filas, Christy Gutowski, David Kazak, Joel Reese, Stacy St. Clair, and Shamus Toomey, "In the Path of Killers—Twists of Fate Put Workers in Brown's That Night," Daily Herald, January 8, 2003.
48. Mary Jane Crow, "I Want America to Know Who Michael Was," Chicago Sun-Times, May 19, 2002.
49. People v. Degorski, September 3, 2009, transcripts.
50. People v. Degorski, September 8, 2009, transcripts.
51. People v. Degorski, September 9, 2009, transcripts.
52. Sara Burnett, Madeleine Doubek, Diane Dungey, Lee Filas, Christy Gutowski, David Kazak, Joel Reese, Stacy St. Clair, and Shamus Toomey, "A Late-Night Meal, Mayhem and Mourning," Daily Herald, January 7, 2003.
53. Sara Burnett, Madeleine Doubek, Diane Dungey, Lee Filas, Christy Gutowski, David Kazak, Joel Reese, Stacy St. Clair, and Shamus Toomey, "A Late-Night Meal, Mayhem and Mourning," Daily Herald, January 7, 2003.

Chapter 6—Eileen

1. Obituary of Patricia Ellen Kroll, Daily Herald (via Legacy.com), https://www.legacy.com/us/obituaries/dailyherald/name/patricia-kroll-obituary?id=20289018.
2. Crystal Rednak and Diane Rado, "Brown's Secret Haunted Women," Chicago Tribune, June 9, 2002.
3. Ibid.
4. Tom Biesty, Linas Kelecius, Dave Daigle, Palatine Police Department, "Police and Trial Prosecutors' Opposition to James Degorski's Petition for Executive Emergency Clemency," June 30, 2021.
5. Ibid.
6. Stacy St. Clair and Joseph Ryan, "Luna Gave Her 'Heebie-Jeebies'," Daily Herald, April 18, 2007.
7. People v. Degorski, September 9, 2009, afternoon transcripts, page 8.
8. Tom Biesty, Linas Kelecius, Dave Daigle, Palatine Police Department, "Police and Trial Prosecutors' Opposition to James Degorski's Petition for Executive Emergency Clemency," June 30, 2021.
9. People v. Degorski, September 9, 2009, afternoon transcripts, page 8.

10. Tom Biesty, Linas Kelecius, Dave Daigle, Palatine Police Department, "Police and Trial Prosecutors' Opposition to James Degorski's Petition for Executive Emergency Clemency," June 30, 2021.
11. Ibid.
12. Rebecca Carr, "Pain, Questions Replace Shock—Healing Eludes," Chicago Sun-Times, January 9, 1994.
13. Dennis Shere, The Last Meal: Defending an Accused Mass Murderer, (Titletown Publishing, 2010), pages 2-10.
14. "Daughter testifies in Brown's trial," Chicago Tribune, September 15, 2009.
15. Diane Dungey, "Brown's Tragedy Builds Cultural Bridges," January 31, 1993.
16. Maurice Possley, The Brown's Chicken Massacre, (Berkley Books, 2003), page 5.
17. Joseph Kirby, "Brown's Cook Saw His Job as a Chance for Something Better," Chicago Tribune, January 10, 1993.
18. Joel Reese, "Palatine Man Was Seen as Peaceful, Thoughtful Soul," Daily Herald, January 9, 2003.
19. Joel Reese, "Palatine Man Was Seen as Peaceful, Thoughtful Soul," Daily Herald, January 9, 2003.

Chapter 7—Jane

1. People v. Luna, April 13, 2007, opening statement transcripts.
2. Dennis Shere, The Last Meal: Defending an Accused Mass Murderer, (Titletown Publishing, 2010), page 4.
3. Tom Biesty, Linas Kelecius, Dave Daigle, Palatine Police Department, "Police and Trial Prosecutors' Opposition to James Degorski's Petition for Executive Emergency Clemency," June 30, 2021.
4. People v. Luna, April 13, 2007, opening statement transcripts.
5. Peter Kendall & Michael Lev, "Murder Mystery Deepens with Each Passing Day," Chicago Tribune, January 18, 1993.
6. People v. Luna, April 13, 20007, opening statement transcripts.
7. Ibid.
8. Ibid.
9. "A Late-Night Meal, Mayhem and Mourning," Daily Herald, January 7, 2003.
10. Ibid.
11. ABC 7 Eyewitness News, ABC, January 10, 1993.
12. People v. Luna, April 16, 2007 transcripts, volume 2.
13. Chris Hedges, correspondence with author, February 24, 2023.
14. People v. Luna, April 16, 2007 transcripts, volume 2.
15. Burt Constable, "Brown's Case Has Aged, but Wounds Still Fresh," Daily Herald, April 17, 2007.

[16] People v. Luna, April 16, 2007 transcripts, volume 1.
[17] Chris Hedges, correspondence with author, February 24, 2023.
[18] Tom McNamee, "Many Questions, Few Answers," Chicago Sun-Times, January 17, 1993.
[19] Barbara Vitello, "Deputy Testifies About Bloody Footprints," Daily Herald, September 11, 2009.
[20] People v. Luna, April 16, 2007 transcripts, volume 1.
[21] People v. Luna, April 16, 2007 transcripts, volume 2.
[22] Stacy St. Clair, "How Forensics Found the DNA," Daily Herald, April 17, 2007.
[23] People v. Luna, April 16, 2007 transcripts, volume 3.
[24] Bob Susnjara, "From Garbage to Vital DNA Evidence," Daily Herald, May 20, 2002.

Chapter 8—Martin

[1] ABC 7 Eyewitness News, ABC, January 10, 1993.
[2] Lou Ortiz & Phillip O'Connor, "Freed Suspect Still a Puzzle," Chicago Sun-Times, January 12, 1993.
[3] ABC 7 Eyewitness News, ABC, January 10, 1993.
[4] Ibid.
[5] Scott Fornek & Rebeccca Car, "Elgin Man Had Reputation as a Partier," Chicago Sun-Times, January 11, 1993.
[6] Lou Ortiz & Phillip O'Connor, "Freed Suspect Still a Puzzle," Chicago Sun-Times, January 12, 1993.
[7] ABC 7 Eyewitness News, ABC, January 10, 1993.
[8] Scott Fornek & Rebeccca Car, "Elgin Man Had Reputation as a Partier," Chicago Sun-Times, January 11, 1993.
[9] Lou Ortiz & Phillip O'Connor, "Freed Suspect Still a Puzzle," Chicago Sun-Times, January 12, 1993.
[10] Scott Fornek & Rebeccca Car, "Elgin Man Had Reputation as a Partier," Chicago Sun-Times, January 11, 1993.
[11] ABC 7 Eyewitness News, ABC, January 10, 1993.
[12] Dennis Shere, The Last Meal: Defending an Accused Mass Murderer, (Title Town Publishing, 2010), page 17.
[13] Scott Fornek & Rebeccca Car, "Elgin Man Had Reputation as a Partier," Chicago Sun-Times, January 11, 1993.
[14] ABC 7 Eyewitness News, ABC, January 10, 1993.
[15] Maureen O'Donnell, "Blake's Friends Say He Told of 'Good Alibi'," Chicago Sun-Times, January 13, 1993.
[16] Sara Burnett, Madeleine Doubek, Diane Dungey, Lee Filas, Christy Gutowski, David Kazak, Joel Reese, Stacy St. Clair, and Shamus Toomey, "The Long Wait for One Call," Daily Herald, January 7, 2003.

[17] Lou Ortiz & Phillip O'Connor, "Freed Suspect Still a Puzzle," Chicago Sun-Times, January 12, 1993.
[18] Sara Burnett, Madeleine Doubek, Diane Dungey, Lee Filas, Christy Gutowski, David Kazak, Joel Reese, Stacy St. Clair, and Shamus Toomey, "The Long Wait for One Call," Daily Herald, January 7, 2003.
[19] Teresa Mask, "The Guy Who Didn't Do It," Daily Herald, June 2, 2002.
[20] Peter Kendall & Michael Lev, "Murder Mystery Deepens with Each Passing Day," Chicago Tribune, January 18, 1993.
[21] Peter Kendall & Michael Lev, "Murder Mystery Deepens with Each Passing Day," Chicago Tribune, January 18, 1993.
[22] "A Late-Night Meal, Mayhem and Mourning," Daily Herald, January 7, 2003.
[23] Teresa Wiltz, "Man Suing Palatine for False Arrest," Chicago Tribune, January 9, 1994.
[24] Dennis Born, interview with author, October 14, 2023.
[25] Teresa Mask, "The Guy Who Didn't Do It," Daily Herald, June 2, 2002.
[26] Ibid.
[27] ABC 7 Eyewitness News, ABC, January 10, 1993.
[28] Lou Ortiz & Phillip J. O'Connor, "Freed Suspect Still a Puzzle," Chicago Sun-Times, January 12, 1993.
[29] Peter Kendall & Michael Lev, "Murder Mystery Deepens with Each Passing Day," Chicago Tribune, January 18, 1993.
[30] Sara Burnett, Madeleine Doubek, Diane Dungey, Lee Filas, Christy Gutowski, David Kazak, Joel Reese, Stacy St. Clair, and Shamus Toomey, "A Late-Night Meal, Mayhem and Mourning," Daily Herald, January 7, 2003.
[31] Dennis Born, interview with author, October 14, 2023.
[32] ABC 7 Eyewitness News, ABC, January 11, 1993.
[33] Martin Blake, interview with author, February 15, 2023.
[34] Sara Burnett, Madeleine Doubek, Diane Dungey, Lee Filas, Christy Gutowski, David Kazak, Joel Reese, Stacy St. Clair, and Shamus Toomey, "Now, Another Kind of Waiting Begins," Daily Herald, January 8, 2003.
[35] Peter Kendall & Michael Lev, "Murder Mystery Deepens with Each Passing Day," Chicago Tribune, January 18, 1993.

Chapter 9—Michelle

[1] V. Dion Haynes, "Brown's Murders Prime Cub Reporter's Career," Chicago Tribune, January 20, 1993.
[2] Michelle Parke, interview with author, December 5, 2023.
[3] "Club Treasurer Stole Before, Attorney Says," Chicago Tribune, February 8, 1991.
[4] Nancy Robb, interview with author, February 17, 2023.

5. Rebecca Carr & Frank Burgos, "Key Suspect Held in Murder Probe—Palatine Tries to Cope with Seven Killings," Chicago Sun-Times, January 11, 1993.
6. Susan Kuczka & Louise Kiernan, "Basketball Game Lets Students Share Grief," Chicago Tribune, January 10, 1993.
7. Rebecca Carr, "High School Mourns—and Waits for News," Chicago Sun-Times, January 12, 1993.
8. Ibid.
9. Nancy Robb, interview with author, February 17, 2023.
10. Michelle Parke, interview with author, December 5, 2023.
11. V. Dion Haynes, "Brown's Murders Prime Cub Reporter's Career," Chicago Tribune, January 20, 1993.
12. Ibid.
13. Sheri Vazzano, "School Paper Helps Mollify Tragedy," Daily Herald, January 23, 1993.

Chapter 10—Anne

1. People v. Luna, April 24, 2007, volume 1.
2. Frank Main and Carlos Sadovi, "Brown's Chicken Murder Mystery—Thrill Kill," Chicago Sun-Times, May 18, 2002.
3. People v. Luna, April 24, 2007, volume 1.
4. Dennis Shere, The Last Meal: Defending an Accused Mass Murderer, (Titletown Publishing, 2010), page 159.
5. Frank Main, Steve Warmbir, Carlos Sadovi, and Robert C. Herguth, "Brown's Defendant Hit in Jail—Guard Could Lose," Chicago Sun-Times, May 21, 2002.
6. People v. Luna, April 24, 2007, volume 1.
7. Jake Griffin, "'I Could Have Done It Earlier': Brown's Murders Witness Feared Killer Before Coming Forward," Daily Herald, January 9, 2023.
8. Melissa Benz, interview with author, August 5, 2004.
9. Jake Griffin, "'I Could Have Done It Earlier': Brown's Murders Witness Feared Killer Before Coming Forward," Daily Herald, January 9, 2023.
10. People v. Luna, April 24, 2007, volume 1.
11. Tom Biesty, Linas Kelecius, Dave Daigle, Palatine Police Department, "Police and Trial Prosecutors' Opposition to James Degorski's Petition for Executive Emergency Clemency," June 30, 2021.
12. Sara Burnett, Madeleine Doubek, Diane Dungey, Lee Filas, Christy Gutowski, David Kazak, Joel Reese, Stacy St. Clair, and Shamus Toomey, "The Long Wait for One Call," Daily Herald, January 7, 2003.
13. Dave Newbart and Andrew Herrmann, "Ex-Girlfriend Shows 'Courage'," Chicago Sun-Times, May 19, 2002.
14. Tom Biesty, Linas Kelecius, Dave Daigle, Palatine Police Department, "Police and Trial Prosecutors' Opposition to James Degorski's Petition for Executive Emergency Clemency," June 30, 2021.

15. James Degorski, "Chapter 2," JamesDegorski.com.
16. Tom Biesty, Linas Kelecius, Dave Daigle, Palatine Police Department, "Police and Trial Prosecutors' Opposition to James Degorski's Petition for Executive Emergency Clemency," June 30, 2021.
17. People v. Luna, April 13, 2007, opening statement transcripts.
18. Stacy St. Clair, "Jury Watches Videotaped Confession," Daily Herald, April 26, 2007.
19. People v. Luna, April 13, 2007, opening statement transcripts.
20. Ibid.
21. Ibid.
22. Tom Biesty, Linas Kelecius, Dave Daigle, Palatine Police Department, "Police and Trial Prosecutors' Opposition to James Degorski's Petition for Executive Emergency Clemency," June 30, 2021.
23. People v. Luna, April 26, 2007, transcripts.
24. People v. Luna, April 13, 2007, transcripts.
25. Tom Biesty, Linas Kelecius, Dave Daigle, Palatine Police Department, "Police and Trial Prosecutors' Opposition to James Degorski's Petition for Executive Emergency Clemency," June 30, 2021.
26. Shamus Toomey and Rhonda Sciarra, "Brown's Suspects Had Plans to Do 'Something Big,' Authorities Say," Daily Herald, May 19, 2002.
27. Tom Biesty, Linas Kelecius, Dave Daigle, Palatine Police Department, "Police and Trial Prosecutors' Opposition to James Degorski's Petition for Executive Emergency Clemency," June 30, 2021.
28. People v. Luna, April 17, 2007, transcripts, volume 1.
29. Ibid.
30. Bryan Opitz, interview with author, September 15, 2023.

Chapter 11—Jerry

1. "Ehlerty Found Guilty of Drowning Baby Daughter in Salt Creek," Chicago Tribune, February 13, 1993 (updated August 10, 2021), https://www.chicagotribune.com/1993/02/13/ehlert-found-guilty-of-drowning-baby-daughter-in-salt-creek/.
2. "Doctor Committed for Killing Family," UPI, December 6, 1989, https://www.upi.com/Archives/1989/12/06/Doctor-committed-for-killing-family/6087628923600/
3. Doug Ray, "Chief Bratcher Will Face New Challenges in Palatine," Daily Herald, December 12, 1973.
4. Brad Grossman, interview with author, October 20, 2023.
5. Walt Gasior, interview one with author, October 9, 2023.
6. Brad Grossman, interview with author, October 20, 2023.
7. Walt Gasior, interview two with author, October 9, 2023.
8. Bryan Opitz, interview with author, September 15, 2023.

[9] Walt Gasior, interview one with author, October 9, 2023.
[10] Sara Burnett, Madeleine Doubek, Diane Dungey, Lee Filas, Christy Gutowski, David Kazak, Joel Reese, Stacy St. Clair, and Shamus Toomey, "The Long Wait for One Call," Daily Herald, January 7, 2003.
[11] Rebecca Carr, "Palatine Link Explored in Slaying Probe," Chicago Sun-Times, April 24, 1993.
[12] Flynn McRoberts & Michael Lev, "Seven Massacred in Palatine," Chicago Tribune, January 10, 1993.
[13] ABC 7 Eyewitness News, ABC, January 14, 1993.
[14] Dr. Henry Lee and Jerry Labriola, Dr. Henry Lee's Forensic Files: Five Famous Cases, (Prometheus, 2006).
[15] Sara Burnett, Madeleine Doubek, Diane Dungey, Lee Filas, Christy Gutowski, David Kazak, Joel Reese, Stacy St. Clair, and Shamus Toomey, "The Long Wait for One Call," Daily Herald, January 7, 2003.
[16] Ibid.
[17] Maurice Possley, The Brown's Chicken Massacre, (Berkley Books, 2003), page 66.
[18] Maurice Possley, The Brown's Chicken Massacre, (Berkley Books, 2003), page 67.
[19] Maurice Possley, The Brown's Chicken Massacre, (Berkley Books, 2003), page 138.
[20] People v. Lee Harris, Circuit Court of Cook County, post-conviction petition.
[21] Rebecca Carr, "Pain, Questions, Replace Shock—Healing Eludes," Chicago Sun-Times, January 9, 1994.
[22] Ibid.
[23] Susan Kuczka, "Palatine Task Force Shrinks Operations," Chicago Tribune, June 09, 1993.
[24] People v. Luna, April 24, 2007, volume 1.; see also Eric Herman, "Experts: Print, DNA Are Luna's—Both on Evidence," Chicago Sun-Times, April 20, 2007; Diane Dungey and Sandra Lawhead, "Brown's Task Force Hits Another Wall," Daily Herald, March 22, 1994.
[25] Rebecca Carr and Phillip J. O'Connor, "Palatine Suspect Held—Chicago Man Questioned," Chicago Sun-Times, March 21, 1994.
[26] Diane Dungey and Sandra Lawhead, "Brown's Task Force Hits Another Wall," Daily Herald, March 22, 1994.
[27] Ibid.
[28] Rebecca Carr and Jim Casey, "Fingerprint Controversy Adds to Palatine Puzzle," Chicago Sun-Times, March 23, 1994.
[29] Diane Dungey and Sandra Lawhead, "Brown's Task Force Hits Another Wall," Daily Herald, March 22, 1994.

SOMETHING BIG

Chapter 12—Rita

1. 1989 Municipal Election Results, Chicago Tribune, https://www.chicagotribune.com/1989/04/06/cook-county-1549/.
2. "Allstate Gives Out Benefits," Daily Herald, January 12, 1993.
3. Rita Mullins and Amber Mullins, interview with author, June 23, 2024.
4. People v. Luna, April 13, 2007, opening statement transcripts.
5. ABC 7 Eyewitness News, ABC, January 12, 1993.
6. Sue Ellen Christian and Ted Gregory, "Families Lay Aside Questions to Say Farewell," Chicago Tribune, January 13, 1993.
7. ABC 7 Eyewitness News, ABC, January 12, 1993.
8. Joel Reese, "Nellsen Was Making a New Start on Management Track," Daily Herald, January 9, 2003.
9. Steve Zalusky, "'I Can Remember the Sound of His Voice': Daughter of Brown's Victim Now a Correctional Officer," Daily Herald, January 8, 2023.
10. V. Dion Haynes and Janan Hanna, "Mourners Search in Vain for Peace," Chicago Tribune, January 14, 1993.
11. Stacy St. Clair, "Move to America Brought Teen's Dreams Within Reach," The Daily Herald, January 9, 2003.
12. Sue Ellen Christian and Ted Gregory, "Families Lay Aside Questions to Say Farewell," Chicago Tribune, January 13, 1993.
13. ABC Nightly News, ABC, January 12, 1993.
14. Rebecca Carr, "Students Gather Strength, Bid Farewell to Classmates," Chicago Sun-Times, January 14, 1993.
15. Rebecca Carr, "Daughters Express Thanks, Vow to Reopen Restaurant," Chicago Sun-Times, January 15, 1993.
16. CBS 2 Chicago News, CBS, January 19, 1993.
17. ABC 7 Eyewitness News, ABC, January 14, 1993.
18. Sara Falwell, "Palatine Ready to Leave Stigma of Slayings Behind," Daily Herald, May 11, 2007.
19. Kimberly Pohl, "What About the Reward?," Daily Herald, October 1, 2009.
20. Rita Mullins and Amber Mullins, interview with author, June 23, 2024.
21. Ibid.
22. David Silverman, "Palatine Mayor Joins Push for Gun Control," Chicago Tribune, January 19, 1993.
23. Melissa Benz, interview with author, August 5, 2004.

Chapter 13—Chuck

1. "The Parents Who Left Their Kids 'Home Alone' to Vacation in Mexico: The Oprah Winfrey Show," posted December 11, 2020, by OWN, YouTube, https://www.youtube.com/watch?v=SuWbRtWcAlQ.
2. Chuck Goudie, interview with author, September 1, 2024.
3. Ibid.

4. Eric Zorn, "Who's Running This Murder Case?," Chicago Tribune, January 19, 1993.
5. Chuck Goudie, interview with author, September 1, 2024.
6. Eric Zorn, "Who's Running This Murder Case?," Chicago Tribune, January 19, 1993.
7. Flynn McRoberts and John O'Brien, "Palatine Cops Have 300-Pound Question," Chicago Tribune, January 20, 1993.
8. Diplomas Honor Puplis for Staying Straing, Chicago Tribune, February 19, 1993.
9. Flynn McRoberts and Mark Shuman, "Man Charged with Giving Cops False Lead in Palatine Murders," Chicago Tribune, March 18, 1993.

Chapter 14—Frank

1. The Chicago Traveler, "Weather Bell," 2007, https://www.thechicagotraveler.com/2007/12/weather-bell/.
2. Michael Martinez & John O'Brien, "Palatine's Police Chief Fires Back Brown's Investigators Weren't Lax, He Says," Chicago Tribune, November 30, 1995.
3. Dick Portillo & Don Yeager, Out of the Dog House (Triumph Books, 2018), 26; Elaine Poffeldt, "Frank Portillo Had It All—Until a Brutal Murder Drove His Chicago Chain to the Brink of Bankruptcy." CNN Money, October 14, 2002.
4. Diane Dungey, "Families' Agony Still Haunts Portillo," Daily Herald, February 25, 1993.
5. Flynn McRoberts, "Word Spreads of $100,000 Reward in Slayings," Chicago Tribune, January 28, 1993
6. Ameet Sachdev, "Tighter Security on Restaurant Menus," Chicago Tribune, May 23, 2002
7. Rummana Hussain, "After Massacre: No One Come," Chicago Sun-Times, August 10, 2009.
8. Maurice Possley, The Brown's Chicken Massacre, (Berkley Books, 2003), page 134.
9. Maurice Possley, The Brown's Chicken Massacre, (Berkley Books, 2003), page 134.
10. John Carpenter, "Watchdogs May Review Palatine Task Force," Chicago Sun-Times, November 30, 1995.
11. Jeff Favre, "The Cops' Not-So-Silent Partner Though Its Glory Years Are History, The Chicago Crime Commission Is Ready to Go Like Gangbusters After a New Public Enemy No. 1," Chicago Tribune, March 31, 1995.
12. Diane Dungey, "Portillo to Lead Anti-Crime Group, Daily Herald, April 23, 1993.

SOMETHING BIG

13. Michael Martinez and John O'Brien, "Palatine's Police Chief Fires Back Brown's Investigators Weren't Lax, He Says," Chicago Tribune, November 30, 1995.
14. Stacy Bardo, interview with author, March 10, 2024.
15. Terry Brunner, interview with author, March 12, 2024.
16. Michelle Roberts, "Dispute Snags Panel Studying Probe of Brown's", Chicago Sun-Times, October 4, 1997.
17. Dan Rozek and Sandra Del Re, "Police: Tips Leading to Brown's Suspect Bogus," Daily Herald, November 29, 1995.
18. Tamara Kerrill, "Victim's Dad Files Suit in Palatine Slayings," Chicago Sun-Times, January 7, 1995.
19. Sabrina L. Miller, "Watchdog Is Being Watched," Chicago Tribune, May 6, 1996.
20. Diane Dungey, "Group Reviewing Brown's Investigation Readies Report," Daily Herald, January 9, 1997.
21. Terry Brunner, interview with author, March 12, 2024.
22. Ibid.
23. Maurice Possley, The Brown's Chicken Massacre, (Berkley Books, 2003), page 178.
24. Jim Allen, "Police Still Optimistic on Solving Brown's Murders," Daily Herald, November 23, 1997.
25. Maurice Possley, The Brown's Chicken Massacre, (Berkley Books, 2003), page 179.
26. Becky Beaupre, "Report on '93 Killings to Be Reviewed," Chicago Sun-Times.
27. Dan Rozek, "Report: Palatine Probe Thorough," Chicago Sun-Times, August 30, 2000.
28. "Most Wanted" In Chicago, Chicago Sun-Times, May 9, 1997.
29. John Carpenter, "'America's Most Wanted' to Feature Brown's Case," Chicago Sun-Times, April 25, 1997.
30. Melissa Benz, interview with author, August 5, 2024.

Chapter 15—Casey, Todd & John

1. Casey Sander Haefs, interview with author, June 19, 2024.
2. 1993 press photo (Chicago Sun-Times), Casey Sander, Brown's Chicken Massacre., https://www.ebay.com/itm/375727231228.
3. Joseph Ryan, "Huge Burden Is Lifted with 2 Convictions," Daily Herald, October 4, 2009.
4. Dennis Shere, The Last Meal: Defending an Accused Mass Murderer, (Titletown Publishing, 2010), page 24.
5. Casey Sander Haefs, interview with author, June 19, 2024.

6. Ben Grove, "Investigator Brings Fresh Outlook to Brown's Case," Chicago Tribune, May 5, 1995.
7. Ibid.
8. Ibid.
9. Dennis Shere, The Last Meal: Defending an Accused Mass Murderer, (Titletown Publishing, 2010), page 25.
10. Dennis Shere, The Last Meal: Defending an Accused Mass Murderer, (Titletown Publishing, 2010), page 25.
11. People v. Luna, May 2, 2007 transcripts, volume 2.
12. People v. Luna, May 2, 2007 transcripts, volume 1.
13. Frank Medrys, interview with author, September 7, 2024.
14. "Palatine's Bratcher Is Retired, Not Resigned," Chicago Tribune, August 15, 1999.

Chapter 16—Jennifer, Dana & Joy

1. Julie Irwin, "Brown's Site Is Reborn as Cleaners," Chicago Tribune, October 15, 1994.
2. Andrew Hermann, "Healing Old Wounds," Chicago Sun-Times, June 3, 1997.
3. Julie Irwin, "Brown's Site Is Reborn as Cleaners," Chicago Tribune, October 15, 1994.
4. People v. Degorski, October 2, 2009, morning transcripts.
5. Joseph Kirby and Ted Gregory, "Ehlenfeldt Daughters Pay Tribute to Parents," Chicago Tribune, January 15, 1993; Rebecca Carr, "Daughters Express Thanks, Vow to Reopen Restaurant," Chicago Sun-Times, January 15, 1993.
6. Joseph Kirby and Ted Gregory, "Ehlenfeldt Daughters Pay Tribute to Parents," Chicago Tribune, January 15, 1993; Rebecca Carr, "Daughters Express Thanks, Vow to Reopen Restaurant," Chicago Sun-Times, January 15, 1993.
7. Flynn McRoberts and Peter Kendall, "Dad Wants Brown's Site Demolished," Chicago Tribune, February 24, 1993.
8. Rebecca Carr, "Shrine for Palatine? Victim's Dad Wants to Raze Building, Memorialize Slain," Chicago Sun-Times, February 24, 1993.
9. Flynn McRoberts and Peter Kendall, "Dad Wants Brown's Site Demolished," Chicago Tribune, February 24, 1993.
10. Lee Daniels, "Safe Retail Zones Law Sends Message," Chicago Tribune, February 27, 1993.
11. Flynn McRoberts and Peter Kendall, "Dad Wants Brown's Site Demolished," Chicago Tribune, February 24, 1993.
12. Karen Cullotta Krause, "Ehlenfeldt Daughters Won't Reopen Brown's," Chicago Tribune, December 22, 1993.

13. Carri Karuhn, "Family of Palatine Massacre Victims Settles Suit over Site," Chicago Tribune, May 10, 1995.
14. Martha Russis, "Brown's Chicken Reopens in Village," Chicago Tribune, March 30, 1995.
15. Michael Sneed, Sneed Says, Chicago Sun-Times, January 28, 1998.
16. "Case Chronology," Chicago Sun-Times, May 17, 2002.
17. Maurice Possley, The Brown's Chicken Massacre, (Berkley Books, 2003), page 209.
18. Richard Wronski, "Infamous Brown's Set to Fall," Chicago Tribune, April 27, 2001.
19. Natasha Korecki, "Demolition Opens Old Wounds," Daily Herald, April 28, 2001.
20. Ibid.
21. Ibid.

Chapter 17—Juan & Jim

1. "Luna Eager for His Day in Court," Chicago Tribune, April 13, 2007.
2. Sara Burnett, Madeleine Doubek, Diane Dungey, Lee Filas, Christy Gutowski, David Kazak, Joel Reese, Stacy St. Clair, and Shamus Toomey, "The Long Wait for One Call," Daily Herald, January 7, 2003.
3. People v. Luna, April 13, 2007, opening statement transcripts, page 44.
4. Scott Fornek, "The Loner—James Eric Degorski," Chicago Sun-Times, May 26, 2002.
5. Sara Burnett, Madeleine Doubek, Diane Dungey, Lee Filas, Christy Gutowski, David Kazak, Joel Reese, Stacy St. Clair, and Shamus Toomey, "The Long Wait for One Call," Daily Herald, January 7, 2003.
6. People v. Degorski, October 16, 2009, morning transcripts.
7. Wrongful Conviction with Maggie Freleng, iHeart Radio, October 21, 2024.
8. People v. Degorski, October 19, 2009, morning transcripts.
9. People v. Degorski, October 15, 2009, transcripts.
10. Rummana Hussain, "Brown's Chicken Killer Had Dysfunctional Childhood," Chicago Sun-Times, October 14, 2009.
11. People v. Degorski, October 6, 2009, transcripts.
12. People v. Degorski, October 6, 2009, transcripts.
13. Ibid.
14. Ibid.
15. People v. Luna, April 24, 2007, volume 1.
16. People v. Degorski, October 5, 2009, afternoon transcripts.
17. Steve Warmbir, Dan Rozek, Art Golab, and Dave Newbart, "Flashback to a Violent Past," Chicago Sun-Times, May 18, 2002.

[18] Scott Fornek, "The Loner—James Eric Degorski," *Chicago Sun-Times*, May 26, 2002.
[19] People v. Degorski, October 5, 2009, afternoon transcripts.
[20] People v. Degorski, September 9, 2009, transcripts.
[21] Rummana Hussain, "Ex-Girlfriend: 'I Will Always Love Jim Degorski'," *Chicago Sun-Times*, October 5, 2009.
[22] Andrew Herrmann, Dave Newbart, and Steve Warmbir, "Suspects Had Been Pals Since High School," *Chicago Sun-Times*, May 19, 2002.
[23] Burt Constable, "Conflicting Profiles," *Daily Herald*, May 26, 2002.
[24] People v. Degorski, October 6, 2009, morning transcripts.
[25] Jessen Funeral Home, Official Obituary of Walter D. Hanger, https://www.jessenfuneralhome.com/obituaries/Walter-D-Hanger?obId=26410354.
[26] Sara Burnett, Madeleine Doubek, Diane Dungey, Lee Filas, Christy Gutowski, David Kazak, Joel Reese, Stacy St. Clair, and Shamus Toomey, "The Long Wait for One Call," *Daily Herald*, January 7, 2003.

Chapter 18—Melissa

[1] Melissa Benz, interview with author, August 5, 2004.
[2] Ibid.
[3] Ibid.
[4] Carlos Sadovi, "Ex-Girlfriend of Brown's Defendant Regrets Silence," *Chicago Sun-Times*, June 12, 2002.
[5] Crystal Yednak and Diane Rado, "Brown's Secret Haunted Women," *Chicago Tribune*, June 9, 2002.
[6] People v. Luna, May 9, 2007, volume 1.
[7] People v. Luna, April 24, 2007, volume 2.
[8] Dennis Shere, *The Last Meal: Defending an Accused Mass Murderer*, (Titletown Publishing, 2010), page 33.

Chapter 19—Bill

[1] Barbara Vitello, "Time Tells the Story After 16 Years," *Daily Herald*, August 2, 2009.
[2] People v. Degorski, September 8, 2009, afternoon transcripts.
[3] Dennis Shere, *The Last Meal: Defending an Accused Mass Murderer*, (Titletown Publishing, 2010), page 30.
[4] Dennis Shere, *The Last Meal: Defending an Accused Mass Murderer*, (Titletown Publishing, 2010), page 31.
[5] Dennis Shere, *The Last Meal: Defending an Accused Mass Murderer*, (Titletown Publishing, 2010), page 32.
[6] Linas Kelecius, interview with author, April 6, 2023.
[7] Bryan Opitz, interview with author, September 15, 2023.

8. Dennis Shere, The Last Meal: Defending an Accused Mass Murderer, (Titletown Publishing, 2010), page 31.
9. People v. Degorski, September 8, 2009, transcripts.
10. Dennis Shere, The Last Meal: Defending an Accused Mass Murderer, (Titletown Publishing, 2010), page 35.
11. People v. Degorski, August 9, 2009, transcripts.
12. Stacy St. Clair and Joseph Ryan, "Luna Gave Her 'Heebie-Jeebies'," Daily Herald, April 18, 2007.
13. People v. Luna, April 18, 2007, transcripts.
14. People v. Luna, April 24, 2007, volume 2; Dennis Shere, The Last Meal: Defending an Accused Mass Murderer, (Titletown Publishing, 2010), page 32.

Chapter 20—Alesia

1. Jim Degorski, "Chapter 7," JimDegorski.com.
2. Dennis Shere, The Last Meal: Defending an Accused Mass Murderer, (Titletown Publishing, 2010), pages 37–8.
3. People v. Degorski, September 8, 2009, transcripts.
4. Dennis Shere, The Last Meal: Defending an Accused Mass Murderer, (Titletown Publishing, 2010), page 39.
5. Tom Biesty, Linas Kelecius, Dave Daigle, Palatine Police Department, "Police and Trial Prosecutors' Opposition to James Degorski's Petition for Executive Emergency Clemency," June 30, 2021.
6. People v. Degorski, September 8, 2009, transcripts.
7. Dennis Shere, The Last Meal: Defending an Accused Mass Murderer, (Titletown Publishing, 2010), page 39.
8. Dennis Shere, The Last Meal: Defending an Accused Mass Murderer, (Titletown Publishing, 2010), page 38.
9. Dennis Shere, The Last Meal: Defending an Accused Mass Murderer, (Titletown Publishing, 2010), page 38.
10. People v. Luna, April 25, 2007, transcripts.
11. People v. Luna, April 25, 2007, transcripts.
12. People v. Luna, April 13, 2007, transcripts.
13. Stefano Esposito, "Brown's Chicken murder confession was all lies, defendant says now," Chicago Sun-Times, July 7, 2005.
14. Eric Herman, "They Were Yelling 'Don't Shoot Me'," Chicago Sun-Times, April 26, 2007.
15. People v. Luna, April 25, 2007, transcripts, page 79.
16. Eric Herman, "They Were Yelling 'Don't Shoot Me'," Chicago Sun-Times, April 26, 2007.
17. People v. Degorski, September 8, 2009, transcripts.

[18] Dennis Shere, The Last Meal: Defending an Accused Mass Murderer, (Titletown Publishing, 2010), page 39.
[19] Rummana Hussain, "Degorski: Victims Were 'Nice People'," Chicago Sun-Times, September 9, 2009.
[20] Sara Burnett, Madeleine Doubek, Diane Dungey, Lee Filas, Christy Gutowski, David Kazak, Joel Reese, Stacy St. Clair, and Shamus Toomey, "Now, Another Kind of Waiting Begins," Daily Herald, January 8, 2003.
[21] Dave Orrick, Natasha Korecki, and Shamus Toomey, "After 9 Years, a Break," Daily Herald, May 18, 2002.
[22] Michael Higgins and Richard Wronski, "Palatine Police Are Due Apology from BGA, Ally Says," Chicago Tribune, May 21, 2002.
[23] Stacy St. Clair, "Stolen Lives: Couple Left Legacy of Service, Civic Duty," Daily Herald, January 9, 2003.
[24] Mickey Ciokajlo, "Palatine Promotes Acting Police Chief," Chicago Tribune, December 28, 2001.
[25] Village of Mount Prospect, "2021 Unsung Hero Award – John Koziol," YouTube, https://www.youtube.com/watch?v=ug_Gd_Mz2hQ&t=139s.
[26] Shamus Toomey and Rhonda Sciarra, "Brown's Suspects Had Plans to Do 'Something Big,' Authorities Say," Daily Herald, May 19, 2002.
[27] Carlos Sadovi, "Ex-Girlfriend of Brown's Defendant Regrets Silence," Chicago Sun-Times, June 12, 2002.
[28] Shamus Toomey and Rhonda Sciarra, "Suspects Could Face Death Penalty," Daily Herald, May 19, 2002.
[29] Carlos Sadovi, "Ex-Girlfriend of Brown's Defendant Regrets Silence," Chicago Sun-Times, June 12, 2002.
[30] Ibid.
[31] Eric Krol, "Witness Says She's Sorry She Waited 9 Years," Daily Herald, June 12, 2002.
[32] Dave Newbart and Andrew Herrmann, "Ex-Girlfriend Shows 'Courage'," Chicago Sun-Times, May 19, 2002.
[33] Maurice Possley, The Brown's Chicken Massacre, (Berkley Books, 2003), page 242.
[34] Ibid.
[35] Shamus Toomey and Rhonda Sciarra, "Brown's Suspects Had Plans to Do 'Something Big,' Authorities Say," Daily Herald, May 19, 2002.
[36] Maurice Possley, The Brown's Chicken Massacre, (Berkley Books, 2003), page 244.
[37] Christy Gutowski, "DNA, Ex-Lovers Often Help Crack Those 'Cold Cases'," Daily Herald, May 20, 2002.
[38] Jamie Sotonoff, "Relatives of Victim Thank Police with Banners," Daily Herald, May 31, 2002.

39. Grace Chung Becker, Patrick J. Fitzgerald, "Re: Cook County Jail," July 11, 2008, https://www.justice.gov/sites/default/files/crt/legacy/2011/04/13/CookCountyJail_findingsletter_7-11-08.pdf.
40. Frank Main, Steve Warmbir, Carlos Sadovi, and Robert C. Herguth, "Brown's Defendant Hit in Jail—Guard Could Lose," Chicago Sun-Times, May 21, 2002.
41. Ibid.
42. People v. Degorski, September 14, 2009, morning transcripts.

Chapter 21—Vincent

1. Carlos Sadovi, "Suspects Enter Not Guilty Pleas in Brown's Murders," Chicago Sun-Times, July 4, 2002.
2. Vincent Michael Gaughan, interview with author, September 6, 2024.
3. Carlos Sadovi, "Suspects Enter Not Guilty Pleas in Brown's Murders," Chicago Sun-Times, July 4, 2002.
4. Lou Longhitano, interview with author, April 21, 2023.
5. Frank Main, Steve Warmbir, Carlos Sadovi, and Robert C. Herguth, "Brown's Defendant Hit in Jail—Guard Could Lose," Chicago Sun-Times, May 21, 2002.
6. "Judge Rejects Review of Death Penalty," Chicago Tribune, January 7, 2004.
7. Dennis Shere, The Last Meal: Defending an Accused Mass Murderer, (Titletown Publishing, 2010), page 79.
8. Alan Spellberg, interview with author, November 2, 2023.
9. Stephen Richards, interview with author, October 27, 2023.
10. Stacy St. Clair and Erin Holmes, "Jury Still Debating if Luna's Eligible for Death," Daily Herald, May 15, 2007.
11. "Judge Rejects Review of Death Penalty," Chicago Tribune, January 7, 2004.
12. Stephen Richards, interview with author, October 27, 2023.
13. Stefano Esposito, "Brown's Chicken murder confession was all lies, defendant says now," Chicago Sun-Times, July 7, 2005.
14. Stacy St. Clair, "Jury Watches Videotaped Confession," Daily Herald, April 26, 2007.
15. Vincent Michael Gaughan, interview with author, September 6, 2024.
16. Ibid.
17. Stefano Esposito, "Public Polled Before Brown's Trial," Chicago Sun-Times, August 3, 2006.

Chapter 22—Juan

1. Joseph Ryan and Stacy St. Clair, "Luna's Family Prays for 'Mercy, Understanding'," Daily Herald, May 13, 2007.

2. Tara Malone and Stacy St. Clair, "A Plea for His Father," Daily Herald, May 17, 2007.
3. Carlos Sadovi, "Luna, family eager for Brown's trial to get under way," Chicago Tribune, April 13, 2007.
4. Carlos Sadovi, "Luna, family eager for Brown's trial to get under way," Chicago Tribune, April 13, 2007.
5. Dennis Shere, The Last Meal: Defending an Accused Mass Murderer, (Titletown Publishing, 2010), page 111.
6. Burt Constable, "Brown's Case Has Aged, but Wounds Still Fresh," Daily Herald, April 17, 2007.
7. Stacy St. Clair, "Duty-Bound 150 People in Court Learned They Could Be Jury For Sensational Brown's Case," Daily Herald, March 29, 2007.
8. Eric Herman, "Brown's Chicken Trial Times Upset," Chicago Sun-Times, March 29, 2007.
9. People v. Luna, April 26, 2007, transcripts, volume 2, page 21.
10. Stacy St. Clair, "Duty-Bound 150 People in Court Learned They Could Be Jury For Sensational Brown's Case," Daily Herald, March 29, 2007.
11. Vincent Michael Gaughan, interview with author, September 5, 2024.
12. People v. Luna, April 13, 2007, opening statement transcripts.
13. John Gorman, interview with author.
14. People v. Luna, April 13, 2007, opening statement transcripts.
15. Alan Spellberg, interview with author.
16. People v. Luna, April 16, 2007, transcripts, volume 1.
17. People v. Luna, April 16, 2007, transcripts, volume 2.
18. Karl Reich testimony.
19. Stacy St. Clair, "Not All DNA on Dinner Was Luna's," Daily Herald, April 19, 2007.
20. Burt Constable, "Brown's Murder Trial Brings Out Best in Key Witness," Daily Herald, May 3, 2007.
21. Stacy St. Clair and Joseph Ryan, "Luna Gave Her 'Heebie-Jeebies'," Daily Herald, April 18, 2007.
22. Ibid.
23. Steve Zalusky, "'I Don't Think Any of Us Really Had Closure': Brown's Murder Victim's Sister Recalls Toll on Family," Daily Herald, January 8, 2023.
24. Henry Lee, interview with author, January 19, 2023.
25. Eric Herman, "Expert: Chicken Bones Had 'Mixture of DNA'," Chicago Sun-Times, April 19, 2007.
26. Dennis Shere, The Last Meal: Defending an Accused Mass Murderer, (Titletown Publishing, 2010), page 157.
27. Linas Kelecius, interview with author.
28. Alan Spellberg, interview with author.
29. Linas Kelecius, interview with author.

30. Eric Herman and Rummana Hussain, "Grisly Details Emerge," Chicago Sun-Times, April 25, 2007.
31. Stacy St. Clair and Joseph Ryan, "DNA Experts at Odds as Testimony Wraps Up," Daily Herald, May 4, 2007.
32. Stacy St. Clair, "In Closing: Look at Evidence," Daily Herald, May 10, 2007.
33. Alan Spellberg, interview with author.
34. Ibid.
35. People v. Luna, May 9, 2007, transcripts.
36. People v. Luna, May 9, 2007, transcripts, volume 2.

Chapter 23—Juror 56

1. Izabela Milott, interview with author.
2. Tara Malone, Erin Holmes, and Eric Krol, "Murder Trial 'Took Toll on Us All'," Daily Herald, May 18, 2007.
3. Kristen Kridel, "Juror Stood Firm, Alone," Chicago Tribune, May 20, 2007.
4. Stacy St. Clair and Joseph Ryan, "Luna Guilty After Hours of Jury Deliberations," Daily Herald, May 11, 2007.
5. Ibid.
6. Ibid.
7. Erin Holmes and Tara Malone, "Families' Reactions Reflect Differing Views of Justice," Daily Herald, May 18, 2007.
8. Stacy St. Clair, "Victim's Family Stands Beside Luna at Rally," Daily Herald, May 16, 2007.
9. Ibid.
10. Stacy St. Clair and Erin Holmes, "Jury Still Debating if Luna's Eligible for Death," Daily Herald, May 15, 2007.
11. Tara Malone and Stacy St. Clair, "A Plea for His Father," Daily Herald, May 17, 2007.
12. Vincent Michael Gaughan, interview with author.
13. Eric Herman, "Luna Weeps During Son's Testimony," Chicago Sun-Times, May 17, 2007.
14. Tara Malone and Stacy St. Clair, "A Plea for His Father," Daily Herald, May 17, 2007.
15. Stacy St. Clair, "Circle of Grief—Luna Eligible for Death Penalty," Daily Herald, May 16, 2007.
16. Ibid.
17. Leonard N. Fleming, "Inside Jury Room: Pain, Tears—Lone Juror Upset," Chicago Sun-Times, May 20, 2007; Izabela Milott, interview with author.
18. Leonard N. Fleming, "Inside Jury Room: Pain, Tears—Lone Juror Upset," Chicago Sun-Times, May 20, 2007.

[19] Eric Herman, Leonard N. Fleming, and Rummana Hussain, "Single Juror Spares," Chicago Sun-Times, May 18, 2007.
[20] Dennis Shere, The Last Meal: Defending an Accused Mass Murderer, (Titletown Publishing, 2010), page 201.

Chapter 24—Jim

[1] Burt Constable, "Brown's Murder Trial Brings Out Best in Key Witness," Daily Herald, May 3, 2007.
[2] People v. Degorski, August 31, 2009, morning transcripts.
[3] Rummana Hussain, "3 Clear Jury Hurdle in Brown's Case," Chicago Sun-Times, August 11, 2009
[4] Matthew Walberg, "Degorski's Presence at Palatine Massacre Disputed," Chicago Tribune, September 1, 2009.
[5] People v. Degorski, September 15, 2009, morning transcripts.
[6] Matthew Walberg, "Degorski's Presence at Palatine Massacre Disputed," Chicago Tribune, September 1, 2009.
[7] Rummana Hussain, "Brown's Chicken Suspect Degorski Paid $15 for Gun," Chicago Sun-Times, September 9, 2009.
[8] People v. Degorski, October 20, 2009, morning transcripts.
[9] People v. Degorski, September 29, 2009, transcripts.
[10] People v. Degorski, September 29, 2009, transcripts.
[11] People v. Degorski, October 14, 2009, transcripts.
[12] "Sentencing Phase of Degorski Trial Under Way," ABC 7 Chicago, October 5, 2009, https://abc7chicago.com/archive/7049384/.
[13] Barbara Vitello, "Degorski's Life Sentence Entered," Daily Herald, November 5, 2009.
[14] "Partners in Crime Solving It's Been a Decade Since", Daily Herald, March 25, 2007.
[15] "Two Women Sharing Brown's Chicken Reward Money," NBC 5 Chicago, March 2, 2010, https://www.nbcchicago.com/news/local/browns-chicken-palatine/1868640/.

ACKNOWLEDGMENTS

This book is far from the first thing written about the Brown's Chicken case. News outlets covered the story closely for decades. Other authors have written books. And there are podcast episodes produced nearly every month on this saga. Despite this, there were a few important people in this process who believed, like myself, that there was still more to be said.

There is no way I could have completed this book without the love and support of my husband, Chris Chaffee. He was the first look at draft chapters, my finest editor, and the person who championed me throughout. Thank you for your patience and endless encouragement.

I want to also express my appreciation for the team at Post Hill Press and, in particular, Debra Englander and Caitlin Burdette, for seeing potential in this project. Thank you to my agent, Leslie York, for the countless hours she spent going back orth and her zeal in representing me.

thank you to the people who spoke with me
This was a difficult subject to speak about,
ed over phone calls, Zoom sessions, or
lar, I am grateful to the families who
who were willing to open up to
ory.

ABOUT THE AUTHOR

Patrick Wohl is an author and lawyer originally from Illinois. He received his law degree from Georgetown University Law Center and attended The George Washington University. His first book, *Down Ballot*, tells the story of a campaign for state representative that drew national attention because it was viewed as a proxy battle for larger political issues.